JAPAN'S TRADE FRICTIONS

Also by Ali M. El-Agraa

ASPECTS OF THE WORLD ECONOMY
*BRITAIN WITHIN THE EUROPEAN COMMUNITY: The Way
  Forward (*editor*)
*INTERNATIONAL ECONOMIC INTEGRATION (*editor*)
*PROTECTION, COOPERATION, INTEGRATION AND
  DEVELOPMENT (*editor*)
THE ECONOMICS OF THE EUROPEAN COMMUNITY (*editor*)
THE THEORY OF INTERNATIONAL TRADE
THEORY OF CUSTOMS UNIONS (*with A. J. Jones*)
*TRADE THEORY AND POLICY: Some Topical Issues

*Also published by Macmillan

Japan's Trade Frictions

Realities or Misconceptions?

Ali M. El-Agraa
Senior Lecturer in Economics
University of Leeds, and
Visiting Professor of International Economics
Graduate School of International Relations
International University of Japan

MACMILLAN
PRESS

First published 1988

Published by
THE MACMILLAN PRESS LTD
Houndmills, Basingstoke, Hampshire RG21 2XS
and London
Companies and representatives
throughout the world

Typeset by Latimer Trend & Company Ltd, Plymouth

Printed and bound in Great Britain at
The Camelot Press Ltd, Southampton

British Library Cataloguing in Publication Data
El-Agraa, A. M.
Japan's trade frictions: realities or
misconceptions?
1. Japan—Economic conditions—1945–
I. Title
330.952′048   HC462.9
ISBN 0–333–45986–5

Contents

Preface and Acknowledgements

Visiting Japan from Western Europe, one cannot help but notice the overwhelming publicity given to Japan's trade relations-cum-frictions with the USA. Of course, the daily papers do mention the trade frictions-cum-relations between Japan and Western Europe, ASEAN nations, the People's Republic of China, etc., but the statements made in this regard are completely dwarfed by those made on the US–Japan relationship. As an economist who has devoted a large part of his academic career to date to the problems of West European integration, I have inevitably taken great interest in Japan's trade relations with the European Community (EC) and the European Free Trade Association (EFTA). It seemed strange, therefore, that Japan's global trade relations should be so eschewed towards its bilateral exchanges with the USA. Of course, Japan and the USA have a very 'special relationship', hence the one-sided nature of the discussion may be a mere reflection of this simple reality. However, the US also has a 'special relationship' with Western Europe through the Atlantic Alliance and NATO. Although the decline in the importance of the 'special relationship' between the USA and Western Europe relative to that between Japan and the USA may explain the extent of publicity given to the latter, it remains a fact that that relationship has not been severed, and, in particular, the relationship between Britain and the USA has remained very close indeed: witness the support extended to President Reagan by Prime Minister Margaret Thatcher for the recent bombing of Libya. There is, therefore, a need for a discussion of Japan's trade frictions with the outside world within a global trade context, rather than in purely bilateral terms. The purpose of this book is to do precisely that.

The book is aimed at those specialising in international economics; hence the reader is assumed to be familiar with the technical aspects of balance of payments theory, trade performance, protectionism, international economic integration, etc. However, while assuming that the reader is familiar with this theoretical background, Chapter 7 is devoted to a comprehensive analysis of neo-protectionism which is still not well-understood by the profession and is of particular relevance to this book. I have nevertheless sought to write in a style which should be intelligible to most economists. As a matter of fact, the style should make most of the book intelligible to all those concerned with Japan's trade frictions-cum-relations, be they businessmen, diplomats, politicans or simply informed laymen. Indeed, Chapters 2, 5 and 6 contain information which should be of interest to all. Of course, writing in such a style incurs the risk of the reader believing that economics is no more than simple common sense, but that is the risk I take in full awareness that the 'fallacy of composition' (adding up a number of independent measures, each with well-defined consequences, will not in fact produce the desired overall impact) is not confined to professional economists alone.

I would not have had the inspiration to write this book had I not had the chance to stay in Japan from August 1984 to August 1986. As Visiting Professor of International Economics, West European Integration and Middle Eastern Economy with the Graduate School of International Relations (GSIR), International University of Japan (IUJ) – 'kokusai daigaku' – I was given the opportunity to participate at an early stage in the development of this unique Japanese educational institution; it is unique in that it is the only Japanese university which is strictly for graduates, instructs mainly in English, has a large percentage of overseas students (about 30 per cent, aiming at 50 per cent) coming from all parts of the globe and visiting professors from such countries as Australia, Canada, the UK and the USA. It is also unique in that it has been located, since the time of its official inauguration in 1982, in a rural part of Japan which has only recently been connected to Tokyo via the 'shinkansen' or 'bullet train', thanks mainly to ex-Prime Minister Kakuei Tanaka whose constituency and birthplace are in this part of 'snow country'. Moreover, and most importantly for the purposes of this book, IUJ is unique in that the majority of the Japanese students are employees of the private companies who set up the university with the support of the Japanese Ministry of Education: these students have an average of four or five years of work experience after graduating from distinguished Japanese universities and are set to be the business leaders of the future, hence they are ripe material for information on Japanese work habits, life perceptions, thoughts on internationalisation, etc. Although I did not use any formal questionnaires to solicit information, I had many discussions with the students which helped me to corroborate (or otherwise) certain features which are supposed to be peculiar to the Japanese.

Being at IUJ also gave me the chance to discuss matters concerning

Japan's international trade with such distinguished Japanese authorities as Professors Saburo Okita (President of IUJ, Chairman of the Institute for Domestic and International Policy Studies, ex-Foreign Minister, ex-member of the Japanese Economic Planning Agency (EPA), etc.), Hiroshi Kitamura (ex-Professor of two distinguished Japanese universities, ex-Head of the Research and Planning section of the United Nations' Economic and Social Commission for Asia and the Far East – ECAFE, now ESCAP – and the first Dean of GSIR, IUJ, Chihiro Hosoya (Vice-President of IUJ, Director of its Centre for Japan–US Relations, ex-Professor of Hitotsubasḷi University and chairman/president of numerous committees both in Japan and abroad), Toshio Shishido (now retired Vice-President of IUJ, aeronautics engineer before turning to economics through his ex-membership of the EPA and member of so many distinguished Japanese committees and institutions), etc. The list is really too long to allow mention of all by name; however, I wish to record my gratitude not only to the above, including my students of four semesters, but also to all of those at IUJ who made my stay so enjoyable and fruitful, especially those in the international economics, international management, international politics and Middle Eastern sections, particularly Professors Seigen Miyazato (Dean, GSIR, 1984–6), Chung-hsun Yu (Dean, GSIR, 1986–), Toshio Kuroda (Director, Institute of Middle Eastern Studies), Ichiro Inukai (Head, International Economics section), Toshiyuki Otsuki (Head, International Management section), Susumu Ishida (Middle Eastern Studies), Naoki Maruyama (Middle Eastern Studies), Masaru Yoshimori (International Management), Kazuhiko Okuda (North American Studies), Sumimaru Odano (International Economics), Yoshitaka Okada (Sociology) and Teruji Sakiyama (Development Economics).

As mentioned above, one of the advantages of being at IUJ was to meet a number of distinguished visiting professors. In connection with this book, I benefited greatly from the insight of Robert Gilpin, Eisenhower Professor of International Relations at Princeton University and Lewis Freitas, Professor of International Finance, University of Hawaii. I wish to record my deepest gratitude to both of them.

While with IUJ, I had the chance to deliver lectures at a number of other places. This gave me the opportunity to meet a number of distinguished Japanese economists. At Osaka National University, the distinguished Department of Economics provided a good forum for testing the ideas contained in this book. I am extremely grateful to all its members and graduate students, especially to Professor Hirofumi Shibata. At Okayama National University, I benefited a great deal from discussion with its economics professors, especially Professor Yoshizo Hashimoto, an old friend from his days on sabbatical leave at Leeds University. One of my most memorable connections is that with Fukuoka University where I delivered a number of papers as well as offered a short intensive course to some of the graduate students. The members of the economics department there were so forthcoming with constructive ideas and guidance; I am grateful to all of them, especially my esteemed friend Professor Toyo Yamanaka. Last but by no means least, the opportunity to teach two intensive courses at the International Development Centre of Japan gave me the chance to meet students with a similar background to those at IUJ, some of whom came from government departments (hence providing me with the bureaucratic side of the picture), and also the chance to meet the Centre's Director of Research and Planning, the distinguished Professor Kazushi Ohkawa, as well as my colleague from IUJ, Professor Otsuki, disguised as course director. I learnt a great deal about Japan talking with Professor Ohkawa, his colleagues and students over lunches.

Dr Kenichirou Sasae, Deputy Director of the First International Organisations Division, Ministry of Foreign Affairs, Tokyo, was generous enough to devote not only his own time but also that of his staff to checking the information and tables in Chapter 6. Dr Sasae is the most informed Japanese on matters concerned with market-opening since he is probably instrumental in all that is contained in them, and, as his title indicates, his Office is directly involved in dealing with the Action Programme of 1985. I wish to record my special gratitude to him and his staff.

While with IUJ, I had the opportunity to go to Tokyo twice every month for research purposes. This allowed me not only to use the extensive library facilities of different universities and institutes but also the chance to meet a large number of business people through the activities of the International House of Japan, 'kokusai bunka kaikan'. I am grateful to all the friends I made there especially to Katsuyoshi Saito, Chairman, East–West Discussion Group.

I am of course grateful to my university, the University of Leeds, England, without whose approval to take up my position with IUJ I would not have been able to visit Japan over such a long period.

Also, I wish to express special gratitude to my friends the distinguished economists Professor Hiroshi Kitamura and Dr Fred V.

Meyer for their thorough reading of the entire manuscript and for their constructive comments on it.

As usual, I am extremely grateful to my wife, Diana, for all her help and moral support and for her negotiating some impossible situations through her quick grasp of some of the basics of the Japanese language; travel in the rural parts of Japan would have been impossible otherwise. Finally, I am also extremely grateful to my son, Mark, and daughter, Frances, for making us enjoy Japan so much – the Japanese simply adore children and families – and for mastering the language so quickly as to give us the confidence that all is not yet lost for my wife and myself to pursue its study.

ALI M. EL-AGRAA

The author and publishers are grateful to the following for permission to reproduce copyright material:

Basil Blackwell for Tables 2.13, 2.14, 4.1 and Chart 3.3.
Brookings Institute for Table 2.8.
Foreign Policy for extracts from I. M. Destler, 'Protecting Congress or Protecting Trade?' from *Foreign Policy* 62 (Spring 1986). Copyright 1986 of the Carnegie Environment for International Peace.
Institute for International Economics, Washington, DC, for Tables 3.3 and 8.1. © Institute for International Economics. Reproduced by permission from *The United States–Japan Economic Problem* by C. Fred Bergsten and William R. Clive.
Japan's Economic Planning Agency for Tables 2.2 and Charts 2.1, 3.1 and 3.2.
Journal of Common Market Studies for Table 7.1.
Littlewood, Adams & Company for Chart 4.1 from Table 5.1, 'Japanese Industrial Policy since 1946', from John Pinder (ed.), *National Industrial Strategies and the World Economy* (Totowa, NJ: Allanheld, Osmun, 1982), pp. 126–7.
Oxford University Press for Table 2.3.

Every effort has been made to trace all the copyright-holders, but if any have been inadvertently overlooked the publishers will be pleased to make the necessary arrangement at the first opportunity.

1 General Introduction

The nature of Japan's trade frictions with the outside world, particularly with the EC and the USA, is rather complicated since there is no single or simple way of explaining them. From an economic point of view, at least two 'scenarios' can be entertained. The first is concerned with the mere existence of trade imbalances which is too simplistic an explanation since economists have long recognised a 'balance of payments stages theorem' which depicts that countries are bound to experience trade surpluses during particular phases in the development of their economies; these aspects are dealt with in Chapter 3. The second scenario digs deeper below the surface and considers a multiplicity of factors which might explain the tension, such as the particular characteristics of the Japanese market, the differences between the Japanese and other members of the OECD, etc.; this scenario is tackled in Chapter 4. There is a third scenario which is purely political, but since this book is basically concerned with economic arguments or political arguments based on economic factors, there is no place for a whole chapter on pure politics; therefore, I will discuss this scenario briefly in this Introduction. However, Chapter 7 is devoted to a comprehensive analysis of neo-protectionism, with a whole section on its political economy foundations; political economy is what the book is all about.

A meaningful discussion of the two economic scenarios cannot be contemplated without some understanding of the basic characteristics of the Japanese economy. It is therefore wise to devote the second chapter to a comprehensive but brief review of the basic features of the Japanese economy, especially its international sector.

Of course, no matter what scenarios can be advanced to explain the nature/causes of Japan's trade frictions, it is vital to learn, firstly, about the demands that have been made on Japan to open up its markets and to eliminate its trade surpluses and, secondly, about Japan's response to these demands. These two aspects are dealt with, respectively, in Chapters 5 and 6.

The concluding chapter deals with some macroeconomic misconceptions regarding the nature of the demands for market opening: sector-specific approaches (now referred to as MOSS – 'market-oriented sector-specific') are futile unless they change the basic savings/investment behaviour of the Japanese since trade imbalances

1

are no more than mirror-images of the difference between savings and investment. The chapter also contains a section dealing specifically with a practical but complex and demanding proposal designed to alleviate Japan's fears regarding its heavy dependence on imported crude oil and raw materials within a context which tackles the country's trade frictions with the outside world. This approach may aggravate those political historians who believe that 'bilateral' imbalances are central to the current political debate and cannot be wished away unless popular perceptions are drastically changed, but the reality of the world suggests that no fundamental change will come about unless a *multilateral* solution is sought; hence, it is pointless to pursue this narrow bilateral line only to please those who hold 'popular' views – the world is not led by those who 'follow the people', and one must always remember that there is a great deal of truth in Henrik Ibsen's notion that 'the minority may be right; the majority is always wrong'.

A POLITICAL SCENARIO

A very simple political scenario is one which is specifically geared to tackling Japan's trade frictions with the USA. Its proponents claim that, particularly when election time is approaching in the USA, one very easy way to secure re-election is to bash the Japanese for running such a huge trade surplus with the USA. This election ploy is very effective particularly in states which produce cars and are now experiencing a combination of a high level of unemployment and surging imports of Japanese cars. It is equally effective as a pure election ploy because the US President has the right to veto any legislation in that spirit, unless it is passed by two-thirds of the legislators after he activates his veto. With President Reagan speaking openly against protectionism and the securing of a two-thirds majority a near impossibility given the political party persuasions of those in the Senate and House and their realisation that protectionism is no panacea for trade imbalances, the ploy is truly effective since no actual harm is likely to arise from it!

Destler (1986, pp. 97–8) gives a clear background to this phenomenon:

Consistently since the early 1930s, Congress has employed four principal devices to avoid having to fix the level of import protection for individual commodities. First, Congress delegated authority over [US] trade barriers. Through the Reciprocal Trade Agreements Act of 1934 and successor bills it allowed presidents to negotiate "reciprocal" tariff reductions with [US] trading partners. In 1974, legislation also authorized the president to negotiate agreements reducing nontariff barriers to trade. The second mechanism has been the rules: the quasi-judicial procedures through which particular trade-injured industries could obtain limited import relief by going downtown to the International Trade Commission or the Department of Commerce and proving their eligibility under current statutes.

Especially powerful industries like textiles were enticed away from forming broad, trade-restrictive coalitions through a third device: Congress pressed the executive branch to arrange nonstatutory deals, usually in the form of "voluntary export restraints" enforced by the seller country. And finally, Congress created and nurtured a special official in the White House, currently called the [US] trade representative (USTR), to act as overall trade broker, to balance competing interests – domestic and bureaucratic as well as international – to manage trade issues, and to draw some of the heat away from Capitol Hill.

For Congress and its committees with primary trade jurisdiction – the House Ways and Means Committee and the Senate Finance Committee – these four means constituted a system to cope with pressures for trade restrictions, one that diverted them, channeled them, and created pro-trade counterweights. *The system allowed members so inclined to advocate, even threaten, trade restrictions, while nicely relieving them of the need to deliver on their threats. Indeed, its main result was not protection for industry but protection for Congress – insulation of its members from trade pressures.* Or to employ a more flattering phrase, Congress, recognizing its vulnerability to industries seeking import restrictions, opted to exercise "voluntary legislative restraints" (italics added).

Moreover, it is also felt that Japan may take this US political game seriously and undertake measures which will directly influence the size of the USA's trade deficit with Japan. If that were to actually materialise, the political ploy would become doubly effective: it would ease the tension by reducing the size of the trade balance; and the legislators could claim that this was brought about by their strong stance against the unfair Japanese practices which had created the unemployment, thus indicating to their electors the extent of their devotion to their task as well as their strong sense of patriotism – note how Senators Danforth and Packwood became household names, not only in the USA but also in Japan.

Simple as it is, this political scenario has a great deal of support both in terms of the number of bills that have been passed (or were promised resolution) by the US Congress in the full knowledge that the US President was going to veto them and that there was never any possibility that they would secure the two-thirds majority the second time round, and also in terms of the view held of Japan by the average US citizen. With regard to the former point, recall: Senator Danforth's 1985 resolution advocating retaliation against imports of Japanese telecommunications, debated in the Senate Finance Committee; the 1985 approval of a Senate Finance Committee (chaired by Senator Packwood) bill, subject to Congressional approval, instructing President Reagan to reduce US imports of Japanese products if restrictions of US exports to Japan were not lifted within ninety days; the House Rostenkowski bill proposing a 25 per cent tariff on any country whose exports to the USA exceeded its imports from the USA by 50 per cent and whose global exports exceeded its global imports by 65 per cent; the March 1986 Senate endorsement by 92 votes to nil of a resolution demanding retaliation against Japan; the passing with a comfortable majority by both Houses of a proposal to curtail textile imports; etc. Regarding the latter point, when Potomac Associates/ Gallup Polls asked the US citizens to choose the five countries they believed to be 'specially trustworthy', 23 per cent cited Japan, ranking it seventh out of a total of thirty countries. That was in 1983; in 1978, only 13 per cent regarded Japan as especially trustworthy, but although the image had improved between these two periods, the overall view is not very impressive. It should be pointed out that when the *Yomiuri* newspaper has asked the same question of the Japanese over a number of years (this is now an annual poll), the USA has come consistently at the top. When one side is ranked highly by a side it does not think much of, some would suggest that such a position is ripe for exploitation by the former. Hence, anti-Japanese sentiments can easily be politically exploited by US Congressmen coming from states with high unemployment, particularly where a large number of people drive Japanese cars; indeed, in August 1985, a Texan Democrat used the imports issue to win a close race for an open House seat.

The case of Japan and the EC deserves separate treatment. According to Hosoya (1979), the trade imbalance between the EC and Japan emerged as a serious political problem as a conscious 'tactical ploy' on the part of the EC. He claimed that the issue of the trade deficit with Japan had already become a problem whose solution was of vital importance as early as December 1975 and June 1976 at the high-level official consultations between Japan and the EC, at the OECD ministerial conference in June 1976, and also on the occasion of the visit to Japan of EC Commissioner Gundelach in July 1976. The lack of a satisfactory response from Japan must have brought home to the EC the need to take drastic measures. The Japanese would seem not to have had sufficient awareness by then of the political nature of the problem as far as the member countries of the EC were concerned; the Japanese side saw the deficit from an economic point of view, stressing the fact that the trade deficit should be considered in the context of the overall balance of payments and the principle of free trade. Moreover, the mechanism of foreign policy making, strongly constrained by the bureaucratic structure and lack of a strong leadership, was such that policy changes were not easily made. The EC seemed to have arrived at the conclusion that, in order to elicit a response to their complaints, it would be necessary to bring external pressure to bear on the Japanese policy-making mechanism when the opportunity presented itself. Perceived from the EC's point of view, this opportunity presented itself with the European visit of the Dokō mission. After all, it was a mission led by the President of the Japan Federation of Economic Organisations (*Kaidanren*), which is the very core of Japanese business and was regarded by the EC as having great influence on the government's policy-making process. Hence, it was not surprising that they calculated that using the mission as a channel of communication and feeding in a large amount of intensive criticism and censure would have the effect of applying pressure on the Japanese government. At the same time the occasion was probably also seen as a highly useful opportunity to draw the attention of Japan's news media to the trade problems between Japan and the EC, and to get a widespread understanding among all strata of the Japanese people of the political nature of the issue. 'The politicization of the trade dispute came about as a result of the tactical manoeuvre based on this assessment of the situation' (Hosoya, 1979, p. 167).

Hosoya also claimed that, apart from settling the problem of trade imbalances, the tactical politicisation of the trade issue was intended to make Japan fully recognise the EC as a corporate body 'not as a legal fiction but as an actually existing entity', and to accept the EC Commission as the only negotiator for the EC in matters concerning international trade. The former point was due to the fact that until the mid-1970s, Japan's attitude towards the EC was somewhat ambiguous: Japan found it easier to deal with nations on the grounds of 'familiarity, tradition, the emotional factor, and organizational considerations' (Hosoya, 1979, p. 168); hence the need to conclude a comprehensive trade agreement with the EC as a whole to replace the agreements that had been in force with individual member nations of the EC created a real dilemma for Japan. However, the EC did not actually succeed in persuading Japan to deal with it as a corporate body until much later. The success was achieved only after the bizarre 'Poitiers' incident: in 1982, the French government did not know what to do in the face of the 'Japanese invasion' of the French VTR market, so they adopted the tactic of requiring all Japanese VTRs to go to Poitiers for customs inspection. Poitiers was a town almost completely lacking in staff trained in the procedures of customs inspection; hence, a 'go slow' tactic had been adopted, ensuring that Japanese VTRs reached the consumer at a much reduced pace. This was a bizarre incident simply because the French knew very well that their tactic was clearly against the rules of GATT – human ingenuity in the creation of non-tariff trade barriers makes the mind boggle! Be that as it may, what is of significance for our purposes is that before that incident, the Japanese government was adamant that it should deal with each member nation of the EC as a separate entity, but while the incident was taking place, the Japanese authorities approached the EC Commission and asked: 'What can we do in order to solve this problem which is detrimental to our industry?' (Anouil, in an address to the Nihon EC Gakkai – Japan-EC Study Association – Conference held at Waseda University, Tokyo, in November 1984; reproduced in the Conference Proceedings in 1985). One should hasten to add that the President of the EC Commission was the only major participant in the Tokyo Summit of May 1986 who was not a head of state in the traditional sense.

CONCLUSION

Although the politicisation of trade frictions between Japan and the EC is different from that between Japan and the USA, it should be clear that both are based on pre-conceived perceptions about the influence of the Japanese government and industrial organisations on national policy/decision making. The bases of these perceptions should be investigated; hence the pre-conceived ideas should not be taken for granted. Therefore, to assume that these bases are purely political is to fall into the trap of thinking that the trade frictions can be explained in purely political terms. This is the reason why this book does not contain a chapter specifically devoted to this issue, and also why its chapters do not dwell on this matter unless the political manifestations emanate from or impinge on economic or other factors that can be rigorously analysed.

2 The Japanese Economy

GENERAL CHARACTERISTICS

Japan comes second in the league of national economies. In the early 1960s, its GNP was only 5 per cent of that of the USA, but by 1965 it had reached just over 13 per cent. In 1970 it amounted to about 20 per cent and in 1982 it reached over 35 per cent (see Table 2.1) before dropping slightly to 32.5 per cent in 1983. Japan has a growth rate which, after the two oil crises, has continued to be higher than the average for the OECD. However, the real rate of growth of GNP was a modest 3.3 per cent in 1982 and 3.4 per cent in 1983, but the average for 1980–85 was 3.9 per cent. To the casual observer, the driving force for the economy seems to be mainly export growth rather than domestic demand; the latter is usually the case within the rest of the OECD. Japan's domestic demand registered growth rates of 2.1, 2.8, 1.8, 3.8 and 3.7 per cent respectively for the years from 1981 to 1985. (See Table 2.2 for trends in the major indicators of the Japanese economy.)

The point about the Japanese obsession with export growth needs careful examination. Boltho (1975) writes:

> it is commonly thought that production for export is the primary occupation of most Japanese firms; and foreign trade is frequently seen as the engine which propelled the country's economic growth. But many of these arguments ... tend to stem from pressure groups in America or Europe defending particular sectors threatened by Japanese competition, rather than from economic analysis ...
>
> For a nation supposedly devoted almost solely to foreign trade, the weights of exports and imports in total output are surprisingly low. Table [2.3] ... shows that Japan's share of foreign trade in GNP is well below that of other countries for which figures are provided. Indeed, within the O.E.C.D. area, only the United States has lower foreign trade proportions. Outside the O.E.C.D., a few more examples can be found but, apart from the Soviet Union, these are all developing countries and relatively large economies (e.g. Argentina, Brazil, India, China). Thus, despite the fact that Japan has become the world's single largest importer of raw materials and the third largest exporter, it remains one of the

Table 2.1   Japan's output relative to that of the World, the USA and West Germany

	World	Japan		USA		W. Germany	
	($m)	($m)	(%)	($m)	(%)	($m)	(%)
1970	3 136 300	203 569	6.5	989 513	31.6	184 508	5.9
1979	10 177 400	997 609	9.8	2 388 402	23.5	759 662	7.5
1980	11 439 900	1 040 452	9.1	2 606 625	22.8	814 829	7.1
1981	11 552 500	1 145 098	9.9	2 933 460	25.4	682 562	5.9
1982	11 313 900	1 062 867	9.4	3 052 088	27.0	658 879	5.8

Source: Yearbook of National Accounts Statistics, 1985.

countries least dependent on external transactions, when 'dependence' is measured in this relatively simple statistical manner ... Exports were very much a resultant of domestic growth – of the growth of a very large market for consumer and investment goods ... and of the growth of a highly productive capital stock (constantly embodying new techniques) ... Both these allowed the attainment of scale economies and cost reductions, which in turn permitted a successful growth of exports. Even in these periods of domestic recession when exports directly stimulated renewed growth, it was not foreign demand but internal supply which was the initiating force. To be sure, rapid export growth must also have encouraged investments – directly through demand effects and indirectly by raising business confidence. But the overall contribution of exports to economic growth (abstracting, of course, from their role of financing import requirements), does not seem to have been fundamental.

Thirlwall (1983) has observations, derived from his own statistical analysis, which are not so easy to interpret in the context of the contention of Japanese export-led growth, but they are worth considering in order to have some perspective. He states:

No country can grow faster than the rate of growth consistent with balance of payments equilibrium on current account unless it can finance an ever-growing absolute deficit by capital inflows, which is extremely unlikely over the long-run unless the country issues a

Table 2.2 Trends of major economic indicators

Items	Period									1983			1984	
---	FY 1976	FY 1977	FY 1978	FY 1979	FY 1980	FY 1981	FY 1982	FY 1983	Apr.–June	Jul.–Sept.	Oct.–Dec.	Jan.–Mar.	Apr.–June
GNP													
Gross national product (nominal)	12.2	10.9	9.5	7.4	8.5	5.7	5.0	4.1	1.1	1.2	0.9	2.0	
Gross national product (real)	5.1	5.3	5.1	5.3	4.6	3.5	3.3	3.7	1.1	1.5	0.8	1.8	
Contribution ratio of domestic demand to GNP	3.6	4.2	6.9	4.8	1.4	1.8	2.9	1.9	0.5	0.9	0.7	1.0	
Contribution ratio of private demand to GNP	3.2	2.3	5.0	4.7	1.2	1.3	2.7	1.5	-0.0	0.7	1.1	0.9	
Production													
Industrial production	10.8	3.2	7.0	8.0	2.2	2.0	-0.6	6.4	1.9	2.6	2.9	3.2	(P) 2.6
Industrial shipment	9.8	3.3	6.1	7.1	0.4	1.5	-1.1	6.0	1.7	2.5	2.0	3.2	(P) 1.0
Producers' inventory–shipments ratio of finished goods from mining and manufacturing (1980=100)*	105.3	103.0	93.8	93.4	7.6	104.6	102.4	93.5	100.8	93.6	93.2	93.5	(P) 97.6
O Index of operating rates of manufacturing industries (1980=100)*	92.3	91.2	95.6	101.2	98.3	95.2	91.9	96.2	92.5	94.4	97.8	100.0	
Prices													
O Wholesale price	5.5	0.4	-2.3	13.0	12.8	1.3	1.0	-2.3	-2.0	-2.8	-3.3	-1.3	-0.4
O Consumer prices	9.4	6.7	3.4	4.8	7.8	4.0	2.4	1.9	2.1	1.4	1.7	2.4	2.1
Private demand													
Personal consumption expenditure (real)	3.7	3.7	5.5	4.7	0.9	1.3	4.6	2.9	0.2	0.8	0.5	1.1	
O Nationwide department store sales	7.9	6.0	7.4	8.3	8.0	6.3	2.3	3.1	1.2	2.5	3.4	5.1	4.5
Private housing investment (real)	3.5	3.0	3.1	-0.1	10.0	-1.9	1.3	-7.3	-12.7	3.4	5.7	-2.3	
Plant and equipment investment by private enterprises (real)	1.8	2.3	9.7	10.3	7.6	4.8	2.8	3.8	0.9	1.7	2.1	3.0	
Public finance and money supply													
Public fixed capital formation (real)	0.0	15.8	14.4	-0.9	0.4	1.4	1.1	-0.1	5.0	0.9	-2.9	-2.6	
O Disbursements of public works appropriations	5.9	29.1	24.0	8.7	7.5	2.0	3.1	-3.0	-3.4	-8.8	1.9	2.0	-0.0
O Average balance of money supply (M₂ + CD)	14.4	10.9	12.1	11.4	8.4	9.7	8.4	7.5	7.6	7.1	7.2	7.9	

Item														
Circulation yields on government bonds of longest maturity		8.4799	7.0452	6.5519	8.3859	8.4615	8.2319	8.1341	7.6728	7.8743	7.8813	7.5460	7.3897	
Labour														
Aggregate cash wage earnings	O	11.8	8.1	5.9	6.1	6.0	5.1	4.7	3.2	3.9	2.2	3.0	4.2	5.1
Number of regularly employed persons	O	0.8	1.4	1.3	1.2	1.1	0.8	1.3	1.3	1.7	1.9	1.1	0.2	0.5
Effective job openings-to-job-seeker ratio (fold)*		0.64	0.54	0.59	0.74	0.73	0.67	0.60	0.61	0.59	0.59	0.62	0.64	0.64
Number of fully unemployed persons		2.0	2.1	2.2	2.0	2.1	2.2	2.5	2.7	2.62	2.71	2.63	2.71	2.69
Merchandise trade														
Exports (customs clearance; unit sales)		(21.5)	(7.7)	(−5.6)	(8.0)	17.4	8.5	−3.1	12.4	3.4	3.4	1.8	6.4	3.7
Imports (customs clearance; unit imports)		(10.5)	(0.7)	(9.8)	(7.1)	4.4	−0.8	−4.3	7.6	2.9	3.0	7.6	1.2	1.3
Current-account balance (IMF formula, in million dollars)*		4682	13996	11852	−13853	7012	5934	9135	24277	5720	5714	5518	7202	9170
Overall balance (IMF formula, in million dollars)*		3252	12145	−2297	−18951	380	−7859	−1988	2415	1825	−3.6	1222	−674	−5861
Yen rates (inter-bank middle rate of yen to dollar, average rate)		292.43	256.74	201.44	229.50	217.40	227.38	249.66	236.39	237.53	242.60	234.30	231.12	229.29
Business														
Current profit-sales ratio (Mfg firms, %)*		2.92	3.00	3.77	4.60	3.74	3.40	3.19	3.51	3.23	3.08	3.72	3.97	

Notes:

1. Figures given under items bearing the mark 'O' represent percentage changes from a year earlier or from the same quarter of the preceding year, while those given under items bearing an asterisk are those seasonally adjusted. Other figures indicate percentage changes on a seasonally adjusted basis from a year earlier or from the same quarter of the preceding year.

2. Figures for gross national product, personal consumption expenditure, private housing investment, private investment in plant and equipment, public fixed-capital formation are drawn from the 'Report on National Economic Accounts' compiled by the Economic Planning Agency (EPA).

3. Quarterly figures given under the heading of 'Producers' inventory-shipments ratio of finished goods from mining and manufacturing' represent those seasonally adjusted at the end of the given quarters, while the yearly figures represent those seasonally adjusted at the end of the given years.

4. Figures regarding the money supply for FY (Financial Year which begins in April) 1979 and thereafter include CDs.

5. Quarterly and yearly figures given under the headings 'Exports' and 'Imports' are computed on the basis of simple arithmetic averages for monthly indexes of their respective volumes (1980 = 100). Figures given in parentheses are computed on the basis of simple arithmetic averages of indexes of their respective volumes (1975 = 100).

6. Figures regarding the current profit-sales ratio (manufacturing) are drawn from the 'Quarterly Report on Financial Statements of Business Corporations' compiled by the Ministry of Finance (MOF).

Source: Economic Planning Agency's *Economic Survey of Japan 1983–1984.*

Table 2.3   Foreign trade ratios – 1953 to 1972

	Exports[a]	Imports[a]	Trend increase in
	Percentage of GNP at constant prices		combined share[b]
Japan	11.3	10.2	0.33
France	15.2	14.8	0.42
Germany	20.8	18.3	0.85
Italy	17.0	16.2	0.93
United Kingdom	21.3	21.2	0.32
OECD Europe[c]	21.2	20.9	0.67

Notes:
[a] Goods, services, and factor income.
[b] Annual increase in the average of the export and import shares in GNP obtained by fitting linear time trends to the data.
[c] At 1963 prices and exchange rates.

Source: A. Boltho, *Japan: An Economic Survey, 1953–73* (Oxford: Oxford University Press, 1975).

reserve asset. If relative prices in international trade measured in a common currency remain relatively stable over the long term, the balance of payments equilibrium growth rate approximates to the rate of growth of exports. This is the dynamic analogue of the static Harrod trade multiplier result that income is determined by the level of export demand divided by the marginal propensity to import if other sectors of the economy are in balance and other net autonomous expenditure is zero. ... When I fitted the dynamic Harrod trade multiplier to a selection of developed countries over the period 1951 to 1973, a remarkable approximation to the actual growth experience was observed, indicating to me that relative price changes cannot be a very efficient adjustment mechanism in international trade and it is income (and growth) that adjust to bring exports and imports into line with one another in the absence of capital flows ... Japan was the major deviant observation with an actual growth rate substantially below that consistent with balance of payments equilibrium, meaning the accumulation of a large balance of payments surplus and indicative of supply constrained growth (and not surprisingly with *actual* growth averaging over 10 per cent per annum).

Thirlwall's analysis could, of course, be interpreted to mean that the Japanese economy has been mainly geared to export-led growth, implying a rate of growth of exports in excess of the rate of GDP growth.

However, Kitamura (1976), writing simultaneously with Boltho (1975) – these are books – completely endorses the latter's position:

> Unquestionably foreign trade played an important part in supporting the phenomenal growth of the Japanese economy in the past. Japanese industry depends in a vital way on the supply of raw materials from abroad, and as import needs rise *pari passu* with domestic industrial expansion, exports must also expand in order to pay for increased imports. In fact, exports were in the latter part of the 1960s expanding at about 15 per cent per year, twice the rate of increase for world trade as a whole. However, the role of exports in Japan's mechanism of growth can easily be misinterpreted if attention is focused only on the rate of export growth. The degree of export dependence of the economy has remained almost constant, at about 9 per cent over the last decade, and this level is surprisingly low. ... In so far as the sources of a primary autonomous impetus to growth are concerned, therefore, the significant point is that Japan's postwar economic growth has not been of an export-led type, at least until very recently. . . . The basic function of the expansion of exports . . . has rather been a supporting one.

Maybe the best way to conclude this debate on Japan's export-led growth is to give some relevant data for the period 1981–5. According to figures just released by the Japanese Economic Planning Agency, the contribution of external demand to the increase in GNP was 1.5, 0.31, 1.5, 1.3 and 1.0 per cent respectively for these years. However, the contribution of domestic demand for the same years was 2.1, 2.8, 1.8, 3.8 and 3.7 per cent. Do these figures support the assertion that the Japanese economy is driven by export-led growth?

Japan has a very steady and healthy economy when compared with the rest of the OECD. Inflation has remained stable since 1981. It was at the low rate of around 2.8 per cent for the period 1981–5, and, according to World Bank data (which are much higher than the Japanese data), the average for the decade 1973–83 was 4.7 per cent. The 1981–5 equivalent figures for some members of the OECD were 5.5 per cent for the USA, 3.9 per cent for West Germany, 9.6 per cent for France and 7.3 per cent for the UK. It should also be added that the rate of wage increases in the manufacturing sector for the period 1981–5 was the lowest in Japan (4.7 per cent), with 6.5 per cent in the USA, 4.6 per cent in West Germany, 14.4 per cent in France and 10.4 per cent in the UK. At the same time, the level of productivity increase in the manufacturing sector for the same period was very high at 3.2 per cent, only exceeded by the UK at 3.5 per cent, the others recording 2.6 per cent, 2.5 per cent and 2.1 per cent respectively. Unemployment is also very low indeed since it has been about 2.5 per cent (2.9 per cent for the period 1981–5) of the labour force; during the late 1960s, such a low rate was equated with full employment, allowing for structural unemployment. However, many Japanese economists, point out that this low rate of unemployment is deceptive since some of what is classified in Japan as permanent employment would not pass as such in the rest of the OECD. Be that as it may, the equivalent 1981–5 figures for the selected OECD countries were 6.8 per cent for the USA, 9.2 per cent for West Germany and 13.2 per cent for the UK (France's figures are not available).

It should be added here that it is generally believed that Japan practices a system of 'lifetime employment': company employees should, may or even actually remain with the same company for life, entering it immediately after school or university and staying with it until retirement age, which is normally 55. However, 'lifetime employment' is a characteristic of large rather than small firms, and these days large firms employ only about 20 per cent of the total Japanese labour force. Moreover, the firms that practice 'lifetime employment', do not extend it to temporary workers and female employees, the former because they are not regarded as part of the 'family' and the latter because they are assumed to leave the firm at about the age of 25 when they get married. In addition, it is not true to assume that all full-time male employees of large firms stay with them throughout their working life since there is evidence to suggest that, for example, in 1975 about 10 per cent of the males in this category left their company before full retirement – see Clark (1979, pp. 150–2).

It should also be added that Japan has a rate of population growth of six per thousand and has the highest life expectancy in the world, i.e. Japan has now a fast-ageing population. With retirement age being 55, this is creating a real problem regarding a better pension scheme, improved health provision, competition for part-time work, etc. Indeed, the Japanese government is seriously examining the possibility of raising the retirement age.

Japan has a very high savings rate as well as a very high rate of investment. Fixed capital formation is presently about 17 per cent of GNP and has been so for a long time. This has been attributed to a tax system which is predominantly direct and whose rate is lower than in the EC and the USA. It has been further enhanced by the need to take out individual insurance for retirement. However, it has also been argued that there are some fundamental reasons for such a high savings rate which are a manifestation of Japanese society: the savings habit, or rather the mechanism that supports it (poor social security and housing due to a public emphasis on 'productive' investment), results in high savings rates which finance further 'productive' investment without improving social security or housing, making it necessary for people to save rather than spend their incomes. Freitas gives a good account of this:

Analysis of the need for savings for transactions and precautionary balances readily yields the conclusion that Japanese households require substantially higher savings balances to achieve equivalent patterns of consumption. In the case of transactions balances, the lack of synchronization of personal income and consumption over the life cycle has not been offset by as broad a set of institutional practices in Japan. For example, for many American workers it is no longer important to save for retirement years because of social security and private pension plans. In Japan, not only is social security smaller but private pension plans are still relatively rare. In their place is a practice of paying a lump-sum retirement allowance. However, compulsory retirement is still commonly around the age of fifty-five, and with a remaining life expectancy of over twenty years the usual levels of retirement allowance . . . are grossly inadequate. There are two ways in which this problem is addressed: greater accumulation of savings during the years of working as a regular employee and a second career as a nonregular worker following retirement. Nonregular worker categories receive substantially lower salaries . . . and receive few or no fringe benefits, causing great reliance on the accumulation of savings. . . . Some other spending needs in Japan that require greater savings balances are the costs of education . . . , housing . . . and even the cost of wedding (Freitas, 1984).

Since the end of the Second World War, technical innovation has been regarded as a major factor contributing to Japan's phenomenal growth rate: research suggests that its contribution has been equal to half of the growth rate (Mashimoto, 1982). This is in spite of the fact that Japan started as a mere imitator in this field, but as Sato (1985) has demonstrated, Japan's experience with regard to imitation was no different from that of any other nation within the OECD. Hence, the image in the West of Japan as a nation which excels in borrowing technology belongs to the distant past, since Japan today leads in the field of technology in many areas, particularly in technology-intensive industries such as electronics and precision instruments.

Expenditure on R&D is, of course, a major contributor to technological innovation. Japan's gross expenditure on R&D in 1983 was equal to 2.6 per cent of GDP. This compares with 2.7 per cent in the USA, 2.6 per cent in West Germany, 2.5 per cent in Sweden, 2.3 per cent in the UK and 2.2 per cent in France. However, these percentages are deceptive since in Japan R&D expenditure tends to be concentrated in the areas with the highest percentage pay-off: it is a well-known fact that R&D expenditure 'produces results' at a much higher rate in Japan than in the rest of the OECD. The combination of this reality and the actual percentage of GDP spent on R&D means that 'technology in Japan is already at the same level as that in the United States and has surpassed that in the European nations' (Shishido, 1985).

The concentration of R&D efforts in the areas where the potential outcome is one for direct commercial exploitation has paid dividends for Japan. Concentration has been brought about by companies carrying out research in their own laboratories. Hence, the problems faced in the UK, where the fruits of research carried out in the universities are desperately awaiting commercial exploitation, rarely occur in Japan. Moreover, the Japanese educational system has a direct bearing on this achievement: more emphasis is put on the learning of subjects such as science, mathematics, statistics, etc. and on practical experience which is reinforced by immediate training when the graduates join the companies. Education also contributes in a wider respect than is depicted here since in Japan the enrolment ratio at the university level is just over 30 per cent making Japan the second in this league, the USA being at the top with over 50 per cent. The equivalent ratios for France, West Germany and the UK are 25.5, 27.6 and 20.1 per cent respectively – see El-Agraa and Ichii (1985) and El-Agraa (1986b) for detailed information.

Given that research efforts are concentrated in areas of direct commercial exploitation, it should not come as a surprise to learn that Japan still lags behind in terms of general technological 'creativity'. Shishido (1985) pointed out:

Japanese society places great importance on conformity and stifles individual deviance. This ... has played an important role in Japan's imitation of foreign technologies and is the reason for her good performance in economic activities ... Japan is not actually held back by any lack of creativity, but several features which are advantages in imitation may turn into disadvantages when it comes to creating technology. A centralized education system with uniform standards can assure a high average level of skill in the computer age. Such a system may be more acceptable in Japan than in other advanced nations in the information era. However, such uniformity in education which makes society very reluctant to accept the sort of individualistic personalities in which creativity is developed may prove a big obstacle to any improvement in Japanese creativity.

Although about 25 per cent of the national budget for 1983 was financed by loans, and the national debt amounted to 40 per cent of GNP, military expenditure is limited to a ceiling of 1 per cent of GNP (a decision reached in November 1976). In terms of a percentage of GNP, this compares with about 6.7 per cent for the USA, 4.1 per cent for France, 3.4 per cent for West Germany, 2.8 per cent for Italy, 3.2 per cent for Sweden and 5.3 per cent for the UK. This relatively low level of military expenditure is due to both historical and political reasons: Japan's military commitment is to 'self-defence'. To be brief, Japan's defence strategy is 'exclusively defensive', *Senshu-boei* in Japanese. This is based on the constraints of Article 9 of the Japanese Constitution. 'Exclusive defence' is a posture of passive defence which incorporates six elements:

(a) A policy of pacifism reinforced by the right of self-defence which requires the fulfilment of three pre-conditions: a sudden and unjustifiable aggression, the absence of other appropriate means to deal with this aggression and the use of the minimum necessary armed force;
(b) Self-defence capability should be the minimum necessary for self-defence – Japan cannot possess weapons such as ICBMs and long-range strategic bombers since these can be used to attack and destroy other countries;
(c) The prohibition of the dispatch of armed forces overseas;
(d) The prohibition of the exercise of the right of collective self-defence;
(e) The three non-nuclear principles, i.e. Japan will not possess, produce or bring into its territory nuclear weapons;

(f) The three principles prohibiting arms exports, i.e. not to export weapons to countries if they are 'communist', in conflict or designated by the UN not to receive weapons.

Recently, however, there have been some indications to suggest that debate is imminent regarding the raising of this ceiling; a committee was recently set up to look into it. All this is a reaction to US accusations that Japan is a 'free-rider' in the area of defending its national boundaries, but by no stretch of imagination can one see how Japan can increase its defence expenditure far beyond this limit, given its commitment to 'self-defence'.

As to the Japanese welfare system, Kitamura (1976) stated:

Japan's postwar performance seems to have been an outstanding exception to the trend of the Western mixed market economy. Whereas other developed countries generally managed to speed up the pace of economic expansion and attain high levels of prosperity without imposing greater burdens on wage-earners, it was a striking characteristic of the Japanese growth process that the share of income accruing to labour tended to decline over the whole period. Parallel with the shift of functional distribution of income in favour of profits and property incomes, the national level of consumption tended to lag considerably behind the rise in the level of output. This was expressed in the continual decline in the relative proportion of national product devoted to personal consumption and benefits. Although the absolute level of living of the average Japanese must have risen quite substantially during the past twenty-five years, reflecting growing productive capacity of the economy, the rise was hardly commensurate with what the people would have expected as legitimate shares of the fruits of economic growth.

Another aspect of the welfare system is the distribution of income. Writing in terms of regional income disparities, Kitamura (1976) stated that, at the time of writing, incomes were 'almost completely equalized as between the urban and rural areas, partly through the artificially raised price level of agricultural products and partly owing to the tendency of rural households to depend increasingly on non-farm incomes'. With regard to personal income distribution, it may suffice to point to some of today's realities. One of Japan's most distinguished journalists, Yukio Matsuyama (Chief Editorial Staff, *Asahi Shinbun* newspaper), points to the fact that his net salary (he is probably the highest paid journalist in Japan) is only four times that of a new graduate just joining his paper. Statistics indicate that this is the case in practically the whole of Japan. Furthermore, over 90 per cent of the Japanese think of themselves as 'middle class'. Hence, it would seem that the picture has changed much since the time when Kitamura was writing.

However, there is another side to the coin. Consider the question: are the economic gaps among consumers growing wider? The answer requires information regarding income differentials; this is provided in Table 2.4. The table lists indices of income by occupational category and by year, using the national average for non-farm households in the corresponding year as the basis for comparison. Ozawa (1986) pointed to five phenomena that can be observed from the data on the period since the second half of the 1960s: the income gap between farm and non-farm households has widened; the incomes of 'executives' have further outpaced those of other wage and salary earners; the gap has widened between government workers and those in the private sector; the edge over the national average enjoyed by farmers living in the Tokyo area has been enhanced; and the advantageous position enjoyed by wage and salary earners in the Tokyo area has been eroded. Of these five developments, the first four represent a widening in income differentials. Ozawa explains these contradictions to the higher degree of income equalities shown by the decline of the Gini coefficient (which measures inequality) used by the government and other researchers:

First, because data for wage and salary earners' households are easiest to obtain, economists normally use these data alone when calculating the Gini coefficient. This means that the larger disparities of [the first, second and fourth] phenomena above are not reflected.

Second, the Gini coefficient for wage and salary earners ended its decline in the 1960s and has been level for more than a decade. This apparent levelling out, however, probably conceals the widening differentials between government and private-sector workers and the narrowing differentials between Tokyo-area workers and the national average, which have cancelled each other out.

Considering differentials in terms of the stock of personal wealth, using the net financial assets holdings by occupational category given in index form in Table 2.5, Ozawa pointed to three realities: the

Table 2.4 Trends in income differentials. (100 = national average for non-farm households)

	All of Japan					Tokyo area	
	Blue-collar workers	White-collar workers	Government workers	Executives	Farmers	Wage and salary earners	Farmers
1960	78.1	123.2	106.6	265.6	—	—	—
1964	84.3	121.7	108.4	232.3	106.4	124.4	—
1968[a]	87.0	110.8	113.7	187.0	120.6	111.7	116.5[b]
1972	81.1	113.9	110.5	193.8	118.2	110.6	126.9
1976	79.4	107.1	118.3	195.8	124.8	105.3	138.1
1979	81.1	104.8	114.7	201.8	123.3	103.1	128.3
1982	82.5	109.0	116.2	205.5	123.1	105.7	130.3

Data sources: For farm households, *Noka keizai chosa hokoku* (Survey on Farm Finances), Ministry of Agriculture, Forestry and Fisheries; for others, *Chochiku doko chosa hokoku* (Survey on Saving Trends), Management and Coordination Agency.
[a] This year was apparently when income differentials were smallest.
[b] 1967.

Source: M. Ozawa, 'Japanese consumer mysteries', *Economic Eye* (Keizai Koho Centre, Tokyo, June 1986).

disparity between farm and non-farm stocks of assets has widened even faster than that between their respective income flows; wage and salary earners in the Tokyo area hold a relatively low level of assets; and farmers in the Tokyo area have large and growing stocks of assets. Ozawa claims that the widening in the gaps is due to the fact that wage and salary earners have had to pay farmers huge sums of money in order to buy land for housing purposes, and in the Tokyo area, where land prices are extremely high (see Chapter 3), 'enormous' differentials have arisen between farmers and others.

Therefore, it would seem that the picture has changed somewhat since the time Kitamura was writing.

Japan's official development assistance (ODA) stood at 0.35 per cent of GNP in 1984. This compares with 0.53 per cent for the EC as a whole, 0.23 per cent for the USA and 0.39 per cent for all developed and advanced nations. Of course, this falls short of the LDCs' demand for 1 per cent of GNP, but the only countries that come consistently close to this figure are Holland and Norway which sometimes exceed it – see Table 2.6. However, the Japanese government committed itself to an ODA target for the period 1981–5 of $21.36 billion in an effort to double its ODA for the previous five-year period. The net result was a disappointment since what was achieved in 1985 was only $18.07 billion, with the 1985 contribution amounting to a mere 0.29 per cent of GNP. This drop of 12.1 per cent from the previous year was attributed mainly to a sharp drop in multilateral ODA in the form of capital subscription and similar payments to the International Development Association (IDA) and other international financial institutions. One should add that the Japanese government expressed great concern over this development and immediately launched a new programme, submitted in a preliminary report to the Development Assistance Committee (DAC) of the OECD, to double its ODA by 1992; furthermore, calculations by ODA experts at the Japanese Ministry of Finance indicated that a 15 per cent drop in the value of the yen during 1981–5 was the main factor in Japan's failure to achieve its target for 1985.

Although about a dozen major companies (producing mainly cars, cameras, TV sets and other electronic goods) with wide international reputations have become the symbol of Japanese efficiency in trade and industry (such as Mitsubishi, Mitsui, Nissan, Sony, Sumitomo, Toyota, etc.), they represent only the better known part of the country's industrial organisation. There is a large number of small and medium size firms which often act as sub-contractors to the major companies. According to *MITI Handbook* (1985a, p. 325):

Table 2.5   Trends in net financial asset differentials (100 = national average for non-farm households)

	All of Japan		Tokyo area	
	Non-farmers	Farmers	Wage and salary earners	Farmers
1964	100.0	101.6	121.1	—
1968	100.0	116.4	94.3	166.1[a]
1972	100.0	142.7	86.4	231.4
1976	100.0	170.4	94.1	277.3
1979	100.0	203.3	76.1	306.0
1982	100.0	201.3	90.8	306.3

Data sources: For farm households, *Noka keizai chosa hokoku* (Survey on Farm Finances), Ministry of Agriculture, Forestry, and Fisheries; for others, *Chochiku doko chosa hokoku* (Survey on Saving Trends), Management and Coordination Agency.
[a] 1967.

Source: M. Ozawa, 'Japanese consumer mysteries', *Economic Eye* (Keizai Koho Centre, Tokyo, June 1986).

Small and medium sized enterprises occupy an extremely important position in the Japanese economy, employing about 81 percent of the labour force and accounting for some 99 percent of business establishments, 52 percent of the value of shipments in the manufacturing industry, and 62 percent of the value of sales in the wholesale sector. Smaller businesses not only play a big role in the development of the national economy and in the improvement of national welfare but also help to prevent the concentration of economic power. In view of the importance of small business, the Small and Medium Enterprise Agency has been given the duty of establishing adequate conditions for its nurturing by promoting the development of smaller firms and helping them improve their management.

The total number of enterprises in 1981 amounted to about 6.5 million – see Table 2.7 for information on the structure of establishments in Japan. It has to be noted that some of these small firms are very efficient: the co-existence of large and small firms is facilitated by a process whereby the parent companies purchase their parts from the

Table 2.6 Value of development assistance and per cent of GNP by DAC countries

	1983			1984			
	Million US dollars	% of GNP	Per capita (US dollars)	Million US dollars	Growth rate (%)	% of GNP	Per capita (US dollars)
DAC total	27540	0.36	40.5	28647	4.0	0.36	42.1
Japan	3761	0.32	31.8	4319	14.8	0.35	36.7
Australia	753	0.49	49.6	773	2.6	0.45	52.0
Austria	158	0.23	20.9	181	15.0	0.28	24.1
Belgium	487	0.60	48.4	434	−10.9	0.56	44.0
Canada	1429	0.45	58.0	1625	13.7	0.50	67.1
Denmark	395	0.73	77.0	449	13.7	0.85	87.6
Finland	153	0.32	31.7	178	16.3	0.36	37.1
France	3815	0.74	72.2	3790	−0.7	0.77	70.2
Germany (FR)	3176	0.48	51.6	2782	−12.4	0.45	45.1
Italy	833	0.24	14.4	1105	30.1	0.32	19.3
Netherlands	1195	0.91	83.5	1268	6.1	1.02	89.0
New Zealand	61	0.28	19.3	59	−3.3	0.27	18.9
Norway	584	1.09	142.1	526	−9.9	0.99	128.3
Sweden	754	0.84	93.5	741	−1.7	0.80	89.0
Switzerland	320	0.31	49.5	286	−10.6	0.30	41.6
United Kingdom	1610	0.35	28.7	1432	−11.1	0.33	25.0
United States	8055	0.24	34.6	8698	8.0	0.24	37.8

Source: Ministry of Foreign Affairs (Economic Cooperation Bureau) 'Press release'.

sub-contractors and assemble them; hence, in order to maintain the high quality of their products as well as improve their productivity rate, they have to utilise equally efficient sub-contractors – this system has been labelled the 'dual structure of Japanese industry'.

The Japanese distribution system is vertically integrated, with the usual sequence of producer–wholesaler–retailer being interrupted by an extra link between the producer and the wholesaler. This extra link sometimes deals with the distribution of a whole firm's output, hence giving it monopoly of its distribution. Moreover, since in Japan everything is based on personal interaction, it is natural that there is a strong link between the domestic producers and those dealing with

Table 2.7   Establishments and persons engaged by industry (in thousands)

	1954	1963	1972	1981
Total				
Establishments	3309[a]	4016[b]	5309	6488
Persons engaged	18788[a]	30145[b]	43949	51545
Agriculture, forestry and fisheries[1]				
Establishments	—	3	22	26
Persons engaged	—	105	287	308
Mining				
Establishments	8.3	10	8.4	7
Persons engaged	477	370	187	129
Construction				
Establishments	187	245	411	551
Persons engaged	1245	2423	4047	4969
Manufacturing				
Establishments	528	620	794	873
Persons engaged	6196	10462	13336	12896
Wholesale and retail trade				
Establishments	1609	1962	2519	3028
Persons engaged	4963	7997	11721	14897
Finance and insurance				
Establishments	57	56	62	84
Persons engaged	682	963	1417	1711
Real estate[2]				
Establishments	16	82	155	238
Persons engaged	47	185	404	629

Table 2.7 Continued

Transport and communications[3]				
Establishments	77	101	122	161
Persons engaged	1637	2494	3128	3401
Utilities				
Establishments	1.6	12	12	11
Persons engaged	200	235	277	322
Services[4]				
Establishments	825	926	1160	1464
Persons engaged	3341	4910	7597	10548
Government				
Establishments	—	—	44	46
Persons engaged	—	—	1548	1735

Notes:

[1] Until 1966, excluding Veterinary Services.

[2] In 1951, excluding terminal companies.

[3] Until 1966, including Broadcasting Services, and in 1951 also including Veterinary Services, but excluding Broadcasting Services.

[4] Until 1966, including Veterinary Services, but excluding Broadcasting Services.

[a] Excluding Agriculture, Forestry and Fisheries, and Government.

[b] Excluding Government.

[c] The data is based on the latest census of 1981.

Source: Japan Statistical Yearbook, 1985.

distribution, a link which is often reflected in the dependence of stockists on domestic producers. This applies particularly to certain sectors such as household electrical appliances and mass-market electrical goods, where over 60 per cent of stockists depend on domestic producers. This system, however, works against the 'outsiders', and hence it led the British Prime Minister to assert that this immensely complicated Japanese distribution system is deeply rooted in Japanese culture and in 'buy Japanese' tendencies. (For more details, see Chapter 3.)

It is frequently claimed that Japan has a banking system which is compartmentalised and more subject to supervision by the monetary and fiscal authorities than its counterparts in the OECD. It is true that the banking sector was divided into functioning groups (Spindler, 1984): the larger commercial banks (thirteen city banks), long-term credit banks (comprising three long-term credit banks and seven trust banks), regional commercial banks (63), credit associations, foreign banks (71), etc. – see Table 2.8. Some would argue that this was due to the belief that it was better for each group to specialise in the limited services it was assigned and also that the monetary authorities had to effectively control every institution and, if necessary, scrutinise every activity. The monetary authorities tried to manage the banking sector in order to allocate the funds, mostly from the household and business sectors, to certain favourably-designated industries. Spindler (1984) clarifies the complexity of the Japanese banking system:

> Japan's highly centralized government is able to use the Japanese commercial banking sector to serve a range of national objectives. The government has obtained this capability in part through its implementation of a structural policy for the entire banking system and in part through careful ongoing supervision of Japanese

Table 2.8   Structure of the Japanese banking system. Year-end 1982

Institution	Number of organisations	Assets (billions of dollars)	Percentage of system assets
Commercial banks[a]	157	1205.7	45.6
City banks	13	603.8	22.9
Regional banks	63	348.9	13.2
Long-term credit banks	3	135.3	5.1
Trust banks	7	70.9	2.7
Foreign banks operating branches	71	46.5	1.8
Government-owned financial institutions	12	232.6[b]	8.8
Export-Import Bank of Japan	1	25.6[b]	1.0
Japan Development Bank	1	26.9[b]	1.0
Others	10	180.1[b]	6.8
Government	2	397.4	15.0
Postal savings	1	314.4[c]	11.9
Postal life insurance and postal annuity	1	83.0	3.1
Small business financial institutions	1046	484.9	18.4
Mutual savings and loan banks	71	162.9	6.2
Credit associations	456	204.0	7.7
National Federation of Credit Associations	1	18.0	0.7
Shoko Chukin Bank	1	29.3	1.1

Table 2.8 *Continued*

Credit cooperatives	468	45.9	1.7
National Federation of Credit Cooperatives	1	5.0	0.2
Labour credit associations	47	16.3	0.6
National Federation of Labour Credit Associations	1	3.5	0.1
Financial institutions for agriculture, etc.	6131	320.6	12.1
Central Cooperative Bank for Agriculture and Forestry (*Norinchukin*)	1	59.4	2.2
Credit federations of agriculture cooperatives	47[d]	92.0	3.5
Agriculture cooperatives	4359[d]	152.6	5.8
Credit federations of fishery cooperatives	35	5.9	0.2
Fishery cooperatives	1689[e]	10.6[e]	0.4
Total	7348	2641.2	100.0

Notes:

[a] Excludes assets of Japanese banks' foreign branches and foreign subsidiaries. The assets of branches of foreign banks in Japan are based on a summation of 'principal accounts' of those branches. Number of foreign banks operating branches reflects data as of March 1982.

[b] Based on summation of 'principal accounts' for each government-owned financial institution.

[c] Represents balance of postal savings as of September 1982.

[d] As of year-end 1981.

[e] As of November 1982.

Source: J. A. Spindler, *The Politics of International Credit: Private Finance and Foreign Policy in Germany and Japan* (Washington, DC: Brookings Institution, 1984).

commercial banking. The government has obtained a further measure of influence by functioning as a key intermediary itself in Japanese financial markets. Japan's financial system has been categorized as a credit-based, price-administered one, in which the state plays the leading role; this contrasts noticeably with Germany's credit-based, bank-dominated financial system. . . . For the Japanese authorities, the commercial banking sector has proven an important conduit for following and influencing activities in key industries. While the leading banks have tended to exert considerable influence over business, the relationship has had a degree of mutual dependence. One cannot accurately represent Japanese banks as omnipotent over the country's private sector. Still, the banks, responsive to strong central government signals, incentives, and supervision, have served as the most important financiers of Japan's corporate and industrial growth.

The Japanese banking system reflects higher concentration and greater specialization than its American counterpart. The Japanese government has kept concentration from advancing too far, though, and no "Big Three" institutions dominate banking in Japan as do in the Federal Republic of Germany. As a consequence, Japan falls somewhere between Germany and the United States in terms of concentration.

The banking system is, of course, the main pillar of the Japanese financial system; hence, it is important to have some notion about how the financial system as a whole has been liberalised and internationalised over the past decade or so. Chart 2.1 clearly sets out these developments which are self-explanatory. All that one needs to add is that the Japanese government has made great efforts in the area of liberalising and internationalising its financial markets.

Japan has developed a specific system of 'standards' and 'certification procedures' which have been labelled in the West as a 'considerable obstacle to foreign exporters', hence the frequent accusation that Japan's market is relatively uneasy to penetrate by foreign firms. In short, the relative 'unopenness' of the Japanese economy has been attributed to: the homogeneous structure of the Japanese domestic market, in which exclusive loyalties unite groups of banks, manufacturers, sub-contractors, distributors and traders in fierce inter-group competition against newcomers and outsiders; the apparent incapacity of the Japanese distribution system to handle foreign manufactures in large volumes; and the lack of interest of some foreign exporters in a market which has long been protected and is apparently unpromising, at a time when other markets have seemed easier and more lucrative.

THE INTERNATIONAL SECTOR

Given this bird's-eye view of the domestic economy, let us turn to a more detailed review of the country's external trade position. During the late 1960s and early 1970s, Japan had an overall surplus on the current trade account including invisibles. However, since 1973 the picture has changed drastically, arguably due mainly to the oil crises and changes in the cyclical trends in the state of the world economy, but the Japanese economy has shown a remarkable capacity to ride this storm. In short, in 1973, after a long period of surpluses, Japan had a deficit of $1.4 billion. This increased to $6.6 billion in 1974. From 1976 to 1978, Japan had surpluses which rose from $2.4 billion to $18.4 billion. There followed two years of deficits which came with the second oil crisis: $7.5 billion in 1979 and $10.9 billion in 1980. Since then, the tendency has been one of increasing surpluses: $8.6, $6.9, $20.5 and $33.6 billion in respectively 1981, 1982, 1983 and 1984. This information is given in Table 2.9, with Table 2.10 giving a breakdown for the EC, USA and the rest of the world.

However, Japan's balance of transfers and services continues to show heavy deficits, but it is improving in relative terms all the time. This information is provided in Table 2.11, both globally and with the EC and USA. The recent improvement has been attributed to a rapid increase in the income received from Japanese investment abroad.

The inflow and outflow of long-term capital has been on the increase since the late 1970s. This could be attributed mainly to the 'liberalisation measures' that were introduced in 1980 by the 'foreign exchange law'. Japan's capital outflow rose from $5 billion in 1972 to $27 billion in 1982. Over the same period, inflows of foreign capital rose from $0.5 billion to $12 billion. The capital outflows were accounted for mainly by purchases of foreign securities and offshore loans, while the bulk of foreign capital inflows stemmed from purchases of Japanese securities and bonds issued abroad by Japanese companies. As Table 2.11 indicates, the member countries of the EC accounted for a major part of Japan's capital transactions in the form of portfolio investment. In short, in contrast to the trade balance, Japan's long-term capital balance has been deteriorating steadily since 1965, except in 1980.

An important consideration regarding international trade performance is the fluctuation in a country's exchange rate. The yen has fluctuated against both the US dollar and the European Currency Unit (ECU). Against the ECU, the yen appreciated by about 36 per cent between 1980 and 1983. Over the same period, however, the yen depreciated by about 20 per cent against the US dollar. Of course, there are many parameters involved, but it could be argued that the relative weakness of the yen against the dollar could be partly due to capital inflows in the form of portfolio investment which were

Chart 2.1 Chronology of liberalisation/internationalisation of financial markets, etc.

	Short-term financial markets				Portfolio investment, etc.	
	Deposit and inter-bank markets		Loans and open markets			
	Domestic finance	International finance	Domestic finance	International finance	Domestic finance	International finance
1973		11 Partial relaxation of	6 Expansion of public offerings of short-term government securities (diversified periods, issuance of low face-value bonds, etc.).	5 Expansion of foreign currency loans to residents. 11 Virtual prohibition on		5 Raising of the ceiling on stock acquisition by non-residents (pending agreement by the said corporation).

acquiring short-term, foreign securities (6 months or less).
- Relaxation of restrictions on export credit (the ceiling subject to permission raised from $5000 to $10 000).

12 Abolition of restrictions on stock acquisition by non-residents (within the limit of disposure).

1 Self-restraint to maintain zero net increase for foreign securities investment by banks, securities houses,

restrictions on conversion of foreign funds into free yen on accounts for non-residents.
- Approval of forward exchange contract transactions for resident's foreign currency deposits.

12 Reduction of the reserve ratio for the increase in non-resident free-yen debts (50% → 10%).

1 Restrictions on the balance of residents' foreign currency deposit accounts (not exceeding the month-end.

1 Relaxation of restrictions on export credit (the ceiling subject to permission raised from $10000 to $100 000).

1974

Chart 2.1   Continued

Short-term financial markets				Portfolio investment, etc.	
Deposit and inter-bank markets		Loans and open markets			
Domestic finance	International finance	Domestic finance	International finance	Domestic finance	International finance
	average outstanding balance of Oct.–Dec. 1973)		● Prohibition on acquisition of short-term foreign securities (up to one year) by residents. 7 Relaxation of restrictions on export credit (the ceiling subject to permission raised from $100 000 to $500 000). 8 Liberalization of acquisition by non-residents of		investment trust and insurance companies.

1975		9 Discontinuation of the reserve ratio on non-resident free-yen debts	5 Abolition of short-term loans' voluntarily restricted interest rates by the Federation of Bankers' Associations of Japan, etc.	short-term government securities.	
					6 Abolition of self-restraints (except for banks) on foreign securities investment
1976			3 Authorisation of Gensaki transaction		
1977				1 Issuance of discount government bonds	

Chart 2.1 Continued

| Short-term financial markets | | | | Portfolio investment, etc. | |
| Deposit and inter-bank markets | | Loans and open markets | | | |
Domestic finance	International finance	Domestic finance	International finance	Domestic finance	International finance
					3 Abolition of restraints by banks on foreign securities investment
				4 Establishment of more flexible conditions for issuing deficit-financed government bonds (sellable after a year from the date of issuance).	
	6 Transition from restriction on conversion of foreign funds		6 Abolition of restrictions on acquisition by residents of		6 Transition to automatic recognition of acquisition of

stock and bonds by non-residents.		
short-term, foreign securities.		8 Transition to automatic recognition for acquisition of beneficiary certificates with a residual life of less than six months.
into yen to that of spot position. ● Establishment of reserve ratio for the balance of foreign currency deposits and non-resident free-yen debts (0.25 per cent for each). ● Abolition of Article-five yen accounts. ● Abolition of restrictions on the balance of resident foreign currency deposits, etc.		

Chart 2.1 Continued

| Short-term financial markets | | | | Portfolio investment, etc. | |
| Deposit and inter-bank markets | | Loans and open markets | | | |
Domestic finance	International finance	Domestic finance	International finance	Domestic finance	International finance
	11 Establishment of reserve ratio for the increase in non-resident free-yen accounts (50%)	11 Discontinuation of public issuance of short-term government securities.		10. Relaxation of restrictions on government construction bonds (sellable after a year from issuance). 12 More flexible implementation of BOJ's bond operations (from quota system to volume-upon-request system)	

1978					
	3 Raising of reserve ratio for the increase in non-resident free-yen accounts (from 50 to 100 per cent). 4 Expansion of resident foreign currency deposit system (recognition of	3 Resumption of public issuance of short-term government securities.	3 Relaxation of restrictions on terms of import usance facilities extended by banks in Japan (from 120 days to a year for capital goods, etc.). ● Liberalisation of usance in different currencies.	1 More flexible handling of prices of BOJ's bond operations (the basis of listed levels changed to public issuance tender system).	3 Prohibition of acquisition of yen-denominated securities (up to five years and a month) by non-residents 4 Comprehensive permission to reserve foreign future foreign securities owned under

Chart 2.1 Continued

	Short-term financial markets				Portfolio investment, etc.	
	Deposit and inter-bank markets		Loans and open markets			
	Domestic finance	International finance	Domestic finance	International finance	Domestic finance	International finance
		up to ¥3 million in yen as a revenue source).				overseas securities investment.
	6 More flexible management of call rate quotations ● Recognition of reselling/ buying of bills.			6 Relaxation of restrictions on terms of import usance facilities extended by banks in Japan (from 120 days to 140 days).	6 Public issuance tender starts from mid-term (three year) government bonds. ● BOJ begins government bond-buyer operation under tender system. 9 Government bond-buying by Trust Fund Bureau.	

1979	10 Start of seven-day call trading. 11 Start of one-month trading.	1 Lowering of reserve ratio for the increase of non-resident free-yen debts (from 100 per cent to 50 per cent).	10 Expansion of repurchase selling quota for city banks (from ¥5 billion to ¥20 billion).	12 Transition to multiple pricing determination system for BOJ's government bond-buying operation.	1 Partial relaxation of prohibition measures on acquisition of yen-denominated bonds by non-residents (from within five years and a month to within one year

Chart 2.1 Continued

| Short-term financial markets | | | | Portfolio investment, etc. | |
| Deposit and inter-bank markets | | Loans and open markets | | | |
Domestic finance	International finance	Domestic finance	International finance	Domestic finance	International finance
	2 Abolition of reserve ratio for the increase in non-resident free-yen debts.				and one month). 2 Abolition of prohibition measures on acquisition of yen-denominated bonds by non-residents.
4 Abolition of quotation of the call rate. Start of 2- to 6-day call trading. 5 Establishment of CD (free-interest, ceiling 25 per cent of equity capital).		4 Expansion of Gensaki quota for city banks (from ¥20 billion to ¥50 billion).	5 Extension of import usance term from 140 days to 180 days.	4 Establishment of public bond-trust funds. 5 Start of government bond purchase with national debt consolid-	

• ation fund. • Issuance of two year government bonds by tender system. • Mobilisation of BOJ's government bond-buying operation (to be implemented upon necessity, adoption of smaller per-account volume). 12 Changes in assessment methods for bonds owned by financial institutions (from 'cost or market' method only to choice of this method or cost method).	• Abolition of restrictions on export prepayment. • Lifting of prohibition repurchase trading by non-residents. • Lifting of prohibition on short-term impact loans (subject to permission). 12 More flexible management in issuing permission to introduce impact loans.	10 Abolition of (Yamagoe) bill rate.

Chart 2.1 Continued

	Short-term financial markets				Portfolio investment, etc.	
	Deposit and inter-bank markets		Loans and open markets			
	Domestic finance	International finance	Domestic finance	International finance	Domestic finance	International finance
1980	3 Expansion of CD issuance limit (from 25 per cent of equity capital to 50 per cent).	3 More flexible measures implemented to procure overseas funds through head office/branch free yen accounts (exempted from			1 Establishment of mid-term government bond fund. 2 Establishment of central depository system for government bonds.	

restrictions on spot position).
• Liberalisation of interest rates for public authorities' free yen.

4 Abolition of ceilings for city banks on selling repurchase deals.

5 Relaxation of restrictions on selling government bonds (from 'one year after issuance' to 'the time of listing').

6 Issuance of four-year government bonds by tender system.

11 Sell and buy operation of bills and call money

Chart 2.1   Continued

	Short-term financial markets				Portfolio investment, etc.	
	Deposit and inter-bank markets		Loans and open markets			
	Domestic finance	*International finance*	*Domestic finance*	*International finance*	*Domestic finance*	*International finance*
	authorised for local and trust banks. • Authorisation given to four top securities companies to take call money (up to ¥10 billion per company).	12 Transition from non-resident free yen account to non-resident yen accounts system. • Exemption of registration		12 Liberalisation of impact loans. • Liberalisation of import usance (within one year).		12 Liberalisation of acquisiton of securities (excluding direct investment) via nominated securities companies.

<table>
<tr><td>

requirement for major foreign exchange banks regarding issuance of foreign securities (overseas CD) and acquisition of foreign securities (over one year).

● Liberalisation of resident foreign currency deposits for Japanese foreign exchange banks.

1 Raising of reserve ratio for foreign currency deposits, etc. (time-deposit type: 0.25 to 0.5 per cent; others 0.25 to 1.25 per cent).

</td></tr>
<tr><td>1981</td></tr>
</table>

Chart 2.1 Continued

| Short-term financial markets | | | | Portfolio investment, etc. | |
| Deposit and inter-bank markets | | Loans and open markets | | | |
Domestic finance	International finance	Domestic finance	International finance	Domestic finance	International finance
3 Introduction of non-standard loans system.	3 Lowering of reserve ratio for foreign currency deposits (time deposit type: from 0.5 per cent to 0.375 per cent. Others: from 1.25 to 0.5 per cent).			3 Establishment of collateral treatment for BOJ loans of discount government bonds.	
4 Permission call loans by city banks.		4 Establishment of market selling of short-term government securities owned by BOJ.		4 Shortening of selling restriction period for government bonds (from 'up till listing'	

	to three months later). 9 Issuance of non-market type (6-year) government bonds. 10 Establishment of accumulation-type government bond fund.		
		• Authorisation for city banks to make loans by Gensaki transaction.	
1981			12 Expansion of call money procurement ceiling by four major securities companies (from ¥10 billion to ¥30 billion each). • Authorisation of call money procurement by eight medium-class securities companies (¥5 billion each).

Chart 2.1 Continued

| | Short-term financial markets | | | | Portfolio investment, etc. | |
| | Deposit and inter-bank markets | | Loans and open markets | | | |
	Domestic finance	International finance	Domestic finance	International finance	Domestic finance	International finance
1982	1 Additional authorisation for two medium-class securities companies to engage in call money procurement.			6 Authorisation for life insurance	4 Short-term credit dealers start securities operations.	3 Self-restraint on acquisition of zero coupon bonds.

1983	2 Expansion of CD issuance limit (percentage to net worth): Feb.–Mar. 1983: 55% Apr.–Jun. 1983: 60% Jul.–Sept. 1983: 65%		companies to own overseas CD and CP, etc. 7 Authorisation for non-life insurance companies to own overseas CD and CP, etc.	11 Initial treatment of bank debenture fund.	2 Resumption of marketing of zero coupon bonds.

Chart 2.1 Continued

| Short-term financial markets | | | | Portfolio investment, etc. | |
| Deposit and inter-bank markets | | Loans and open markets | | | |
Domestic finance	International finance	Domestic finance	International finance	Domestic finance	International finance
Oct.–Dec. 1983: 70% Jan. 1984 on: 75%		6 Six securities companies begin extending loans with public bonds as collateral.		4 Over-the-counter government bond-selling by banks begins.	5 Initial acquisition of overseas bonds with postal life insurance funds.

51

1984				
1 Lowering of minimum unit of CD issuance (from ¥500 million to ¥300 million).			8 Twenty-year term, fixed rate government bonds issued. ● Release of government bond time-deposit accounts. 9 Release of government bond trust accounts. ● Release of consolidated compound-interest accounts. 10 Establishment of over-the-counter selling of mid-term government bonds. 4 Mid-term government bond funding	4 Start of domestic marketing of
			4 Abolition of the principle of actual demand	

Chart 2.1 *Continued*

	Short-term financial markets				Portfolio investment, etc.	
	Deposit and inter-bank markets		Loans and open markets			
	Domestic finance	*International finance*	*Domestic finance*	*International finance*	*Domestic finance*	*International finance*
		6 Abolition of restrictions on conversion of foreign funds into yen.		concerning forward exchange contracts. ● Extension of import usance term (from one year to two years). 6 Lifting of ban on Euro-yen loans for residents.	marketing initiated by credit associations and securities companies on a combined basis.	overseas CD and CP. 6 Start of dealing by financial institutions in already-issued bonds.

Source: Japanese Economic Planning Agency's *Economic Survey of Japan 1983–1984.*

Table 2.9   Japan's current balance (including invisible trade)
1965–82, in billion US dollars

Year	Exports	Imports	Current balance
1965	8.425	8.169	0.283
1966	9.776	9.523	0.253
1967	10.442	11.663	−1.221
1968	12.972	12.987	−0.015
1969	15.990	15.024	0.996
1970	19.318	18.881	0.437
1971	24.121	19.797	4.324
1972	29.088	23.863	5.225
1973	37.017	38.389	−1.372
1974	55.426	61.982	−6.556
1975	55.729	57.842	−2.113
1976	67.321	64.894	2.427
1977	81.083	71.340	9.743
1978	98.353	79.923	18.430
1979	102.299	109.831	−7.532
1980	130.441	141.295	−10.854
1981	151.495	142.866	8.629
1982	138.403	131.516	6.887
1983	146.928	126.393	20.535
1984	170.114	136.503	33.611

Sources: International Financial Statistics, 1983, Japan Tariff Association's
The Summary Report Trade of Japan, various years and Bank of Japan's
Balance of Payments Monthly.

induced by the differentials in the two countries' interest rates. In addition, the yen's share in world reserves (about 3–4 per cent) is not in proportion to Japan's relative standing in international trade; for example, the Deutschmark has a share of 12 per cent when West Germany accounts for only 9 per cent of world trade.

Table 2.11 does not give all the information which is needed to examine Japan's trade balance by 'area' distribution. This is given in Table 2.12, both in terms of absolute values and percentage share. The table shows quite clearly that Japan has a trade surplus with practically every 'area' except for the Middle East.

Most of Japan's exports tend to be manufactured goods, with cars and electrical and electronic commodities at the top of the list. For example, 97 per cent of Japan's total exports to the EC are in this category and in the USA many Japanese imports are seen as 'highly

Table 2.10 The EC, Japan and the USA's bilateral and global trade imbalances in US$ billion

	Japan			USA			EC 10		
	World	US	EC	World	Japan	EC	World	Japan	US
1973	−1.384	179	1.679	1.863	−1.363	1.140	−7.344	−1.570	−2.497
1974	−6.575	117	2.445	−9.489	−2.796	1.467	−22.039	−2.128	−5.565
1975	−2.110	−459	2.601	4.207	−2.773	5.360	−9.302	−3.633	−9.455
1976	2.427	3.880	4.326	−14.556	−6.778	6.780	−24.646	−4.825	−10.435
1977	9.686	7.321	5.598	−36.348	−9.666	3.756	−14.227	−6.235	−6.197
1978	18.200	10.124	5.890	−39.430	−13.606	1.611	−12.259	−7.361	−6.800
1979	−7.641	5.972	5.788	−37.125	−10.584	7.675	−41.252	−7.795	−12.324
1980	−10.721	6.959	9.317	−32.099	−12.171	16.397	−75.299	−12.140	−24.820
1981	8.741	13.321	10.341	−39.613	−15.789	10.739	−41.467	−11.834	−13.862
1982	6.900	12.151	9.504	−42.610	−16.778	5.423	−34.273	−11.407	−10.701

Sources: EC Delegation in Tokyo, Japan Ministry of Finance and US Department of Commerce.

Table 2.11 (a) Japan's current balance (including invisibles), 1976–82
(*Billion US$*)

	European Community			USA			Rest of the World		
	TB	S/T	CB	TB	S/T	CB	TB	S/T	CB
1976	3.9	−2.1	1.8	5.5	−2.1	3.4	9.9	− 6.2	3.7
1977	4.7	−2.0	2.7	8.7	−1.9	6.8	17.3	− 6.4	10.9
1978	5.5	−2.4	3.0	10.6	−1.9	8.7	24.6	− 8.1	16.5
1979	4.8	−3.4	1.4	7.6	−2.8	4.9	1.8	−10.6	−8.8
1980	9.3	−4.3	5.0	9.8	−3.6	6.3	2.1	−12.9	−10.8
1981	10.8	−6.9	4.0	16.3	−2.4	13.9	20.0	−15.2	4.8
1982	9.9	−5.1	4.8	15.1	−0.8	14.3	18.1	−11.2	6.9

Note: TB = Trade Balance; S/T = Services and Transfers; CB = Current Balance, and the European Community refers to the Nine for the period from 1976 to 1980, but the EC of Ten thereafter.

Source: EC Delegation in Tokyo and *The Balance of Payments Monthly,* (Bank of Japan).

(b) Japan's long-term capital account (US$ million)

	Total	Direct investment	Portfolio investment	Bonds
1975	3392	1768	24	−41
1976	4559	1991	146	−64
1977	5247	1645	1718	735
1978	14872	2371	5300	1897
1979	16294	2898	5865	3385
1980	10817	2385	3753	2996
1981	22809	4894	8777	5810
1982	27418	4540	9743	6076
1983	32459	3612	16024	12505
1984	56775	5965	30795	26773
1985	81815	6452	59773	53749

Source: Ministry of Finance, Tokyo.

visible consumer products, such as automobiles, electronic equipment, and cameras' (United States–Japan Advisory Commission 1984, p. 27). Japan's imports from these two areas are also mainly manufactured products but there are some interesting differences; for

Table 2.12   Japan's external trade balance by area distribution, 1969–84

(a) In thousand million US$

Year	Developed area	Developing countries	Middle East	Communist bloc
1969	0.4	0.6	− 1.4	− 0.1
1970	0.01	0.3	− 1.7	0.2
1971	2.8	1.3	− 2.2	0.2
1972	3.6	1.3	− 2.3	0.2
1973	− 0.7	− 0.3	− 3.2	− 0.3
1974	0.6	− 8.0	− 12.2	0.8
1975	− 0.5	− 3.3	− 10.4	1.7
1976	5.6	− 5.0	− 11.5	1.8
1977	10.6	− 2.4	− 11.6	1.6
1978	12.6	2.8	− 10.0	2.8
1979	5.7	− 15.4	− 18.6	2.0
1980	12.1	− 25.3	− 30.1	2.5
1981	22.3	− 15.4	− 24.9	1.8
1982	19.6	− 13.6	− 20.8	1.0
1983	27.2	− 8.6	− 16.6	1.9
1984	41.7	− 10.7	− 18.9	2.6

(b) In percentages

Year	Developed area		Developing countries		Middle East		Communist bloc	
	Exports	Imports	Exports	Imports	Exports	Imports	Exports	Imports
1969	52.1	52.7	43.1	41.7	3.9	13.2	4.8	5.6
1970	54.0	55.2	40.5	40.1	3.3	12.4	5.4	4.7
1971	54.2	52.1	40.9	43.1	3.4	15.3	4.8	4.8
1972	55.8	52.5	39.1	42.1	4.1	14.9	5.0	5.2
1973	51.6	51.6	43.1	42.4	4.8	12.9	5.3	6.0
1974	47.6	41.5	45.4	53.4	6.6	25.6	7.1	5.1
1975	42.0	41.3	49.6	53.5	10.9	28.5	8.4	5.2
1976	47.1	40.2	46.0	55.4	10.8	28.9	6.9	4.4
1977	47.2	38.9	46.7	56.4	11.0	30.0	6.1	4.7
1978	46.8	33.9	46.4	53.5	11.0	26.2	6.8	4.9
1979	47.3	38.9	45.5	56.2	10.4	26.5	7.2	4.9
1980	47.1	35.0	45.8	60.3	11.1	31.7	7.1	4.7
1981	48.5	35.8	45.3	58.8	11.7	29.8	6.3	5.4
1982	49.0	36.7	45.0	57.7	12.2	28.6	6.1	5.6
1983	52.1	39.0	41.8	55.4	11.7	26.7	6.1	5.5
1984	56.7	40.1	37.1	54.1	8.4	24.2	6.2	5.9

Sources: Calculated from (i) *Statistical Survey of Japan's Economy* and (ii) *Balance of Payments Monthly* (various years).

example, although 77 per cent of Japan's imports from the EC consist of manufactures, the major items being machinery, transport equipment and chemicals, they cover a wide range of products with lower value-added while Japan's exports tend to be concentrated in a few high value-added sectors. It is also interesting to note that about 20 per cent of Japan's imports from the EC are agricultural products. Moreover, the picture is not too different for trade between Japan and the USA, but when it comes to the Middle East, the bulk of trade is imports of petroleum and exports of heavy and light industry products.

OPENNESS OF THE JAPANESE ECONOMY

Since this book is mainly concerned with the international trade relations of Japan, it may be worthwhile to dwell a bit on the openness or otherwise of its economy.

It is generally agreed that one of the most appropriate means of comparing the openness of markets in various countries is the number of commodities subject to 'residual' import quotas and tariff rates. (Under the rules of GATT, specifically Article XI, import quota restrictions should be removed; hence those still imposed are euphemistically referred to as 'residual'.)

According to Okita (1984), in 1981, the Japanese residual import quotas applied in the case of only 27 items and commodity categories (Table 2.13). This number is less than one-third of what it was about a decade or so ago. Note, however, that in 1981, Japan was third in that league, performing only better than Norway and France. But it should be stressed that this number is declining steadily in the case of Japan. It should also be pointed out that Japan's performance in this category is fine when comparison is confined to the 'mining and manufacturing' sector (mainly coal, leather and leather footwear), where the number of items is less than that in the USA. However, when it comes to agricultural products, Japan fares only better than Norway: Japan has a very protective agricultural policy, but so does the EC and the USA, although 'effective protection' may be much higher in Japan where the price of rice is about four times the world price.

With regard to tariffs, Japan has introduced a series of market-opening 'packages' and has reduced its tariff rates on a number of products. Consequently, Japan's tariff burdens (defined as the total tariff revenue divided by the value of total imports) in 1981 were

Table 2.13   Residual import quotas, 1981

	Agricultural products		Mining and manufacturing		Total	
Benelux	2	(10)	3	(4)	5	(14)
Canada	4	(3)	1	(1)	5	(4)
Denmark	5	(62)	0	(2)	5	(64)
France	19	(39)	27	(35)	46	(74)
United Kingdom	1	(19)	2	(6)	3	(25)
Italy	3	(12)	5	(8)	8	(20)
Japan	22	(55)	5	(35)	27	(90)
Norway	48	(54)	1	(1)	49	(55)
Sweden	5	(2)	1	(—)	6	(2)
United States	1	(1)	6	(4)	7	(5)
West Germany	3	(19)	1	(20)	4	(39)

Notes: Figures are as of 31 December 1981. The figures in parentheses are as of 31 December 1970. Agricultural products have been classified in accordance with Customs Cooperation Council Notation 1–24 and mining and manufacturing products in accordance with CCCN 4.

Source: S. Okita, 'Role of the Trade Ombudsman in liberalising Japan's market', *World Economy,* vol. 7, no. 1 (1984).

among the lowest in the world – see Table 2.14. Indeed, according to GATT calculations, when the Tokyo Round agreed tariff reductions are fully implemented, the average tariff for Japan will be 3 per cent, while it will be just over 4 per cent for the USA and just under 5 per cent for the EC. Moreover, in 1984, Japan implemented Tokyo Round tariff cuts for mining and manufacturing products (one year ahead of schedule), lowered tariffs on 47 items of interest to foreign countries (for example, semi-conductors, reconstituted wood, perfumes and bananas) and raised its Generalised System of Preferences (GSP) import ceiling by about 55 per cent. Moreover, Japan has recently taken the initiative of recommending further tariff cuts by bringing forward the implementation of Tokyo Round tariff cuts – these are discussed in detail in Chapter 6.

However, Japan is mostly criticised for its non-tariff barriers. But even here, Okita (1984) claims that Japan has made a number of reforms in its import inspection procedures and has made major progress in making its market more open. For instance, in the case of 'Standards and Certification Systems', the Diet in 1983 enacted amendments to sixteen laws and made them effective from the

Table 2.14   Tariff burdens,ᵃ 1977–81

	1977	1978	1979	1980	1981
Australia	9.1	10.1	9.5	9.5	9.0
Canada	5.1	5.2	4.6	4.5	4.5
European Community	3.3	3.7	3.3	2.8	2.6
Japan	3.8	4.1	3.1	2.5	2.5
United States	3.4	4.1	3.9	3.1	3.2

Note: ᵃ Defined as the total revenues from tariffs and customs duties divided by the value of total imports.

Source: S. Okita, 'Role of the Trade Ombudsman in liberalising Japan's market', *World Economy,* vol. 7, no. 1 (1984).

beginning of August 1983. The object of the amendments was to permit self-certification by foreign corporations and to make the inspection and certification procedures essentially the same for both Japanese and foreign firms. These amendments 'institutionalised the principle of non-discrimination for a wide range of products, including foodstuffs, pharmaceuticals, chemicals, fertilizers, home electrical appliances, automobiles and agricultural machinery' (Okita, 1984).

In addition to the enactment of these amendments, other improvements have been made in the areas of cars, pharmaceuticals and household electrical appliances. These include:

(a) Enhanced 'transparency', i.e. soliciting the opinions of foreign experts during the drafting of standards as well as making more information available regarding the standards and their establishment;

(b) 'Harmonisation' with internationally-agreed standards and 'participation' in efforts to draw up international standards when needed;

(c) More 'acceptance' of foreign test data;

(d) 'Simplification and streamlining' of certification procedures.

Another area of contention is the Japanese distribution system; most foreign firms believe it is an irrational and unnecessarily complicated one. It is claimed that it leads to higher distribution costs due to its complexity and 'multi-layered' nature. There are essentially two aspects to this complaint: that there is an excessively large number of small retail outlets; and that there are various distribution channels even at the wholesale level, with the large commissions to be paid at each stage leading to excessive distribution costs.

Apart from the distribution system, Japanese commercial practices are criticized for being exclusive. Moreover, the associations between Japanese firms are seen by foreign corporations as an element designed to exclude them from the Japanese market.

Okita (1984) responds to all these criticisms in the following manner:

> The existence of many retail outlets ... does not inherently mean a complex distribution system and it is very much in the Japanese consumer's interest to have large numbers of retail outlets ... [;] it is true that Japanese distribution is multi-layered and that many layers do tend to drive up distribution costs. But it is not only foreign products or foreign companies which pay the high costs resulting from complexity in the distribution system. Japanese products are subject to the same costs. The only difference, if any, is that it may take foreign companies longer to understand the Japanese distribution structure and to devise ways of using it to their best advantage ...
>
> Although foreign companies may see the close personal relations between manufacturers and distributors as abnormal, these are not exclusory. Rather they are the natural result of any long-term business relationship and a foreign company which has been in Japan a long time would most likely develop the same kind of close personal relations with its Japanese distribution (as, in fact, many have) ...
>
> Industry associations ... are primarily for friendship and networking of information; they are not where trading actually takes place. Even if they were, foreign firms are free to join Japanese industry associations for the same purposes of friendship and information networking for which Japanese companies use them.
>
> Most of the complaints relating to commercial practices are based upon misunderstandings. Some reflect differences between Japanese practices and those in the United States and Western Europe. Yet the fact that Japanese practices are different is hardly grounds for criticism.

CONCLUSION

The information provided in this chapter is mainly selective except for the more detailed data and discussion of some of Japan's international trade sector-cum-relations; this is deliberate since the book is about Japan's international trade relations. The reader who is interested in detailed information and analysis of the Japanese economy is advised to consult Boltho (1975), Kitamura (1976) and the annual publications by the Economic Planning Agency of Japan, particularly their *Economic Survey of Japan*.

3 Japan's Trade Balance in the Context of the Balance-of-Payments Stages Theorem

The first scenario for explaining Japan's trade frictions with the EC and the USA is the most straightforward since it depends entirely on the information provided in Chapter 2. The brief look at the Japanese economy, especially its trade balance, tends to suggest that Japan has had *many* years of balance of trade surplus while the EC and the USA have had *many* years of trade deficits. Hence, it would seem inevitable to conclude that this has been the main cause of the trade frictions between Japan and these countries, particularly given the information about the inherent difficulties associated with a Japanese market which is supposedly relatively 'impenetrable' by foreign firms. However, such a scenario would be too simplistic as an explanation of Japan's trade frictions: according to the 'balance of payments stages' theorem, Japan is undergoing the same process experienced by the UK from 1800 to 1880 and by the USA from 1915 to 1960.

The aim of this chapter is to: explain the 'balance of payments stages' theorem; examine Japan's trade balance within this context; adjust Japan's trade balance taking into consideration only long-term factors; and document the claim that the trade balance has been the main cause of Japan's trade frictions with the rest of the world community.

THE BALANCE-OF-PAYMENTS STAGES THEOREM

This is a very important theorem; it is therefore appropriate to discuss it in some detail in order to highlight its most salient features. Neo-classical economists originally believed, from statistical analysis, in at least five borrowing-cum-lending stages through which a country may pass. During the very early stages of its development, a country is likely to be a net long-term importer of capital. Net interest and dividend $(i + d)$ payments are short of the country's long-term capital imports. The adjustment mechanism in the balance of payments therefore operates so that the country tends to have a net deficit on current account even excluding i + d payments. The country is a 'young debtor'. Later, as i + d charges on the country's debt mount and surpass net capital imports, the nation enters the second stage. Now it tends to have a net surplus on current account if i + d payments are excluded. However, since net payments on i + d are so large, the current account as a whole shows a net deficit.

Next, the country begins to buy back and redeem its outstanding debt and also starts to lend to other countries. These long-term capital exports exceed long-term capital imports. Thus, the country shifts from being a long-term capital importer to a net long-term capital exporter, but i + d payments still exceed i + d receipts, i.e. the country remains a net international debtor. At this stage the country tends to have a net surplus on current account as a whole. The country is a 'mature debtor'.

In the fourth stage the country has net i + d receipts. It becomes a 'young creditor'. Net receipts of i + d, however, are less than net exports of long-term capital. Therefore, the country tends to have a surplus on current account even excluding net i + d receipts.

Finally, the nation reaches the position in which net i + d receipts exceed long-term capital exports. The country tends to have a net deficit on current account if these net i + d receipts are excluded but a surplus for the current account as a whole. The country is a 'mature creditor'. This stage is fraught with the danger of the country becoming a 'rentier nation', a state of affairs against which Keynes never tired to warn.

This early version of the theorem was later refined in accordance with the availability of more data and sophisticated analysis – see, *inter alia*, Imlah (1958), and Mitchell and Deane (1962). According to the revised version, a country tends to go through six development stages, beginning as an 'immature debtor' and finishing as a 'credit dispositor', with the intervening stages being ones of: 'mature debtor', 'debt repayer', 'immature creditor' and 'mature creditor'. Chart 3.1 clearly portrays these stages together with the corresponding movements in the 'goods and services', 'investment profit', 'current account', and 'long-term capital' (excluding investment profit) balances.

As can be seen from the chart, a nation emerges as an importer of capital due to the inadequacy of domestic savings for development purposes. During this stage, the balance on long-term capital shows a surplus while the current account registers a deficit: the nation

Chart 3.1 Development stages of international balance of payments – Britain, US, West Germany and Japan

	Goods services balance	Investment earnings balance	Current account balance	Long-term capital balance	Prewar (upper lines) / Postwar (lower lines)	Britain Period (year)	Britain Current account balance/ nominal GNP	US Period (year)	US Current account balance/ nominal GNP	W. Germany Period (year)	W. Germany Current account balance/ nominal GNP	Japan Period (year)	Japan Current account balance/ nominal GNP
I Immature debtor	−	−	−	+								1868–1880	−
II Mature debtor	+	−	−	+				1871–1890	−0.6			1881–1914	−
III Debt-repaying country	+	−	+	−				1891–1910	0.7			1955–1964 / 1914–1920	−0.2 / 72
IV Immature creditor	+	+	+	−		1851–1890	3.8	1911–1940	24	1951–1970	1.3	1965–1969	0.8
V Mature creditor	−	+	+	−		1891–1925	3.4	1946–1970	0.6	1971–1982	0.5	1970–1983	0.7
VI Credit disposition country	−	+	−	+		1948–1982 / 1926–1944	0.3 / −2.6	1971–1981	0.4				

Notes:

(a) Basic sources: A. H. Imlah, 'British Balance of Payments and Export of Capital, 1816–1913', in *Economic Elements in the Pax Britannica* (Harvard University Press, 1958); B. R. Mitchell and P. Deane, *Abstract of British Historical Statistics* (Cambridge University Press, 1962); B. R. Mitchell, *Macmillan World History Statistics*; IMF, *Balance of Payments Statistics, International Statistics*; OECD, *National Statistics; OECD Economic Outlook and National Accounts of OECD Countries*; UN, *Yearbook of National Accounts Statistics*; S. Kuznets, *Quantitative Aspects of the Economic Growth of Nations*; Deutsche Bundesbank: *Monthly Report of the Deutsche Bundesbank*; Okawa and others, *Long-term Economic Statistics – National Income*; Yamasawa and others, *Long-term Economic Statistics Trade and International Balance of Payments*; EPA, *Report on National Economic Accounts*.

(b) Because of restrictions on data concerning the prewar current account–GNP ratio, some parts do not always match the gradation of international balance of payments.

Source: Economic Planning Agency, *Economic Survey of Japan* (Tokyo: EPA, 1985), p. 73.

becomes a debtor in terms of both the 'flow' and 'stock' (net external assets as a cumulative total of the current account balance) concepts. The country has a deficit because of payments which exceed the investment earnings balance and also because the performance of the less developed export industries tends to affect the goods and services balance adversely when profits on investment are excluded.

As the process of economic development sets in, the goods and service balance moves into the black, taking the nation to the 'mature debtor' stage. When the surplus in the goods and services balance exceeds the deficit in investment earnings balance, the nation's current account balance also moves into the black, with its long-term capital balance showing a net outflow. Hence, although the country is a debtor in terms of 'stocks', it is a debt repaying country in terms of 'flows'.

When debts are completely redeemed and the current account maintains a surplus, the country becomes a creditor in 'stock' terms with the investment earnings balance then showing a surplus but with long-term capital still in deficit (outflow). In other words, it is the investment earnings balance which determines whether or not a country is a debtor or a creditor.

If, due to the loss in international competitiveness, the deficit in the goods and services balance (leading to the 'mature creditor' stage) exceeds the surplus in the investment profit balance, the current account balance will register a deficit, moving the long-term capital balance into the black. The country has entered the stage of collecting the credits it has accumulated.

It should be apparent from the above that the balance-of-payments stages theorem is a hypothesis for explaining the long-term changes in the pattern and structure of a country's balance of payments. The theory focuses on the fact that the balance of domestic savings and domestic investment in a country tends to change in accordance with its economic development. Moreover, the movements of net external assets depicted by this hypothesis are consistent with the life-cycle hypothesis for households savings behaviour where people borrow at an early age to invest in education and housing, save money to educate their children and cater for old age during their middle-age, and draw on the income from their accumulated assets when old.

HISTORICAL EXPERIENCE

Chart 3.1 also gives some information in terms of the historical experience of Britain, the USA, West Germany and Japan. The chart shows that Britain turned from a debtor to a creditor nation during the Victorian era (1837–1901) while the USA did the same before the First World War. More precisely, Britain's current account balance was in the black from the beginning of the twentieth century. The ratio of the current account surplus to nominal GNP averaged about 3.8 per cent during 1851–90. During this period, Britain's trade balance registered a deficit, but it had a large surplus in the services balance (mainly due to shipping) and in the investment profit balance, which together resulted in a large surplus on current account. It could be argued that this surplus was responsible for a major increase in Britain's long-term capital exports in the 1850s which reached a peak just before the First World War. However, during the 1920s Britain's current account surplus began to decline and recorded a deficit in 1926, suggesting that the country became a 'credit collector' from then until the Second World War. Britain's balance of payments recorded a current account surplus mainly due to the surplus on the investment earnings balance; hence, the nation was a 'mature creditor'. However, the current account reverted to a deficit during the second half of the 1970s, arguably mainly due to a loss in international competitiveness. The discovery of North Sea oil in the late 1970s brought about a surplus on Britain's current account.

With regard to the USA, it had a goods–services deficit until the 1870s, with the deficit on current account continuing into the 1880s. It was after the 1910s that the USA's investment earnings balance moved into the black, i.e. the US became an 'immature debtor' before the 1870s, a 'mature debtor' from the 1870s to the 1890s and a debt-repaying country from the 1890s to the 1910s. The US became an 'immature creditor' in the 1910s when its investment earnings balance went into the black. After the First World War, the USA replaced Britain as the world's major capital and savings supplier. At the end of the 1960s, the USA became a 'mature creditor', maintaining its surplus on current account through its surplus on the investment earnings balance. During the period from 1911 to 1940, the country's ratio of surplus on current account to nominal GNP rose to 2.4 per cent, which is lower than Britain's equivalent percentage.

West Germany became a debt-repaying nation in 1951, having been in a debtor stage before then. It became an 'immature creditor' during the 1970s after registering a surplus on its investment earnings balance. After reaching the stage of 'immature creditor', West Germany's ratio of surplus on current account to nominal GNP declined to 0.5 per cent from the 1.3 per cent of the preceding period; this could be attributed to the first oil shock.

What lessons can be drawn from this for the current discussion regarding Japan's trade frictions? Given the experience of Britain and the USA, it should be apparent that at least three conclusions emerge. Firstly, despite wars, discovery of new natural resources and drastic changes in the two countries' tax systems, they both experienced these balance of payments development stages but to varying extents: the critical period for Britain lasted from 1800 to 1880 and for the USA from 1915 to 1960. Secondly, during the relevant periods when these countries were capital suppliers to the outside world, their current account surpluses amounted to as much as 2.4 per cent of nominal GNP. Finally, the two nations needed a long period to move from the 'immature creditor' to the 'mature creditor' stages.

What about the case of Japan? According to Japan's Economic Planning Agency (see Chart 3.2).

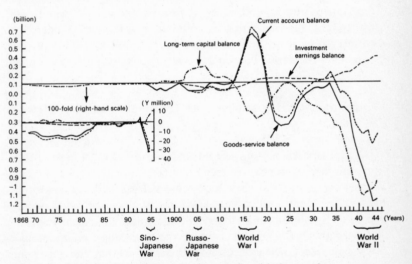

Chart 3.2   Japan's prewar long-term international balance of payments

Notes:
1. From Toyo Keizai Shinposha, 'Long-Term Economic Statistics', *Trade and International Balance of Payments*.
2. Five-year moving averages. Reparations after the Sino-Japanese War are excluded from the current account balance.

Source: Economic Planning Agency, *Economic Survey of Japan* (Tokyo: EPA, 1985) p. 74.

Japan's goods-service balance ran a deficit from the Meiji Restoration (1868) to the 1880s. Japan also registered a deficit in its current account balance, except during the Russo-Japanese War (1894–5) and World War I ... On the other hand, its investment profit balance moved into the black after World War I owing to increased direct investment in mainland China. In this period, the U.S. established its position ... as an "immature creditor" in the world. Japan's experience as an "immature creditor," though temporary, owed much to its export boom during World War I.

After World War II, Japan's "goods-service balance" fell into deficit. It was after 1955 that the balance reached a surplus. Although its investment earning balance was in deficit, Japan's current account balance shifted into the black after 1965. The investment profit balance showed a surplus from the beginning of the 1970s. Namely, Japan started the postwar years as a "debtor," became a "credit-repaying country" in 1965, and an "immature creditor" in the beginning of the 1970s ... [when] the country was hard hit by the two oil crises. Although its current account and investment earning balances immediately fell into deficit, the country was again able to gain and maintain a surplus in both balances (Economic Planning Agency, *Economic Survey of Japan,* 1983/84, p. 76).

Kitamura (1976) has something to say about Japan's experience in this respect:

An export surplus does not necessarily indicate an international disequilibrium; a positive trade and services balance can be fully offset by a negative balance of capital flow. As the economy develops, there tend to be relative shifts in individual items of a country's international payments and receipts. According to a well-established school of thought, a mature debtor nation requires a surplus on current account in order to service and repay past debts. With a still persisting and increasing current-account surplus, the nation shifts to the next stage of a young creditor when it starts lending abroad. At this transitional stage a continued current-account surplus should be regarded as a necessary concomitant to the country's progress to the status of a young creditor rather than a disturbing element in international economic relations.

Available indications suggest that Japan has recently been in such a transitional stage. The significant point is that this transition has been taking place with the same extraordinary rapidity that is characteristic of changes in other aspects of her economic development. The fact is that Japan's economic growth was subject to recurrent balance-of-payments constraints until about the middle of the 1960s; during the entire postwar period she had to continue to rely on substantial capital inflows just to maintain the rather precarious international payments balance. It was as late as 1965 that the continual threat of current account deficits ceased to restrain the expansion of the economy. At the same time Japanese capital outflows began substantially to exceed inflows. Until the mid-1960s, therefore, Japan can be said to have remained a young debtor, still struggling with threatening current-account imbalances. Hardly had she arrived at the stage of an adult or mature debtor, enjoying a surplus in the current payments balance, than her long-term balance began to indicate substantial capital outflows. Indeed, Japan has performed the transition from the stage of a young debtor to that of a young creditor within a few years, virtually skipping over the intermediate stages of an adult and mature debtor.

There are obviously some discrepancies between Kitamura's demarcations of Japan's balance of payments stages and those of the Japanese Economic Planning Agency. This is only natural given the availability of more sophisticated data at a later stage. However, this is irrelevant in the present discussion since what is at issue here is not the actual demarcations (this is attempted below), but rather the simple statement of the fact that many economists advocate the theory of the balance-of-payments stages theorem: to assume that current account surpluses/deficits are the main cause of Japan's trade frictions is to make a judgement which lacks historical perspective.

JAPAN'S TRADE BALANCE

It was stated in the previous section that the Japanese Economic Planning Agency, in its discussion of the balance-of-payments stages theorem in the context of Japan, believed that the current account long-term trend is that depicted in Table 2.1, i.e. Japan's trade surplus is a very recent phenomenon. This point is reiterated by Okita (1984):

Some people have charged that Japan is continuing to accumulate major surpluses in her current account and that these surpluses are having a deleterious impact on industry and employment in other parts of the world economy ... Japan has not consistently been in surplus, the current account having fluctuated between surpluses and deficits [see Chart 3.3].

Until the mid-1960s, the current account was a factor limiting GNP growth, for rapid growth quickly threw the current account into deficit. In the mid-1960s, however, the current account shifted to a surplus position, recording major surpluses in the periods 1971–72, 1977–78 and 1982–83. It is in these three periods that trade friction has been most heated. Because the current-account surplus exceeded 1 per cent of GNP in each of these periods, it can be empirically demonstrated that this 1 per cent of GNP is the threshold of trade friction. At the same time, it should be noted that the current-account deficit was approximately 1 per cent of GNP after the oil 'shocks' of 1973–74 and 1979–80 (Okita, 1984).

Of course, if one simply looked at the stylistic facts (see Table 2.1), it would seem that it is only recently that Japan has started the process of continuing surpluses. However, if one were to seek the true underlying trend for Japan's current account, by allowing for the two oil shocks (after all, every nation, except the oil exporters, was a victim), what would Japan's balance on current account look like? It should be recalled that, since 1969, Japan has been experiencing a surplus except for the two deficit periods of 1973–5 and 1979–80 (see Table 2.1), precisely the two oil shock periods. Hence the question: what would have happened to the current trade balance in the absence of the oil shocks? The answer requires that the current balance be broken down by the appropriate 'area' distribution (see Table 2.9): the bulk of Japan's crude oil imports come from the Middle East, and therefore the oil shocks should not have affected Japan's trade with other 'areas' to an appreciable extent.

Table 2.9 clearly shows that the only major recorded changes concern Japan's trade with the Middle East; the percentages indicate no other significant changes. Since the 'Developed Area' is dominated by North America and the EC, and since neither area supplies Japan with crude oil, it follows that the external trade performance of these two areas is largely due to their own economic 'mismanagement', particularly since the complete elimination of Japan's trade surplus and its proportionate allocation between them would not completely dispose of their problem – see El-Agraa (1985a) and Chapter 4.

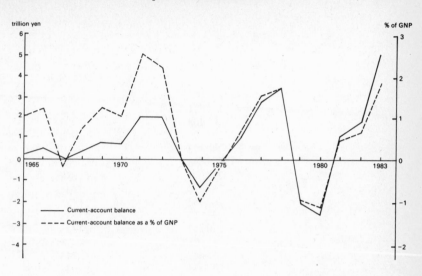

Chart 3.3   Japan's current-account balance compared with GNP

Source: S. Okita, 'Role of the trade ombudsman in liberalising Japan's market', *World Economy*, vol. 7, no. 1 (1984).

With regard to the Middle East, further information about the quantity of imported crude oil is needed, since it is necessary to distinguish between price and quantity changes. Table 3.1 shows that the quantity of crude oil imports declined in 1974 and 1975, reversing a rising trend. The table also shows an increase in 1979 followed by a continuous decline since 1980. Hence, although it is clear that Japan reduced its imports of crude oil after the oil shocks, it would seem that, in the absence of the oil price upheavals, the trend would have been, if not a rising one, at least constant. In the calculations to follow, I shall assume that such a trend would have been a horizontal one, hence my estimates will be on the lower side with regard to the 'positive' impact on Japan's trade balance.

The relevant oil price changes are by now common household figures, but they are portrayed in Chart 3.4. The chart does not include the latest drastic decline in the price of oil simply because it should be obvious that the effects of this are to increase the existing recent Japanese trade surpluses.

Assuming that the bulk of Japan's crude oil imports were subjected to the oil price increases, it follows that, in the absence of the price

Table 3.1   Japan's imports of crude oil, 1969–84

Year	Quantity (000 kl)	Value (US$ million)
1969	167 431	1 907
1970	197 108	2 236
1971	222 492	3 048
1972	249 193	3 927
1973	289 698	6 000
1974	278 393	18 898
1975	263 373	19 644
1976	267 755	21 185
1977	278 017	23 573
1978	270 651	23 433
1979	281 203	33 471
1980	254 447	52 749
1981	227 444	53 343
1982	212 259	46 274
1983	n.a.	40 063
1984	n.a.	39 373

Note: n.a. means not available.

Sources: *Japan Statistical Yearbook,* various years, Statistics Bureau, Prime Minister's Office, and *Balance of Payments Monthly,* various years, Bank of Japan, Tokyo.

upheavals, Japan would have saved two-thirds of its crude oil bill in the five years under consideration. Adding the calculated figures to the actual trade balance (Table 2.1) gives the information in Table 3.2.

In short, Japan would have had a *consistent* balance of trade surplus since 1969. This conclusion remains intact if the calculations are applied to 90 per cent of Japan's total imports from the Middle East, rather than to its imports of crude oil – see the figures given in brackets in Table 3.2.

The fact that Okita tried similar calculations lends support to my assertion:

When oil prices soar, as they did during the two oil crises, Japan's crude-oil import bill also soars and the current account falls precipitously into the red. In the wake of the second oil crisis ... crude oil imports rose by 7 trillion yen ($29 billion) between 1978

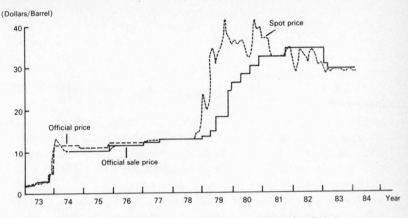

Chart 3.4   Changes in crude oil prices (Arabian light)

Source: *White Paper on International Trade*, Japan External Trade Organisation (JETRO), Tokyo.

and 1980. As a result, the current account slipped from a surplus of 1.7 per cent of GNP in 1978 to a deficit of 1.1 per cent of GNP in 1980. This GNP shift of 2.8 per cent is approximately equivalent to the increase in crude-oil imports (3 per cent of GNP) over the same period. By contrast, the current account tends to go sharply into the black when real oil prices decline, as they have done recently (Okita, 1984).

Table 3.2   Japan's trade balance adjusted for the oil shocks

Year	Calculated trade balance (thousand million US$)
1973	+ 2.624 (1.590)
1974	+ 6.030 (2.987)
1975	+ 10.970 (11.233)
1979	+ 14.760 (10.077)
1980	+ 24.277 (15.819)

Why is it so important to make these adjustments? These are important for two crucial considerations. Firstly, as we shall see below, there are those who believe that it is the *consistent* surpluses in Japan's current account which are the main cause of Japan's trade frictions; they must, therefore, be thinking of the underlying trend, as otherwise their argument would not hold in the context of the stylistic facts. Secondly, as we have seen in the previous section, it is vital to know how long Japan has truly been in current account surplus in order to have some notion about how long it will continue to be so, given the balance-of-payments stages theorem. If the world is to have a sense of perspective, it is important that the world should understand that Japan's trade surpluses (not in their present magnitude – see below) will continue for a while. Regarding the latter point, Okita believes that Japan has been at the 'immature creditor' stage since the late 1970s, and that, as a late-industrialising country, it may be expected to become a 'mature creditor' nation in the early twenty-first century (Okita, 1984). Of course, Okita's assertions are in direct contradiction to those of the Japanese Economic Planning Agency, since they seem certain that Japan has been seen as an 'immature creditor' since 1970 (see Chart 3.1), which is more consistent with my analysis.

It should be added, however, that the duration of the stages, determined according to the theorem, will inevitably become shorter with time due to the continuous development and growth of the world economy. As depicted in Chart 3.1, the duration of the 'immature creditor' stage was 39 years in Britain, 29 years in the USA and eleven years in West Germany. Also, the duration of the 'mature creditor' stage was 26 years in Britain and ten years in the USA, with West Germany not experiencing that stage. Hence, if my assertion that Japan entered the 'immature creditor' stage in 1969 is correct, it follows that Japan is 'naturally' nearing the end of this stage and will be entering the 'mature creditor' stage within the next few years. Therefore, the 'structural surplus' in Japan's goods and services balance should revert to a deficit shortly. There is, therefore, no basis for the statement that Japan should become a 'mature creditor' nation in the early twenty-first century; a difference in forecasts of about a decade is not to be taken lightly. I leave it to the reader to decide whether or not my conclusion is consistent with that of such distinguished institutions as the Industrial Bank of Japan (1984) and the Nomura Research Institute (1985): they claimed that Japan will continue to run current account surpluses averaging about $50 billion annually throughout the 1980s and will become a net creditor country of $500 billion by the early 1990s.

This conclusion is also supported by the realities of the international economy: there is no place for more than one dominant economy undergoing these stages so obviously. This is because, as more and more countries become developed and continue to grow, these stages will become unclear and may eventually disappear altogether: when the whole world has become developed, the theorem will no longer hold. The evidence for this is the case of West Germany where the 'mature creditor' stage was squeezed out due to the fast development of Japan. If this is too hard to swallow, an analogy may help here: when Rostow (1960) first advanced his doctrine of 'stages of economic growth', development experts immediately applied it without serious qualification, but it soon became apparent that, *on the whole*, the later developers had access to knowledge and technical know-how which greatly shortened the duration of such stages. The predictions of the balance of payments stages theorem are no different.

THE SCENARIO

Having established that Japan has been running a true surplus on current account since 1969, we can return to the first scenario by stating that the position of the EC and the USA has been the reverse. As Table 2.7 clearly demonstrates, the EC has been having a consistent deficit in its trade balance since 1973, both with Japan and globally. The table also shows the USA to be in a similar position except for 1973 and 1975 when it had a global trade surplus.

Now, since the world deems it appropriate for countries to correct their trade deficits, it is implicitly assumed that trade surpluses must also be corrected: trade deficits in some countries cannot be eliminated if other nations continue to have trade surpluses. Keynes, of course, believed that these two sides of the same coin should be explicitly recognised by the world trading community by stating that countries with trade surpluses are also in 'imbalance' and should be obliged to take measures to restore balance; indeed, he spent a great deal of effort trying to establish the principle of 'equal responsibility' as the basis for the creation of the IMF. It is ironic that the 'White' Proposal, which was put forward by the USA, won the day: this proposal put the onus entirely on countries with trade deficits. If the concept of equal responsibility is acceptable, it follows that we have a

clear indication of the reason for the trade frictions between the EC
and the USA and Japan. This would be consistent with the argument
put forward by the United States–Japan Advisory Commission:

> *The growing trade imbalance is regarded by Americans as the most
> serious cause of friction between the two countries* (1984, p. 27; their
> italics).

The EC Delegation in Tokyo, speaking on behalf of the EC, put
forward a similar argument:

> The Community's trade deficit with Japan has been growing
> steadily since the 1970s, a source of recurrent, sometimes sharp
> tensions (1984).

However, this scenario is neither a subtle nor a complete one. The
reason is that, apart from the balance-of-payments stages theorem, if
continuing bilateral trade imbalances are the true cause of the trade
frictions of Japan with the EC and the USA, then it must follow that a
correction of these imbalances would help eliminate the tension. No
international trade theorist in his right mind would advocate such a
solution: the aim should be to balance the country's *overall* trade
account; *bilateral* balancing would be a direct negation of the principle of 'comparative advantage', defined in the dynamic sense. Of
course, comparative advantage can be achieved by means other than
'natural advantage', but there is no reason to believe that Japan is
unique in 'making' comparative advantage (see Cooper (1986) and the
following chapter). Moreover, there are those who would argue that
even overall trade balances should not be the goal, only the overall
balance of payments. Such an argument would be misguided since it
would exhibit no understanding of the mechanisms whereby imbalances can be identified even though the balance of payments is
automatically in balance (due to the double-entry accounting system
employed): the distinction between 'autonomous' and 'accommodating' transactions.

In the case of Japan, the implications of its asking the countries of
the Middle East to take immediate measures to correct their bilateral
trade surplus would no doubt warrant a whole book, on both the
economics and politics of the situation. If overall balancing is all that
matters, it would not require much imagination to see that if Japan
took measures to correct its overall surplus and distributed this in

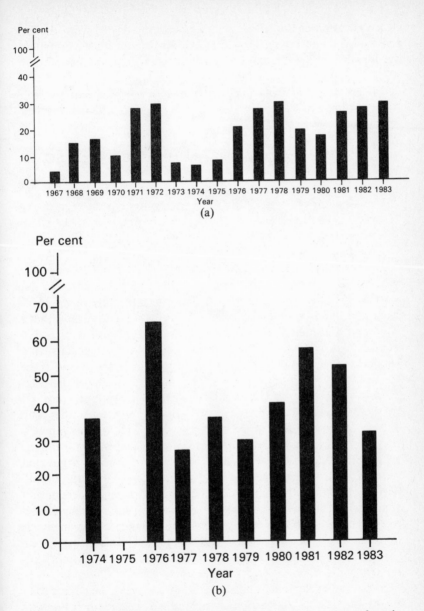

Chart 3.5 (a) US–Japan bilateral trade deficit as a percentage of total bilateral merchandise trade. (b) US–Japan bilateral merchandise trade deficit as a percentage of global US deficit

Source: US Department of Commerce trade statistics.

Table 3.3 Trade balances for 25 major trading nations, total and with United States, 1980–81 to 1984

Country	Bilateral US[a] 1984 level				Change, 1980–81 to 1984				Total non-oil[b] change 1980–81 to 1984	
	Million dollars	Rank	Percentage of bilateral turnover	Rank	Million dollars	Rank	Percentage of bilateral turnover[c]	Rank	Percentage of total country turnover[d]	Rank
Argentina	141	20	7.3	18	1.549	17	48.5	2	38.8	2
Australia	−908	22	−10.5	22	1.015	20	15.5	19	−3.1	22
Austria	365	18	33.9	9	446	23	41.2	6	3.0	15
Belgium	−2.014	23	−23.5	23	1.991	15	24.1	15	1.9	16
Brazil	5.633	7	51.6	3	5.282	6	47.5	3	32.5	3
Canada	20.387	2	18.0	14	13.453	2	9.5	22	0.8	20
Denmark	913	14	43.0	6	955	21	45.5	4	1.0	19
France	2.479	11	17.0	15	4.048	8	28.9	12	1.1	18
Germany	8.726	4	32.4	10	7.257	5	26.0	13	1.4	17
Hong Kong	5.837	6	48.8	4	3.105	12	14.9	20	6.2	10
Italy	4.129	8	32.1	11	4.446	7	35.1	9	12.2	6
Japan	36.795	1	43.8	5	21.664	1	17.6	18	5.1	11
Korea	4.044	9	25.3	12	3.991	9	24.7	14	5.0	12
Mexico	6.275	5	20.7	13	9.319	3	30.9	11	39.7	1
Norway	1.145	13	40.0	7	−625	24	−10.2	24	6.8	9

Netherlands	−3.224	24	−27.1	24	3.131	11	31.1	10	3.4	14
China, PR	337	19	5.9	19	2.443	13	44.9	5	7.3	8
Romania	720	15	59.1	1	857	22	71.7	1	15.4	4
Singapore	446	17	5.7	20	1.374	18	23.9	16	−6.2	24
Spain	66	21	1.3	21	2.009	14	40.5	7	12.5	5
Sweden	1.805	12	37.9	8	1.941	16	39.5	8	4.1	13
Switzerland	636	16	11.0	16	1.352	19	22.8	17	0.8	21
Taiwan	11.065	3	52.2	2	7.391	4	4.7	23	11.9	7
United Kingdom	2.834	10	10.4	17	3.607	10	13.6	21	−5.0	23
Subtotal	108.632	n.a.	n.a.	n.a.	102.003	n.a.	n.a.	n.a.	n.a.	n.a.
United States	−123.209	25	−22.1	25	−85.395	25	−14.4	25	−14.4	25

Notes:

[a] Country exports are from US data on imports, c.i.f.; country imports are from US data on exports, f.o.b. Includes oil.

[b] Based on country's own data on exports, f.o.b. and imports, c.i.f.

[c] 1984 ratio of bilateral balance to bilateral turnover minus average ratio for 1980 and 1981.

[d] Non-oil.

Source: C. F. Bergsten and W. R. Cline, *The United States – Japan Economic Problem* (Washington, DC: Institute for Economic Statistics, 1985) pp. 22–3.

proportions which were consistent with its trade performance with the EC and the USA, the net effect would be no more than a modest contribution. The picture would not be different if Japan were to attain bilateral trade balance with the Middle East and distribute the sum so calculated in accordance with that criterion. Some economists have suggested that Japan and all other nations of the OECD should run trade deficits with the Middle East, but it should be clear, no matter what the merit of such a proposal may be, that this would not alter the relative positions of Japan, the EC and the USA.

If one were to concentrate only on the bilateral trade imbalance with the USA, one would get a very different picture: the net effect on the USA of Japan disposing of its trade surplus and distributing it between the EC and the USA in accordance with the criterion specified in the previous paragraph would be fairly significant but that on the EC would remain small – see United States–Japan Advisory Committee (1984, pp. 27–31) and Chart 3.5.

One possible less simplistic explanation would be that the EC and the USA have trade deficits with countries, other than Japan, which are themselves in overall deficit. Hence, there would be no moral or theoretical justification in asking them to eliminate imbalances with the EC and the USA. Therefore Japan has become the obvious target and this has resulted in the trade frictions. Well, one does not even need any statistics to see that such an argument would not hold much water since the combined deficits of the EC and the USA are of such a magnitude as to render this an impossibility; recall that Japan's trade surplus is far short of the combined deficit of the EC and the USA. Furthermore, the USA is not only running a trade deficit with practically every nation with which it is trading, but, as Table 3.3 clearly demonstrates, 'relative to the size of each country's bilateral trade turnover (imports plus exports) with the United States, . . . other major trading nations (Romania, Taiwan, Brazil, and Hong Kong) have larger surpluses with the United States than Japan' (Bergsten and Cline, 1985).

CONCLUSION

It should be apparent that neither recurring nor *persisting* trade surpluses are sufficient justifications for trade frictions. The reason for this is not only the balance of payments stages theorem but also the fact that eliminating Japan's total trade surplus would not solve the problem of trade deficits in the EC and the USA. Considering this and recalling that Japan should have a trade surplus given the present stage in the development of its balance of payments, it is clear that 'economic mismanagement' has a key role to play in explaining the trade deficits of the EC and the USA (more on this in later chapters). Hence, a more convincing scenario for the trade frictions has to be sought.

4 A More Plausible Explanation of the Trade Frictions

The previous chapter was devoted to a careful consideration of Japan's trade balance within the context of the 'balance-of-payments stages' theorem. The conclusion reached there is that, apart from the fact that that is the only context within which to examine Japan's trade frictions with the outside world, consistent and persistent trade imbalances cannot explain why trade frictions prevail. Hence, a more convincing argument requires an analysis which digs deeper under the surface. The purpose of this chapter is to do precisely that.

There are many possible avenues here, but it may be wise to concentrate on only three.

NATURE OF THE JAPANESE MARKET

Whether for genuine reasons or not, the Japanese market for manufactures has proved relatively more difficult to penetrate by foreign firms. It is not clear whether the reasons are genuine simply because it could be asserted (United States–Japan Advisory Commission, 1984, p. 37) that in Japan:

(a) High tariff barriers persist for some products, particularly those with high value-added content, despite low average tariff levels.
(b) Slow customs procedures, for example, item-by-item inspection of products rather than spot inspection or the holding of air cargo until laborious paperwork is completed, add to import costs.
(c) Rigid and discriminatory standards and certification requirements contrast with simpler procedures in the United States. For example, foreign companies are required to pay for overseas travel expenses of Japanese inspectors, implementation of new measures is slow or inconsistent, and clinical testing done outside Japan is not accepted.
(d) A relatively small amount of foreign telecommunications equipment is procured by the public Nippon Telephone and Telegraph

Corporation, and foreign cigarettes are discriminated against by the Japan Salt and Tobacco Corporation, despite liberalisation in both instances.

The Joint Commission's Report does not leave us much the wiser since its recommendations (United States–Japan Advisory Commission, 1984, pp. vii–ix) seem to be consistent with the above:

* It is in Japan's own national interest to make the further opening of the Japanese market a high priority. ... Although Japan has made a series of unilateral trade concessions, there remain specific difficulties to market entry in Japan which call into question Japan's commitment to free or fair trade. Some of the systematic problems underlying complaints include difficulty in obtaining access to information on Japan's bureaucratic policymaking and implementing processes, a strong bureaucratic tradition conducive to a reactive rather than initiative policy, and a propensity for Japanese to make a distinction between insiders and outsiders.

But it hastens to add:

Positive efforts by Japan to open its markets must be matched by a more positive U.S. export strategy at both governmental and private levels to *take advantage of new opportunities*. The United States also has barriers to market entry which should be reduced, although in view of the generally more open U.S. market, Japan cannot expect full reciprocity for its market-opening measures.

The EC Delegation in Tokyo is more forthcoming since it lists as explanations for the 'import imperviousness' (an utterly and misleadingly incorrect term since Japan does have substantial imports) of the Japanese economy, in addition to the item on the homogeneous structure of the Japanese domestic market referred to above, Japan's geographical position (no tradition of trade with neighbouring countries having a comparable level of development), and its recent history (the 'export or die' mentality of the early post-war years): growing industries were protected in the 1950s and 1960s through an apparatus of tariff and non-tariff barriers and controls; Japan was a latecomer to GATT and has only gradually taken steps to liberalise its tariffs, quotas and investment restrictions; etc. (EC Delegation in Tokyo, 1984).

The point to stress is that this is a genuine area for research since all we seem to have from these two important sources (the EC Delegation in Tokyo and the Joint US–Japan Advisory Commission) is allegations with counter-allegations coming from Japan, even though Japan has equal representation on the Joint Commission. A proper analysis should find out whether or not Japan's domestic market is relatively more difficult to penetrate because of hidden barriers or whether it is foreign firms who do not have the ingenuity and patience to work hard at capturing a share of Japan's market. One must hasten to add that such an analysis must also find out whether any Japanese practices in this respect are more or less protective (effectively) than those practised by other member nations of the OECD.

In the meantime, some information can be obtained from available studies. For instance, Okita (1984) states:

> Most foreign companies have trouble with the Japanese market because they approach it in the wrong way. The first problem is generally the lack of a long-term export strategy. It is obviously impossible to hope for stable long-term expansion of exports unless the target market is studied thoroughly and products are developed which satisfy customer requirements. Taking the simple example of the placement of car steering wheels, Japanese drive on the left-hand side of the road and, therefore, the steering wheel in Japanese cars is on the right. Most cars imported to Japan, however, come with the steering wheel on the left. This demonstrates a lack of commitment and willingness to adapt to market conditions . . .
>
> The second problem is that foreign firms tend to price high in order to generate large commissions. This is especially pronounced in automobiles, whisky, brandy, cosmetics, sports equipment and clothing. While high prices and large profit margins may be successful in the short term by creating an image of quality and exclusiveness, most of these companies have found that their growth potential is limited, that they are unable to compete in price and that they get squeezed out of the market.
>
> The third problem is the lack of sales effort. Foreign firms are quick to criticise the so-called exclusory nature of the Japanese market, but they are far less anxious to discuss their own sales efforts. Looking at the number of overseas offices and overseas personnel as two measures to export sales effort, foreign firms have only an eighth as many offices in Japan as Japanese firms have

overseas and only one twentieth as many people stationed in Japan as there are Japanese stationed overseas [Table 4.1]. American and West European firms are just not making the same effort in exports that Japanese firms are.

Nevertheless, there are numerous companies which have studied the Japanese market and have adopted successful marketing strategies in Japan, among them being IBM (computer equipment), BMW (automobiles), Schick (men's razors), Braun (electric shavers) and Max Factor (cosmetics).

The question regarding non-tariff barriers is very complex indeed; the number of means is unimaginable and human ingenuity seems to suggest new means when old ones have been discovered and tackled in whatever way deemed appropriate (see Baldwin, 1971). Maybe the best way to illustrate non-tariff barriers is to concentrate on 'industrial policy'. Of course, it is well known that industrial policy has no

Table 4.1 Japanese trading offices overseas and foreign trading offices in Japan

	Japanese trading offices overseas		Foreign trading offices in Japan[a]	
	Offices	*Employees*	*Offices*	*Employees*
United States	986	33 464	170	1 551
European Community	703	14 636	79	667
United Kingdom	151	4 294	28	189
West Germany	256	5 857	24	293
France	80	1 455	9	89
Italy	47	495	4	11
South-east Asia	1 370	33 437	175	1 444
Other regions	1 364	28 427	95	1 478
Total	4 423	109 964	519	5 140

Notes:
The figures are as of 31 March 1981, except for British trading facilities in Japan, which are as of 31 March 1980.
[a] Foreign trading facilities in Japan are those facilities of foreign corporations and Japanese corporations in which foreign investors hold a majority interest.

Source: S. Okita, 'Role of the trade ombudsman in liberalising Japan's market', *World Economy*, vol. 7, no. 1 (1984)

clearly defined boundaries since it embraces all acts and policies of the state in relation to industry. Such policy can be either 'positive' or 'negative', i.e. positive in relation to government participation in, or control of, industry; or negative, to the extent that it might be the industrial policy of the government to minimise intervention in industry. Positive industrial policy covers such areas as: the distribution of resources between industries (including such areas as energy, pricing, monopolies and restrictive practices); the structure of industry (including such areas as the degree of concentration, its location, government aids towards declining and expanding industries, the public sector); industry and the environment; conditions of employment; and fiscal and monetary policy. In other words, industrial policy embraces all aspects of government attitudes towards industry in its economic, social and environmental setting (Bayliss, 1985). However, generally speaking, it can be taken to mean any government policies that exert an impact on the structure of output, or, less generally, any 'government policies whose intended purpose is to affect the structure of output' (Cooper, 1986).

Industrial policy in Japan

In the case of Japan, industrial policies have changed substantially over the past two and a half decades, and 'some of the measures most frequently cited in fact belong largely to the past' (Cooper, 1986). It is therefore wise to follow the existing literature by describing Japanese industrial policies within four eras: 1946 to 1955 (the post Second World War restoration period); 1956 to 1965 (the industrial upgrading period); 1966 to 1975 (the transition period to liberalisation); and 1976 to date (the internationalisation period) – see Hosomi and Okumura (1982). Chart 4.1 sets out the main features of Japanese industrial policy during these periods. However, a more convenient classification of the last three periods may be that adopted by Cooper: 1952 to the early 1960s (end of post-war price controls with the object of establishing the groundwork for a modern industrial economy), 1960 to 1972 (removal of foreign exchange controls with the aim of enhancing export performance) and 1972 to date (with the purpose of shifting the structure of the Japanese economy from capital-intensive to knowledge-intensive industries) – see Namiki in Warnecke (1978), Yakushiji in Aoki (1984), Yamamura (1982) and Cooper (1986). It should be noted that the dividing line between these periods is not as clear cut as may be suggested here since continuity in policies and practices can be observed in all three periods. It should also be noted that during the first period industrial policy was directed mainly towards the restoration of the Japanese economy after the devastation of the war, hence the instruments adopted during this period are as self-explanatory as their titles suggest (Chart 4.1); therefore, the discussion will concentrate on the three periods adopted by Cooper (1986).

The 1950s

During the early 1950s, the Japanese wanted to create a modern industrial nation to be based, as much as possible, on the existing foundations which had been built up during the Second World War: a skilled work-force in the steel-making, ship-building and optics (for binoculars) sectors. To achieve this, they drew on their eighty years' experience with powerful governmental guidance in modernisation. Critical industries were identified, demand forecasts were made and industries were encouraged to plan their investment along these guidelines. In 1951, a rationalisation programme for steel was introduced. 'Special industry promotion laws' were passed for: synthetic fibres in 1953, petro-chemicals in 1955, machinery in 1956, synthetic rubber in 1957, electronics in 1957 and aircraft in 1958. Car assembly was given priority in 1952 (Warnecke, 1978). The 'Anti-monopoly Act', which had been enacted by the Occupation forces, was amended to allow for the creation of 'recession' and 'rationalisation' cartels with government approval with the object of preventing cut-throat price competition and inducing an orderly reduction in capacity during periods of slack demand, for example immediately after the Korean War, when the amendments were ratified. In 1953, the 'Export Import Trading Act', which permitted cartels to fix prices and limit imports, was passed. By 1971 there were 195 legally sanctioned cartels under the 'Export Import Trading Act', 13 under the 'Anti-monopoly Act' and 23 under separate legislation pertaining to the machinery, electronics and fertiliser industries (Yamamura, 1982), registering a decline in number of about 20 per cent from the mid-1960s (Caves and Uekusa, 1976).

It was during this period too that the 'Fiscal Investment and Loan Programme' (FILP) was created. This enabled the channelling of postal savings accounts (historically an important depository of household savings) and public pension reserve funds into a number of trust funds (standing at about forty today) for the promotion of public policy.

Chart 4.1 Japanese industrial policy

	Restoration period after World War II (1946–55)		Internal consummation period (1956–65)	
	Recovery from war damage (1946–50)	Adjustment of system (1951–55)	Promotion of priority industries (1956–60)	Enriching business power (1961–65)
Economic phenomena	IIP dropped to 20% of 1944 level	Serious shortage of foreign currency ($200–300 million US)	Annual growth rate of GNP is 7.4%	9.7% (higher economic growth). Foreign currency reserves. $180 million Surplus trend of trade balance. Sharp increase in CPI, 6% and over.
Problems in private sector	Shortage of production capacity, raw materials and funds Prevention of import and foreign funds Amelioration of the quality of products		Relative shortage of funds Dual structure Belated start in technology	Scale merit Strengthen an international competitiveness.
Trump cards in policy execution	Raw materials quota—(abolishment of the *Adjustment of the supply and Demand of Good Temporary Act*) Appropriation of government funds Foreign exchange allocation (import permission) Prevention of import and foreign funds		(Amplification of private funds and strengthened business powers)	

Industrial policy		Transition period to open market system (1966–75)		Internationalization (1976–)
		Reorganization under scale merit (1966–70)	Turning point of industrial policy (1971–75)	Groping years (1976–)
Basic policy	Maintenance of production Financial complement Prevention of imports, restriction on foreign funds, foreign currency control Adjustment of basic resources Acquisition of foreign currency; import substitution Adjustment of quality and standard			Unification of quality and standard Acquisition of foreign currency and intensification of competitiveness Adjustment and development of technology
Structural policy	Promotion of industrial rationalization Preference policy for certain industries			Fostering industries for strengthening competitiveness Quality improvement and funds Efficient utilization of goods Adjustment of key industries Amelioration of structure
Organizational policy	Weakening industries Strengthening industries			Amelioration of dual structure
Economic phenomena		Annual growth rate of GNP 12.4% Annual growth rate of IIP 15.1% (scale merit)	GNP, 5.1% Foreign currency reserves, $16.7 billion (in 1971) Rapid rise in CPI	GNP, 5.7% Foreign currency reserves, $29.2 billion
Problems in private sector		Increases in prices Problems of pollution, etc. Inquietude in energy supply	Countermeasures to appreciation of yen's current value Increasing unemployment	Trade conflict Depression, increasing unemployment

Chart 4.1 Continued

Industrial policy

Trump cards in policy execution	Allocation of oil
	Mass media
	(Abolition of foreign currency concentration system)
	↑ ↑ Liberalization of technological introduction
	1st liberalization of capital
	Liberalization of capital
	(entire liberalization of foreign funds)
	Supervision of import
	Revision of the *Foreign Exchange Control Act*
	Protection of consumption basis
	Development of energy
Basic-policy	Prevention of nuisance
	Protection of consumption basis
	Procurement of energy
	Measure to counter depression and unemployment
Structural policy	Shift from quantity to quality
	Promotion of knowledge-intensive course
	Intensive research and development
	High-degree assembly
	Fashion
	Knowledge industry
Organizational policy	Promotion of reorganization
	Restriction of entry by large companies into the fields in which small and medium sized companies are already active.
	Placing of public sector contracts with small and medium-sized companies and securing employment.

Source: J. Pinder (ed.), *National Strategies and the World Economy* (New Jersey: Allanheld, Osmun; Beckenham, Croom Helm, 1982)

Among these trust funds are the Japan Development Bank (JDB) and the Export-Import Bank of Japan (EIB).

Investment by the designated industries was encouraged by special tax incentives and by loans from the JDB. Japanese industry drew 13 per cent of its external financing from the JDB during 1952 and 1955, and another 15 per cent from other FILP programmes (these figures had declined to respectively 4 per cent and 10 per cent by 1971–5). Four key selected industries (electric power, shipping, coal and steel) received 24 per cent of their external financing from the JDB and another 13 per cent from other FILP programmes in 1952–5 (Noguchi in Yamamura, 1982). Cooper (1986) argues that this public finance was a key instrument of policy and that a JDB loan often provided a signal for lending (at commercial terms) by the quantitatively more important private banks, on the grounds that the designated firms were likely to involve lower risk than other business loans.

Moreover, foreign exchange controls prevailed throughout this period and import licences were used to further industrial policy. For example, imported cars were more durable and commodious than Japanese domestic cars, and when the taxi industry revived and thrived, its demand for imported cars (including used cars from the US forces resident in Japan) increased. The purchase of such cars was limited under the 1951 foreign exchange regulations. However, car imports were liberalised in 1952 only to be tightened again in early 1954, with the taxi-cab companies commencing a 'buy Japanese' campaign. Japanese production with better quality needed foreign technology. In 1952, the Japanese Ministry of International Trade and Industry (MITI) promulgated guidelines for car assembly licensing agreements which, among other things, stipulated that, after a period of time, eleven key car parts must be produced in Japan (Yakushiji, 1984). Also, foreign exchange regulations were employed to restrict imports in many other industries as well as to shape the development of each favourably designated industry.

The 1960s

Japan gave importance to exports in 1949 when 'export promotion' was MITI's main objective. However, the 1950s was predominantly a decade of 'import substitution' due to the production in Japan of more sophisticated commodities leading to a reduction in the import of these products. In 1960, because of pressure from the US and Western Europe on Japan to adopt currency convertibility and to fully endorse the obligations of GATT (which it joined in 1955), Japan introduced wide-ranging liberalisation in trade and foreign exchange. This was to enable Japan to prepare for its admission to the OECD, which it joined in 1964. This gesture entailed the removal of exchange controls and the general use of explicit import restrictions as major instruments of industrial policy, 'although some approved cartels continued to limit imports, presumably with MITI knowledge' (Cooper, 1986). Also, as the private banking sector became both powerful and more assertive, the importance of the JDB diminished drastically.

The relaxation of the foreign exchange regulations and the powerful growth of domestic sources of credit in Japan meant that MITI had to rely more on moral suasion, less on directives. However, this did not always work:

An effort to pass a new law supporting selected industries unexpectedly failed due to domestic opposition in the early 1960s, and in 1965–66 the Sumitomo steel company flouted MITI's administrative guidance to cut back steel production. The growth of independent banks inhibited the development of "national champions" in Japan, since each bank wanted to have within its "family" of firms a representative from each major industry. The degree of competitiveness among major Japanese banks and firms, and the difficulty it sometimes poses for government, was already encountered in 1955 when a MITI plan to create a single small, inexpensive "People's" car (along the lines of Volkswagen) to open the mass market was leaked to the press (Japan's press is more competitive and more aggressive than that in the US) and created a storm of protest from the actual and would-be car makers. The plan was abandoned and vigorous competition developed among Japan's car makers.

A general policy can continue in the face of even major exceptions and derogations. But it is also likely that such exceptions remind the officials, if they need reminding, that there are distinct limits to their authority, and they therefore influence what MITI calls for, and what industry calls on MITI to call for if the industry is not unanimous. It is not true, as foreigners are sometimes led to believe, that Japanese business leaders are unwilling to take risks on their own and to stand out from the crowd (Cooper, 1986).

The steel and ship-building industries became commercially successful by the 1960s. Relative significance then shifted towards the machine-tool industry which was deemed, like steel, to be a prerequisite for a modern industrial economy, given US experience in this respect. The encouragement given to the machine-tool industry included tax breaks, modest subsidies and favourable procurement.

The 1970s

In the early 1970s, Japanese industrial policy showed a marked shift in a number of respects. The Japanese people had become anxious about growing industrial pollution, the inadequacy of their welfare system and about having to pay relatively higher prices for Japanese products than did customers abroad (this was especially so with regard to television sets). Moreover, MITI as well as officials elsewhere, even before the first oil 'shock' in 1973, became concerned about Japan's rapid growth in oil imports. The government responded by establishing a more generous social security system in 1972 and by introducing very strict pollution standards. As a reaction to the dollar crisis of 1971–2, Japan initiated a number of measures to liberalise imports and direct investment inflows and began to monitor exports with the aim of curtailing unduly fast growth. Japan also abolished its 'buy only Japanese' policy in the area of public procurement and subjected loans under FILP to Diet approval, 'something which had not been required before 1972 and which greatly reduced their flexibility as an instrument of industrial policy' (Cooper, 1986).

MITI, realising that the future lay in 'knowledge-intensive' industries, emphasised their importance by encouraging Japanese industry to move in that direction. The Agency for Industrial Science and Technology (AIST) was established within MITI with the purpose of financing research projects in ceramics, computers, sea-bed mining and flexible computer-aided manufacturing systems. AIST supported projects where the product under consideration was not yet on the commercial market and where the research was too large or too risky for private firms to undertake solely. An early success was a desalination process that was later commercialised by private firms and sold in the Middle East. In 1983, MITI's total budget for R&D amounted to about $250 million and it was spent on MITI's own 15 laboratories and on assisting R&D by private firms; the total annual expenditure on R&D by private firms was about $10 billion.

Two of the most heavily publicised instances of MITI assistance for R&D were: the VLSI (very large-scale integrated circuit) project which commenced in 1976 and to which the government extended about $120 million in conditional loans (repayable only when there was commercial success) between 1976 and 1979, and the so-called fifth generation computer in the early 1980s. Moreover, assistance to high technology industries is not confined to research grants and conditional loans: the Japanese National Aeronautics and Space Development Agency has given preference in its procurement to satellites with high local content, which now exceeds 60 per cent. However, the US–Japan Trade Study Group (1984, p. 54) stated that Japan's semi-conductor market was in 1984 completely open to US-owned companies.

Japan does not only assist the commodities of the future. Since 1978 it has had a programme for restructuring Japanese industries that are depressed, 'for whatever reason' (Cooper, 1986). Firms which produce two-thirds of the output of a depressed industry can petition the government for a 'restructuring plan'. This involves an agreed reduction in capacity, with loan guarantees and tax benefits accruing to firms that scrap capacity under the plan. In mid-1984, there were 22 officially-designated industries, of which five (paper, ethylene, compound fertiliser, polyolefins and PVC resin) had formed legal cartels to restrict output and price competition (US–Japan Trade Study Group, 1984, p. 64). This means that there has been a substantial decline in the use of cartels from two decades ago. In addition, FILP support for Japanese industry is very much less (proportionately) than it used to be and the government loan rate differential below market rates dropped from around 3 per cent in the early 1960s to about 1 per cent in the early 1980s (Noguchi in Yamamura, 1982). Cooper (1986) is sure that:

> in general, Japanese government involvement in determining industrial structure is far less than it once was – in part because the two instruments of foreign exchange licensing and credit control are now unavailable for disciplining large firms. But it continues to provide hortatory guidance in MITI's "Visions" and other government pronouncements, and to back these up with direct or indirect funding on a modest scale and with directed government procurement.

Now, before one jumps to the conclusion that, despite the relative decline in the protective nature of Japanese industrial policy, its mere existence lends enough support to the argument that Japan's market is unfairly shielded against the outside world, it is vital to ask: what of industrial policy in the EC and the USA? The answer is that industrial policy does play an important role in both Europe and the USA. Indeed, the European and American industrial policies are not only similar to that of Japan but are also generally more extensive (Cooper, 1986). First, consider Europe.

Industrial policy in Europe

Western Europe is the 'classic' area of industrial policy. As Hager (1982) argues, it would take a whole book to simply describe the industrial policies of the individual nations of this region, particularly since the practices in each country are as complex as those of any major OECD partner. However, since this area is well documented in standard works (see, for example, Pinder (1982) and Jacquemin (1983)), it should be sufficient to give only a very brief sketch of the forms of industrial policies pursued by the Western European nations.

A brief background to the Western European industrial policies is given by Hager (1982):

It is difficult to sketch the history of industrial policy in Western Europe, not least because, until the seventies, structures and policies diverged widely. The story begins in the late forties, with the perceived need to manage scarcity and rebuild key industries. In the French case, this was from the beginning coupled with a long-range development plan, whose concrete result was, [*inter alia*], the modernization and electrification of the railways. The Marshall Plan, initially intended to provide a Euro-American framework for integrating planned economies, rapidly became a force for trade liberalization. This reflected a shift in thinking in northern and northwestern Europe in matters of economic and industrial policy toward a greater reliance on market forces. In the fifties, however, Germany among others continued systematic and concentrated aid toward industrial reconstruction, coupled with a certain resistance toward trade liberalization. In Britain, industrial policy followed a basically liberal path, in line with the early adoption of Keynesian thinking in that country. There were two major exceptions to the British neglect of industry as a subject for public policy. One concerned the Labour Party's policy of owner- ship of the "commanding heights," notably steel; the other was the massive support, by the then prevailing standards, of high technology as part of the big power posture of the country.

After the end of the Second World War, Italy and France saw themselves as relatively underdeveloped agricultural economies. One manifestation of this underdevelopment was the lack of risk-oriented capital markets, with preference given to secure low-rate-of-return investment, such as in real estate, as against investment for 'productive' purposes. Also, both these countries were dominated by small family firms which failed to exploit new technologies. The need for the Italian government to take over, during the inter-war period, some of the major banks and their industrial holdings due to their collapse, and the take-over by the French government of credit institutions before the Second World War, gave both governments 'new tools with which to practise venture capitalism' (Hager, 1982).

Contrary to the case in Italy, in France the role of the government as an entrepreneur was coupled with planning which was characterised by a 70 per cent state ownership and a loose control of sources of finance. Whereas in Italy, the Istituto per la Ricostruzione Industriale (IRI) assisted, among others, in establishing a modern heavy and light engineering industry, the French initially relied on modernising those few sectors that could either be classified as infrastructure, such as railways and electricity, or as intermediate inputs for the rest of industry, such as coal and steel. When trade was being liberalised through the OEEC and later the European Community, France decided to create industries capable of out-competing their international counterparts. Since France was well aware of the slow pace of industrial change, the government took a very active part to help speed up the process by: inducing small firms to merge, supplying capital to industries which needed to replace obsolete capital, providing technological know-how from government research establishments, etc.

Through the National Economic Development Council (NEDC), the Industrial Reorganisation Corporation (IRC) and subsequently other institutions, Britain tried, but cautiously, to establish 'state capitalism' during the 1960s. The aim was to rejuvenate industry and enhance the country's rate of economic growth.

In Britain, France and Italy, and other Western European nations, 'state venture capitalism' is still a powerful instrument of industrial development. Particularly since the 1960s, one 'variant of such policies has been widely used in Europe: the more or less enforced merger of firms whose size was deemed insufficient to allow them to operate profitably and keep abreast of the latest technology' (Hager, 1982). Aircraft production, automobiles, computers, electrical engineering, heavy engineering, metal smelting, shipyards and steel have been some of the industries rationalised by 'state intervention'. Three instruments were used for this purpose: the provision of credit for modernisation, especially in countries with powerful public banking sectors like Italy and France; the threat of withholding credit facilities to near-bankrupt industries as in, among others, Britain and Sweden; and the use of the near monopoly of governments over certain procurement markets like in the aircraft industry in West Germany.

The ability of the big West German banks to have detailed knowledge of all major firms in the key sectors of the economy (through their representatives in the boards of directors) and their willingness to go for long-term capital gains rather than short-term high dividends are 'examples of the many fortunate historically derived arrangements that lessen the need for active industrial policies in that country' (Hager, 1982). Another such circumstance is the comparatively even distribution of industrial activity, allowing the concentration of regional policies in just a few areas.

Concentration of financial resources has also been typical of both positive and defensive policies in West Germany. Of the latter, coal and shipbuilding have been the major beneficiaries as well as, periodically since the 1950s, steel. Among the positive policies, that devoted to nuclear power has been the major effort since the early 1960s. More recently, the aircraft, computer and ocean-related industries have benefited from government aid.

A good deal of West German industrial policy is carried out at the state, not the federal, level:

> The Lander, more than the Federal government, have the ability to give free land, tax holidays, housing grants for workers, etc., and to provide credit guarantees to attract new industries or to preserve old ones. ... Since no aggregate statistics are available, one can only guess at the scale of these efforts, but it is at least equal to all expenditure for industrial purposes by the government. As in the United States, the relative weakness of central policies fosters a myth that exaggerates the extent to which industry operates independently of public authorities (Hager, 1982).

In short, in Britain, France and Italy there are organisations similar to the JDB, channelling funds raised by the government to the private sector. The three European countries extend special tax concessions to encourage investment in general and particularly investment in favourably-designated industries, both by industry and region. These nations have extensive public-owned industrial corporations (a rare occurrence in Japan) which are granted periodic infusions of new 'equity' capital, 'which are difficult to distinguish from subsidies when the firms are running operating losses' (Cooper, 1986). All three have provided extensive support to their steel and textile industries with the aim of consolidating operations and scrapping obsolete capital. Britain, France and West Germany have also extended public support to cushion falling demand in their shipbuilding industries. In the field of high technology, all three have given extensive public funding and preferred government procurement in aerospace, computers and telecommunications – see Carmoy in Warnecke (1978) for details of actions taken. For example, public Post, Telephone and Telegraph (PTT) corporations in these nations very rarely buy equipment made by other countries, and national power-generating organisations rarely purchase foreign-made heavy electrical-generating equipment.

Industrial policy in the United States

The USA does not have an industrial policy as such. However, it has many measures which directly or indirectly assist US business. One of the US's most distinguished economists writes:

The US government has had, and continues to have, extensive sectoral involvement in the US economy. For example, in the nineteenth century it gave land grants to the railroads and more recently it has constructed a vast highway system to open up areas of the country and provide cheap inland transport. It provides cheap, under-priced water to irrigate Arizonan and Californian farms, producing the citrus which growers complain about being unable to sell "fairly" to the Japanese and Europeans. It has extensive R&D and development programmes by the Department of Defence and by the National Aeronautics and Space Administration which generate commercially valuable spin-offs such as jet engines, helicopters and the Boeing 747 [see Nelson *et al.*, 1982]. It is true that the Europeans and the Japanese exaggerate the quantitative importance of the commercial impact of defence R&D, but most American analysis of foreign government policies is also

qualitative, leaving the impression of greater quantitative importance than is generally warranted. Extensive charitable deductions
under the US tax system permit the US to provide higher education
to a much larger percentage of the labour force than the Europeans
could afford with their tax supported systems and in "unfair
competition" with the private universities of Japan.

... the US government engages in a host of actions that
influence the competitiveness of American exports, ranging from
direct actions to encourage exports through activities to stimulate
production and general support for business activity to actions
which by discouraging certain industries lead indirectly to encouragement of others (Cooper, 1986).

Consider some concrete examples (see Cooper in Warnecke, 1978
and Cooper (1986) for a detailed specification):

(1) Economic and military assistance to the LDCs tied to the
procurement of US goods. In this case the US government in effect
buys the American goods and gives them away, or lends them on very
easy terms. Foreign aid represents an extreme form of export subsidisation but it is accepted as contributing to economic development or
national security, and the importing countries in this case would be
unlikely to hold the US accountable for unfair import competition or
to impose countervailing duties. But third countries may lose export
orders because of foreign aid shipments tied to US procurement. The
subsidisation of American exports would cease if foreign aid grants
and loans were freely usable for the purchase of goods and services
anywhere, as is the case with loans from The World Bank. US foreign
assistance and military credit sales amounted to about $15.5 billion in
1982, or about 4.5 per cent of total US exports of goods and services.

(2) Under US tax laws until 1984, corporations that derived at least 95
per cent of their gross receipts from exports could qualify as domestic
international sales corporations (DISCs) and could defer payment of
corporate profits tax until dividends were remitted to the parent
corporation. This provision, with cost in excess of $1 billion in annual
revenue foregone in the mid-1970s, amounted to an interest-free loan
from the government for expenditures involved in the promotion of
exports. The subsidy element – about $60 million a year – was
thought to be much less than the foregone revenues, since the taxes
would have eventually to be paid. In fact, in the 1984 Tax Act which
eliminated the DISC and permitted in its place the Foreign Trade

Corporation, many of the unpaid taxes were waived, so the interest-free loan turned out *ex post* to be a direct subsidy.

(3) US government subsidises both the construction and operation of merchant vessels under US registry. Construction subsidies do not increase exports since such subsidies are available only to purchases by US flag companies, but of course operating subsidies to shipping make it easier for Americans to export shipping services. Both programmes are of long-standing, and in the mid-1970s the operating subsidy amounted to $200 million a year. Ship construction and shipping services generally involve heavy government involvement throughout the world.

(4) The Export-Import Bank provides medium-term credit for American exports. For a number of years the interest rates were below market rates, so a direct subsidy was involved. More recently, the Bank has tried to keep its lending rates above its borrowing rates by enough to cover its operating costs, except when necessary to meet foreign competition. The subsidy to American exports is thus now the more subtle (and smaller) one which arises from the use of US government credit in borrowing in the capital market plus the absence of a requirement to pay dividends on the Bank's capital.

(5) Until 1973 the Commodity Credit Corporation (CCC) gave substantial subsidies to US exports of many agricultural products, the counterpart of a system of high domestic price supports combined with the view that in the absence of agricultural policy the US would be a substantial exporter of agricultural products, especially grains, cotton, tobacco, etc. The high price supports stimulated output, so the programme also involved limitations on acreage. This system was reinstituted on a lesser scale in the early 1980s. It is difficult to say whether agricultural exports are larger or smaller than they would have been in the absence of the government support programmes since the support prices and the acreage controls could be expected to have opposite effects on farm production.

(6) Investment in plant and equipment in the US enjoys a 10–25 per cent tax credit. The credit in effect lowers the cost of domestic investment by that amount, and thus stimulates the productive capacity of the economy. The credit operates for all investment, however, so it is not obvious whether on balance exports or imports are stimulated more by the tax credit. The first round effects of increased production and income could go either way. The major

long-run effect of the investment tax credit is to make American industry somewhat more capital-intensive than it would be without the credit, both in each industry taken separately and in its overall industrial structure. In addition, since 1981 there have been extremely generous write-off provisions for the depreciation of new investment. These provisions have a similar effect to the investment tax credit.

Depletion allowances for oil and other minerals have the effect of stimulating domestic production of such products and thus serve to reduce imports or to increase exports of these products. Until 1975, this tax privilege was available to American-owned mineral investment anywhere in the world, but now it is limited to production in the US.

(7) There are many areas of direct government expenditure for activities that support business enterprise. Examples are federal spending, net of user charges, for: airports and air traffic control; dredging rivers and harbours; and providing the postal service. Government funds by the billion have been devoted to the development of water resources, which provide both cheap hydroelectric power in the areas covered by them, and cheap water for irrigation in the southwestern part of the country, resulting in a great stimulation of agricultural output there. In addition, the Rural Electrification Administration has subsidised the electrification of the rural parts of the American economy for nearly fifty years, at low interest rates, thus making farming somewhat less costly than it would otherwise be.

(8) Price controls on domestically produced natural gas cheapen energy for Americans with access to the price-controlled gas, and hence provide 'subsidies' (but not revenue-reducing ones) for American exports as well as for domestic sales of products that require the use of gas in their production. In 1985 some, but not all, gas price controls were removed, so this 'subsidy' will diminish in importance over time. For nearly a decade before 1981 US oil prices were also held below world market prices, with similar effect.

(9) Government expenditures on R&D help to cover the initial cost of new economic activities, which often later lead to exports. The classic example is agricultural research, which has been financed by government for over a century and which has led to vast improvements in the productivity of American agriculture and to improvements in the quality of agricultural products. Sometimes too, large export sales are a distant by-product of military R&D and development expenditures,

as was the case with the jet engine. Currently, the government is spending substantial sums on R&D in the energy sector, both on nuclear power and on such possibilities as liquefaction of coal. To the extent that the last proves to be economically feasible, it may augment future exports of American coal.

(10) Extensive government purchases sometimes lead to the development of products which are highly competitive in world markets, by helping private firms to spread their own R&D costs as well as other overhead expenditures over a larger number of sales. The list of products here in principle is a long one, but the point is quantitatively important in relatively few industries, such as military equipment, avionics, some kinds of telecommunications equipment and ground tracking stations for satellites.

(11) The most pervasive influences, and quantitatively probably the most important stimulus to exports of particular goods, but also the least obvious, are the host of government regulations on US production which have been introduced to improve the working environment or the natural environment. Such items as effluent controls, safety regulations, minimum wage legislation, and restrictions on child labour can have a profound effect on the competitiveness of particular industries, hence on the relative competitiveness of other industries less directly affected. Since most observers would not mention such government actions in a list of export 'subsidies' – and indeed they do not normally give rise to a loss of government revenue, except where the government occasionally incurs some of the costs, for example, of anti-pollution actions – it is worthwhile to trace through the influence on exports of one of these regulations, the minimum wage. The key assumptions in this analysis are that over time balance is maintained in international payments, for example by movements in the exchange rate of the dollar, and that the government takes whatever steps are necessary to assure full employment of the labour force. So we are looking here for the sectoral effects, the relative stimulation or retardation of production in particular sectors of the economy which arise from the regulation in question.

The minimum wage, if set high enough to exceed the wages that would otherwise be paid in some industries, reduces the international competitiveness of those industries by raising their costs. The industry will find it more difficult to compete with products from abroad. Imports will rise, and restoration of equilibrium in the balance-of-payments will require some depreciation of the dollar relative to what it would otherwise be. The depreciation, in turn will *increase* the competitiveness of all sectors where wages are not influenced by the minimum wage. Put more concretely, it is likely in the US that the minimum wage discourages the production of apparel (which is displaced to some extent by imports) and encourages the production and export of machinery. Thus in an indirect fashion, via adjustment of the exchange rate, the export of machinery is 'subsidised' (but again not in a fashion that reduces revenue to the government). A similar argument holds, *mutatis mutandis*, for other government regulations. For example, meeting required safety standards will raise costs more in some industries than in others, and via adjustments in the exchange rate will increase the competitiveness of industries or firms whose costs for safety have increased least. (See Kalt (1985) for a finding that environmental regulations have had a discernible effect on the composition of US trade.)

The US (like Australia, Canada and West Germany) has a federal government structure. The US federal government accounts for only about one-third of total government expenditure and for about one-fifth of total civilian public employment. For the most part, the influence of state and local governments on the structure of production and costs falls into (7) and (11) in the above list: expenditures which support business enterprise in a general way and regulations on the conditions of production or marketing. In addition, local governments sometimes support particular firms in the form of cheap land, low utility rates or cheap credit. Commencing in the 1950s, a number of localities used their privilege of floating tax-exempt securities to provide cheap credit to new firms through the issue of so-called industrial development bonds, a practice which still continues today. Of course, the business enhancing activities of state and local governments are not aimed at encouraging exports from the US, but rather from the particular state or locality to the rest of the US, only incidentally to other countries.

It should be added that other examples may work in a manner contrary to that of minimum wages: discrimination in favour of certain firms or industries automatically involves discrimination against firms and industries that are not so favoured. If subsidies or tax breaks or below market credits are extended to favoured firms, others have to make up the difference by paying more taxes or more credit than would be true in the absence of the discriminatory measures. The national currency will have to appreciate to the extent that exports are stimulated, thus putting others at a disadvantage with respect to foreign competition. For example, when Japan allows the formation of cartels in periods of recession or for industrial restructuring, the impact of which is to hold domestic prices above what they would otherwise be, this represents a negative action for those that buy from the cartel. Where consumers are made to bear the additional cost, as in the colour TV case, exports are not adversely affected. However, where the cartel raises the price of steel, industrial chemicals, machinery or a number of other products, this represents increased costs for the downstream purchasers. (Note that for domestic prices to stay above world market prices, some form of import restriction must prevail.) It may also be true that the possiblity of creating recession cartels has generated higher capacity than otherwise would occur by removing from investing firms some of the risk of a major downturn in the market; this excess capacity in turn encourages exports at something below average costs – see Yamamura, 1982. In that case, the yen will be stronger and cartellisation will put other firms at a disadvantage.

A similar argument applies to required procurement of domestic products. An enduring complaint of the US heavy electrical generating equipment industry is that potential buyers in other major industrial countries purchase exclusively domestic products, regardless of cost. This is the case especially in Europe where the supply of electricity is typically provided by public authorities. However, it is also true in Japan, which, like the US, has extensive private utilities. In contrast, the US market for heavy generating and transmission equipment is relatively open, with about 20 per cent of US purchases coming from abroad, mainly from Japan. However, the requirement by foreign utilities to buy domestic in general will raise the costs of generating electricity there and those costs must be either subsidised by the government or passed on to the consumer, including industrial consumers. Hence, while the US heavy electrical equipment industry suffers from this practice, the rest of US industry in general benefits by virtue of paying lower electricity charges than their foreign competitors. Similar arguments apply to the requirement in some countries that computers should be purchased locally. Over time, unless the local computers are competitive in both price and quality, the (mostly state-owned) enterprises that are burdened by this obligation will suffer in competitiveness.

Industrial policies in the NICs and LDCs?

It is not just Europe, Japan and the USA that have industrial policies; the newly industrialising countries (NICs) and the LDCs also have them. The LDCs protect most industries on the grounds that they are 'infants', particularly when the industries are of the import-substitute type, but protection is afforded sometimes even for labour intensive industries and frequently for capital and technology intensive ones such as car assembly and shipbuilding. Of course, international trade theorists have for a long time conceded the 'infant industry' argument as the only exception to free trade (see El-Agraa, 1983b), but this concession depends on very specific provisos: the country must lack sophisticated tax-cum-revenue systems and capital markets, and must also be deficient in the necessary skills to operate such industries, indicating the importance of learning by doing. What is most important, however, is the condition that 'infants' must grow so that protection is only temporary, but the reality is very different since there is no evidence to suggest that any country has succeeded in withdrawing the protection even in such countries as Turkey – see Krueger and Tuncer (1982).

Another aspect of industrial policy in the LDCs is the Generalised System of Preferences (GSP) which enables certain LDCs to export some of their manufactured and semi-manufactured products to the countries of the advanced world at a preferential access to their advanced markets without any kind of reciprocity. Again, this is a type of support which is general and is granted by the advanced nations concerned, but it is a type of industrial policy in that it is a subsidy to the relevant industries in the LDCs.

Finally, a specific case of industrial policy occurs in Bahrain where the aluminium smelter industry enjoys an exceptionally cheap price for natural gas. However, this is a 'delicate matter, because there is no established international price [for natural gas] in Saudi Arabia and Bahrain. . . . Thus it is not possible to judge whether the present price . . . is appropriate and it will only be some time in the future when an international price is set, whether the competitive power of . . . Bahrain . . . can be maintained' (Warnecke, 1978). However, in the meantime, the behaviour of these 'non-economic' smelters is disturbing the world market for aluminium ingots.

With regard to the NICs, apart from the traditional means of restricting the import of commodities which compete with the production of publicly-favoured industries, there are also some elements of industrial policy being practised. For example, when a South Korean shipbuilding company succeeded in obtaining a contract to construct a harbour at Jubail on the east coast of Saudi Arabia, the government of Korea ruled that Koreans who work on contract engineering and construction projects in the Middle East should be exempt from the draft and should be given priority in public housing upon their return to Korea; this is tantamount to stating that the Korean government is 'providing quite effective support to a Korean company without undertaking any additional government expenditure' (Warnecke, 1978).

Empirical evidence?

A thorough analysis of the protective effects of both tariff and non-tariff barriers is impossible to carry out due not only to the multiplicity of the factors that have to be taken into consideration, but also to the vagueness of such factors for quantitative work; how easy is it to formulate these industrial policy aspects into *sensible* hypotheses that can be meaningfully investigated in an econometric model? Realising this, Bergsten and Cline (1985) resorted to commonsensical quantitative approaches to find out about these protective effects. The summary and conclusions of their investigations were that:

> Indirect evidence of intangible protection is complicated both in conceptual terms and in empirical demonstration. We would rely primarily on the ratio of total imports to GDP. Cross-country comparisons of this ratio suggest that Japan shows no special aberration of low imports that might be attributable to high but intangible protection, after taking account of country size, natural resource endowment, and transportation costs. And although the share of manufactures in Japan's total imports is low, there are sound reasons of comparative advantage to expect this pattern. Moreover, Japan is the second largest market for US exports of manufactures; US manufactured exports to Japan compare favorably with those to Germany, even though Germany is generally considered to have a relatively unprotected market. One important study at the level of individual products also appears to confirm the macroeconomic evidence that Japanese protection is not abnormally high.

Back to the scenario

Returning to the first point of this scenario, all one needs to remember is that the Japanese market for manufactures is certainly 'different' from that in the EC or the USA; Table 4.2 clearly demonstrates this. However, apart from the implications of the 'industrial policies' impact on the relative performance of different industries, it should be clear that this 'difference' is no more than a mere reflection of the fact that Japan imports a large amount of raw materials relative to these countries, i.e. Japan has to import fewer manufactures in order to be able to import those raw materials which are vital for its economy – see the previous section.

MEMBERSHIP OF CLUB OECD

Japan is a member of the OECD, but does not play according to the rules of the game: the OECD is a club whose members ought to have certain characteristics which entitle them to be labelled 'advanced nations'. Japan is seen as the 'black sheep' of the family due to a discrepancy between its privileged status as a member of the group and its general pattern of behaviour: Japan is recognised as having

Table 4.2   A comparison of the relative importance of manufactures in the imports of the EC, Japan and the USA

Area	Percentage of imports of manufactures to 1982 GNP[a]	Percentage of imports of manufactures to 1982 total imports	Percentage of internal consumption of manufactured products covered by imports	Per capita value of imports of manufactures in 1982 in US dollars
EC	7.8	41	9.15	467
USA	8.0	57.7	6.32	629
Japan	3.9	22.9	3.9	223

Note: [a] The 1960 equivalent percentages were: 3.3, 2 and 2.4 for respectively the EC, USA and Japan.

Source: EC Delegation in Tokyo.

reached a position of industrial prominence but is still conducting its domestic affairs in ways similar to those of an LDC. It was the norm for a member of the OECD to erode 'workaholism' as it became more affluent. Economic advancement was expected to lead to a multiplicity of interests, values and beliefs in a democratic system, but the 'Japan Inc.' with the one-party system are seen to be in direct contradiction to this. Japan's foreign aid performance is seen as inadequate, its representation at the United Nations and participation in UN projects are considered to be out of proportion with its international status, and it does not allocate what is deemed an adequate percentage of its domestic resources to improving the 'quality' of its domestic environment and working conditions. Moreover, Japan does not even contribute to its international defence; hence it is seen as a 'free rider'.

These points are hinted at by no less a distinguished economist than Kindleberger (1986):

[one] should analyse the question of when a country should, in a normative sense, take on some appropriate (substantial?) share of responsibility for the world economic system. A similar problem presents itself in peace-keeping. Indeed the parallelism between peace-keeping and international economic stability is a close one, both being international public goods that have to be provided in the absence of international government that could use coercion, and both goods that are plagued with "free-riders" ... This is sometimes called the "graduation problem" ...

Like so many young adults, having sown their wild oats, it is time for Japan to settle down and take on world responsibilities. At the least, it should eschew the role of free rider, conform to the Kantian Categorical Imperative, which calls for people and countries to act in ways which can be generalised. It should no longer depend on the forbearance of others to escape the fallacy of composition.

A danger for the World is that the US may perceive Japan as moving by herself in directions inconsistent with world economic coherence and stability and set out to discipline her. Retaliation, trade war, monetary restrictions, more industrial competition extending even to bribery and espionage may follow. The picture is unattractive.

With regard to the general economic parameters, Japan is also seen as an outsider. This is because Japan concentrates all its energies in the export sector to the detriment of other important matters. Hence Japan today has congested housing, an inadequate sewage system, cities and towns with very sub-normal park and sports facilities and a work pattern and style which are unpleasant and allow practically no opportunities for recreational and leisure activities. There is a great deal of truth in this; for example, a survey of the average size of a 'flat' or apartment showed that Tokyo ranked 'startlingly low at 59 square meters, as compared with 200 square meters in New York, 167 square meters in Toronto, 140 square meters in London, and 120 square meters in Dusseldorf' (Ozawa, 1984). Moreover, the lack of adequate public park facilities is acknowledged by all concerned, and even the lack of appropriate protection of the environment is conceded. Finally, the point regarding concentration on exports is substantiated by the published statistics: between 1964 and 1973, Japan's annual average rate of growth of GNP was 10.7 per cent while that of its exports was 15.7 per cent; and between 1973 and 1981, the respective rates were 3.7 and 8.5 per cent. As a digression, it should be added that some economists argue that free trade is only advocated in countries where the growth rate of exports exceeds that of GDP; where the contrary is the case, the protection of the home market takes priority over access to foreign markets.

However, there seem to be some fundamental reasons for the Japanese 'workaholic' mentality. Ozawa argues, in response to the EC Commission's assertion that the Japanese are 'workaholics living in rabbit hutches', that:

the average Japanese work-week is 43 hours, substantially longer than in the United States or Western Europe ... but ... the Japanese work long hours not because they are workaholics but because they are poorer than their American and European counterparts. Average hourly earnings in Japan are only $5.27 per hour, as compared with $8.73 in the United States and $7.08 in West Germany. This means that the Japanese must work more hours than Americans or West Germans in order to make ends meet ... Japan's average of $5.27 per hour is not very different from Britain's $5.30 or France's $5.56. But there is another factor compelling Japanese workers to put in more hours to make more money: the burden of the huge housing loans (Ozawa, 1984).

With regard to the last point, the survey mentioned earlier suggested that the average cost per square metre of land showed Tokyo with $2000, New York with $660, Toronto with $800, London with $920 and Dusseldorf with $1440.

In short, Japan is seen as an industrial giant which directs all its activities towards its export sector much to the detriment of facilities which are the symbol of Club OECD. Moreover, the totality of Japan's trade relations is conducted with this principle in mind: the voluntary export restraints (VERs) made by Japan are meant to ease international tension to pave the way for a further round of export onslaught. There is a wealth of food for thought here, but one should leave it to the reader to decide whether or not Japan is the 'black sheep' of club OECD.

ECONOMIC MISMANAGEMENT IN THE REST OF THE OECD

Both the USA and the EC have been having much higher unemployment rates as well as inflation rates relative to Japan – see Table 4.3. In early 1985, I wrote that:

> The USA has an overvalued dollar relative to the yen and its present interest rates are much higher too (by 50%). The EC's relative position is more complex since the ECU is a basket of currencies, but it has been known for a long time that, until recently, the Pound Sterling has also been overvalued. These facts when put together seem to suggest that the trade imbalances for the USA and the EC are largely due to their own doing. In other words, it is the responsibility of the USA to put its own house in order by lowering its interest rates and depreciating the dollar (El-Agraa, 1985a).

The Japanese Economic Planning Agency, in its *Economic Survey of Japan 1983/84* (published in late 1985), confirmed my assertion:

> If all of the above special factors and economic cycle factors are considered as short-term factors, they constituted a $3.5 billion deficit in . . . 1982 but revived to $10.9 billion surplus in . . . 1983. In other words, short-term factors resulted in an increase of $14.4 billion from . . . 1982 through . . . 1983. A break down of this value shows $2.7 billion attributable to changes in the reduction margin

Table 4.3 Inflation rates and recorded unemployment in the EC, Japan and USA

| | Average annual rate of inflation (%) | | Recorded unemployment (% of civilian labour force) | | |
	1965–73	1973–83	1981	1984	1985
EC9			8	10.9	11.2
Belgium	4.4	6.4	11	14.4	13.2
Denmark	7.6	9.5	9	9.8	—
France	5.3	10.8	8	9.9	10.1
W. Germany	4.7	4.3	5	8.4	9.4
Greece	4.4	16.8	—	—	—
Ireland	8.5	14.5	11	16.5	—
Italy	5.1	17.5	8	11.9	13.0
Netherlands	6.4	6.2	8	14.5	15.4
UK	6.2	14.3	10	11.8	12.9
Japan	6.0	4.7	2.5	2.7	2.4
USA	4.7	7.5	7.6	7.5	7.3

Note: Luxembourg is included with Belgium.
— means not available.

Source: Statistical Abstract of the United States, 1985 and *World Development Report*, 1985.

of oil prices, $5.3 billion to changes in economic situations in Japan and the US, and $6.4 billion to changes in exchange rates.

These three factors (totaling $14.4 billion) can be cited in explaining most of the increase of $15.1 billion in the current account surplus from ... 1982 through ... 1983.

The theoretical foundations for this conclusion are explained in Chapter 8: it is a macroeconomic, not a sector-specific, model.

In other words, $6.4 billion out of the $14.4 billion change in the trade balance between Japan and the USA between 1982 and 1983 was due to the change in the dollar/yen parity. This amounted to about 44 per cent of the trade balance for that period. Hence, in the context of 1986 and the coordinated action by the Group of Five (G5) to appreciate the yen, the Swiss Franc and Deutschmark against the dollar, and other weaker OECD currencies, it is misleading to imply that the purpose of the exchange rate alignment is to completely wipe out the US's trade deficit, since, as argued in Chapter 3, the structural element necessitates a surplus for Japan. Obvious as this may seem, at the peak of the dollar in March 1985, econometric equations were being carried out to determine the necessary percentage drop in the value of the dollar in order to 'balance exports and imports' (Thurow, 1986). Moreover, it should be added that Bergsten and Cline (1985) endorse my assessment since their analysis led to the conclusion that '*the rise in the US–Japanese trade deficit from 1980 to 1984 can be fully explained by changes in the exchange rate and the rates of economic growth*' (their italics), not just the exchange rate; this is in spite of the fact that their estimates did not take the balance of payments stages effects into consideration. Furthermore, the excellent study by Marris (1985) also substantiates this point.

Returning to the main point in contention, given what was stated above regarding the fact that the correction of Japan's trade surplus will not solve the USA's trade deficit, nor that of the EC, it follows that the reason for the trade frictions must be mainly due to the prevalence of protectionist sentiments at a time of high unemployment coupled (see Table 5.3) with imports from Japan which are highly transparent to the average consumer. What really added fuel to protectionist sentiments was the credibility given to them, albeit in macroeconomic terms, by such distinguished bodies as the Cambridge University (UK) Economic Policy Group, but the misconceptions underlying their theoretical structure have been demonstrated elsewhere – see El-Agraa (1984) and Chapter 7.

If this line of reasoning is acceptable, it follows that Japan's trade frictions are essentially a manifestation of a socio-political rather than an economic phenomenon. 'Special interest' groups find it easier to blame outsiders for their plight, and governments, by not deliberately dispelling this idea, tacitly abet with the result that what started as a misconceived notion became a successful political stance. However, one should hasten to add, in response to those who may advance the argument that when Britain, the USA and Germany had their structural surpluses, no country complained because unemployment was not a problem to the relevant 'outsiders', but in the case of Japan unemployment is the problem 'outside' Japan, the structural aspect of the trade surplus is only a small proportion of the total. Hence, the stated conclusion is consistent with that reality.

CONCLUSION

When these three elements are considered together, a less unsubtle explanation of the trade frictions of the EC and the USA with Japan emerges. The nature of the relatively difficult Japanese market for for imports of manufactures, the 'abnormality ' of Japan as an influential member of Club OECD and the prevalence of protectionist sentiments in times of hardship seem to combine in a way which too easily puts the blame on Japan, particularly when it exports perceptible and popular commodities. However, this does not absolve Japan of all guilt since, by not agreeing to revalue the yen until recently, it appeared to deem a trade surplus (above the structural one) to be a kind of source of national wealth; countries must learn to accept the basic reality that one nation's trade surplus is another's trade deficit. Hence it is the responsibility of all nations concerned to make concerted efforts to alleviate the situation. It follows that to describe VERs as concessions is both misguided and misleading.

Perhaps the best way to finish this chapter is to give an example of how the Japanese perceive their relationship with the outside world. Professor Masaru Yoshimori reflects on this with reference to Western Europe:

Europe has rested on its laurels and slept for decades after having dominated the world. This is all too human and understandable. We have seen the same phenomenon in the United States in recent years. And nothing guarantees that Japan could be saved from the same destiny, when she attains one day the same quality of life as the Westerners.

This European sleep has been disturbed by the intrusion of "the damned Japanese". And the Japanese industrial challenge has not been taken up entirely by the Europeans. Will they succeed? The answer is no, if they continue to think that Japanese enterprises are competitive, "because they benefit from the government aids, close their market by all means against foreign products, copy the Western technologies, exploit their workers and subcontractors, etc.".

Even if each of these elements contains a grain of truth they do not explain everything, and the Europeans, if they are objective and well informed, know that well. Western Europe will restore its dynamism and its spirit of enterprise of the past, when it starts looking straight at their problems, without seeking pretexts. For my part, I believe that Europe is in the right direction after years of intense introspection ... I do not think that the Europeans of today are very different from their ancestors who made this modern world what it is today (*Cadres*, special issue, June 1986).

5 Demands for Market Opening and for the Expansion of Domestic Demand

In the previous chapter, it was demonstrated, hopefully convincingly, that Japan cannot be held responsible for the whole of its trade surplus. Due to structural aspects which are determined by the present stage reached in the development of its economy and its balance of payments, Japan is accountable for only about a third of its present trade surplus. Be that as it may, it should be of interest to learn about the demands made on Japan to eliminate its bilateral trade surpluses and to undertake measures to open up its market to foreign goods and services. This is the purpose of this chapter; the responses by the Japanese government to these demands will be tackled in the following chapter.

The chapter commences with a *sample* of earlier demands: a comprehensive coverage would not serve any purpose due to the fact that most of the much earlier demands were either fragmentary or not consistently and persistently repeated by any single country or group of countries. The main body of the chapter is devoted to the most recent demands made on Japan by the Joint United States–Japan Advisory Commission to the President of the USA and the Prime Minister of Japan and by a purely Japanese advisory group which was set up by Prime Minister Yasuhiro Nakasone to report to him with recommendations on the restructuring of the Japanese economy in ways which would enhance Japan's harmony with the international community.

A SAMPLE OF EARLIER DEMANDS

Over the past two decades or so, Japan has undertaken many measures to open up its markets in response to demands made by the EC and the USA. Between December 1981 and April 1984, it declared five main 'packages'. Let us consider only a sample of these demands.

114

In January 1981, France decided (via the EC Commission) to restrict the import of Japanese wooden and other toys, radio receivers and colour TV sets. The EC Commission's approval of the restriction remained in force until the end of June. However, it was extended until nearly the end of 1981 (August for toys and radio receivers and November for colour TV sets). In February 1981, Greece raised its tariff rates on the import of some Japanese cars, and the EC Commission decided to monitor imports of Japanese cars, colour TV sets and tuners and imposed quota restrictions on machine tools. During the same month, Italy restricted imports of Japanese VTRs and Jeep-vehicles through the EC Commission, which approved the implementation of these measures for January–June, with an extension in June to the end of 1981. In March of the same year, Italy announced import quotas for Japanese products for the period from October 1980 to September 1981, restricting specifically, through the EC Commission, the imports of trucks and tuners; the EC Commission approved them and extended the date to June 1981 for trucks and October 1981 for tuners.

In May 1981, Italy announced the revival of the import-mortgage and the EC Council of Ministers made a public statement denouncing Japanese trading practices. In July, the EC Commission reviewed its strategy against Japan and Italy restricted its imports of Japanese piezoelectric crystal elements through the EC, which approved it until the end of the year.

In October, Britain issued a twenty-point proposal with the aim of rectifying the trade imbalance with Japan. This was followed by a fourteen-item proposal by the EC Commission for the expansion of EC exports to Japan. In December, the EC Council of Foreign Ministers declared a list of demands against Japan.

In March of the same year, there were strong demands made in the USA for restricting the import of Japanese cars. In September, the US Administration established the Japan–US Trade Committee. In October, the US Senate passed the Communications Act Revision Bill and the lowest bid made by a Japanese firm in an open tender for the supply of a large-scale optical communications system invited by a US enterprise was rejected. In November, the US Administration demanded the removal of tariffs on 29 products and the easing of non-tariff barriers. Finally, in December, the Sub-Committee of the US House Ways and Means Committee published the third 'Jones Report' (the Gibbons Report).

The year 1981 is by way of a random sample. There is no need to specify all the demands and responses made between 1981 and 1985, let alone over the past two decades – see the introduction to this chapter. However, one should add that demands on Japan were not just made by the EC and the USA; they came from practically all corners of the globe, especially from Korea, Taiwan and members of ASEAN.

RECENT DEMANDS

As stated in the introduction to this chapter, instead of simply describing the latest demands made by all and sundry, it may be wise to concentrate on two types of demand: those made by the United States–Japan Advisory Commission (it being a speaker for both the USA and Japan) and by the Advisory Group on Economic Structural Adjustment for International Harmony (it being a Japanese group established by Prime Minister Nakasone to advise him on measures to be undertaken by his government). In other words, what will be considered in this chapter are not only realistic demands (since in one of these groups, Japan's own voice is included, and in the other all the voices are Japanese), but also comprehensive demands due to the fact that the two sets of demands considered in this chapter are highly representative of the totality of demands made on Japan by the outside world. Hence, the approach adopted here should be more fruitful than a detailed consideration of the specific demands made by single nations or groups thereof.

Demands made by the Joint Commission

The United States–Japan Advisory Commission (1984) made a number of recommendations for actions to be taken by Japan and the USA. Since we are concerned with Japan in this book, it is wise to concentrate on the demands made on it. These can be summarised as follows:

(i) Japan could play a much more positive role in stimulating world economic recovery if its own growth rate were increased with due regard for Japan's fiscal integrity, and if Japan were to reduce its now unprecedentedly high trade and current account surpluses.

(ii) With a savings rate of about 20 per cent of disposable income (three times the equivalent rate in the USA) which is not being absorbed by domestic investment and has to seek investment abroad, Japan has the potential to play a role similar to that of Britain in the nineteenth century or the USA during most of this century.

(iii) The further opening of the Japanese market should be a high priority for the Japanese government. The Joint Commission points out that the primary reason for Japan to improve market access is the same as that for any other country; it is in its own national economic interest to do so since open markets spur competition, increase consumer choice, improve economic efficiency and help to hold down inflation. Moreover, it is also in Japan's economic interest to play a leading role in supporting a more open world trading system since in 1982 it was the world's third largest trading nation, accounting for 8.1 per cent of world exports and 7.3 per cent of world imports, it is critically dependent on imports of raw materials and fuels and its ability to sustain a high standard of living depends upon its continued access to world markets for its manufactured exports.

(iv) A variety of non-tariff barriers remain in Japan. These call into question Japan's commitment to 'free or fair trade'. Behind these barriers lie some broader systemic problems, for example, lack of 'transparency' in Japanese bureaucratic policy-making and implementation procedures, and the tendency of Japanese to distinguish between insiders and outsiders.

(v) Japan should avoid the 'package approach' and adopt a more positive approach to market opening by making market access a national goal. This will require: the setting up of a high-level Special Commission to work out the necessary agenda for measures to be taken by Japan which will be of interest to itself and the world economy; the prevention of the creation of further barriers; the strengthening of the Office of Trade Ombudsman (OTO); the development of an effective and internationally credible procedure for the monitoring of the implementation of measures; and promoting inter-industry cooperation so as to avoid the politicisation of market access matters.

(vi) The settlement of agricultural trade issues must be through compromise, not according to rigid formulae. Japan (and the USA) should support pragmatic, incremental, but continuous steps to increase agricultural trade on the basis of comparative advantage and specialisation.

(vii) It is now widely recognised in Japan that the disparity between the domestic price of rice and the world price should be reduced. This is an imperative to promote structural adjustment and root out inefficiencies that hurt the interests of consumers, taxpayers and farmers alike. Generally speaking, Japan should reassess its food security policies.

(viii) The Japanese government should establish a joint scientific commission with the USA to monitor recent developments related to health, inspection and quarantine rules, anticipating future issues, harmonising standards and procedures and providing guidance to the governments in dealing with crises.

(ix) With regard to agricultural trade issues, the Joint Commission recommends that the Japanese and US governments and their respective agricultural communities should be prepared to accept a continuing liberalising process as a feature of Japanese agricultural policy for beef and citrus fruits. To reduce the impact on less efficient producers, Japan should as a high priority develop and implement effective programmes of long-term adjustment.

(x) In keeping with the dismantling of other trade barriers, Japan should continue to reduce its barriers to processed forestry products, with an ultimate objective of achieving tariff levels equivalent to those of other industrialised nations.

(xi) With regard to trade in services, Japan should strive to conform with the principle of non-discrimination, attempting always to maximise open markets. Over the past few years, considerable progress has been made in Japan in opening banking, insurance and brokerage to foreign participation in national terms. Where discrepancies remain in those or other areas, Japan should attempt to provide practical opportunities for market entry. Some of the same institutional mechanisms established to facilitate trade in goods and help resolve trade complaints should be extended to encompass trade in services. These should include the OTO and opportunities designed to provide transparency in regard to applicable laws and regulations.

(xii) As to exchange rates and capital markets, the Joint Commission stressed that international rules or guidelines should be developed to determine when coordinated interventions are appropriate to contain exchange rate volatility and 'overshooting' with the appreciation of the yen in mind. Moreover, the Japanese government should continue its efforts to internationalise the yen; the measures agreed in May 1984 between the US Treasury Department and the Ministry of Finance relating to the internationalisation of the yen and the liberalisation of capital markets constitute a solid basis for significant progress. Implementation of these measures should be undertaken expeditiously; they should be part of a continuing series of actions to assure that the yen assumes its appropriate role as a major international currency for trade and finance.

Because of Japan's high savings rate, Japan can contribute capital to a world in need of it. However, the lack of integration of its capital markets with world markets inhibits the development of Japan's full potential in this respect. Hence, the Joint Committee regarded capital market liberalisation as a key issue.

The Committee also considered the removal of restrictions on interest rates (due to government intervention) as central to the overall process of financial liberalisation in Japan and felt it important to stress that many steps still remain before Japan's long-term and short-term finances become fully responsive to market forces. Also, financial deregulation should not be viewed in Japan as dictated by foreign countries, but as a desirable path in Japan's own economic interest.

(xiii) Noting that although Japanese investment in the USA has increased dramatically during the past decade (rising from $2.1 billion in 1972 to $8.9 billion in 1980 and $13.9 billion in 1982) and that the USA is by far the largest recipient of Japanese foreign investment, the Joint Commission stressed that Japanese foreign investment amounts to only 9 per cent of total foreign investment in the USA, ranking below investment by the Netherlands, Britain and Canada. Hence, their recommendation was that, since reciprocal investment opportunities are nowhere near being fully exploited, the private sector in each country should more actively explore business opportunities in the other.

(xiv) With regard to industrial policies, the Joint Commission recommended that government-sponsored or government-tolerated cartels, whether for the development of products or restriction of output, should be 'transparent', and that, unless overriding reasons exist, they should be open to foreign firms, especially those located in the country concerned, and should not be aimed at limiting foreign competition. Also, Japan and the USA should take the lead in an effort to establish a fair-practice code with regard to cartels, working within the GATT framework.

(xv) Proceeding on the assumption that viable energy cooperation proposals must have a solid economic base and ultimately be attractive to the private sector in both Japan and the USA, the Joint Commission recommended that as existing contracts for coal and liquefied natural gas (LNG) expire, and as Japanese demand expands, Japan should look to the USA for sources of assured, stable long-term supplies, provided mutually satisfactory arrangements can be made with regard to investment, transportation and delivered price. Moreover, cooperation in coal utilisation technology will not only help sustain long-term Japanese demand, but if applied to the LDCs can result in economies of scale to the benefit of all concerned. Similar considerations apply to LNG, where the US–Japan Energy Working Group has highlighted the potential for marketing Alaskan North Slope gas; a joint feasibility study should be expeditiously undertaken.

(xvi) Finally, in the field of nuclear energy, the Joint Commission suggested that a long-term nuclear cooperation agreement should be concluded without further delay. In so doing, the USA should not ask more of Japan than it does of other close allies; Japan, in turn, should be willing, in the light of its national policy, voluntarily to set a world example for the development and application of safeguards. Moreover, Japan and the USA, on an industry-to-industry basis, should start investigating the next generation of nuclear technology. Furthermore, there should be close technological collaboration about common concerns regarding nuclear waste disposal, and Japan and the USA should consult closely in developing common policies on the export of nuclear technology to third countries.

Demands made by the Maekawa Committee

The Advisory Group on Economic Structural Adjustment for International Harmony (the Maekawa Group) was set up by Prime Minister Nakasone on 31 October 1985, to conduct a study on medium- and long-term policy measures regarding Japan's economic and social structure and management. However, although the aims of the Maekawa Group may seem to be purely domestic, international harmony was its uppermost priority: Nakasone had in mind the Tokyo Summit in May 1986. Indeed, the Maekawa Group submitted its report (Maekawa Report) on 7 April 1986, allowing enough time for enactment before the commencement of the Summit.

The Report sets the scene by pointing out that after forty years of rapid economic growth Japan today occupies an important position within the international community but that Japan's current account has been registering increasing surpluses in the 1980s, with an 'unprecedentedly large' surplus in 1985 (3.6 per cent of GNP). It drew attention to the fact that it is 'imperative that we recognize that continued large current account imbalances create a critical situation not only for the management of the Japanese economy but also for the harmonious development of the world economy'. It concludes that the time has come for Japan to make an 'historical transformation' in its traditional policies on economic management and the nation's life-style; there can be no further development for Japan without this transformation.

The Group recommended that, as a medium-term objective, the Japanese government should declare its resolution, both domestically and internationally, to achieve the aim of 'steadily reducing the . . . current account imbalance to one consistent with international harmony'. This should be done in such a way that simultaneous efforts should be undertaken to 'enhance the quality of the nation's living standards'. Moreover, in so doing, Japan 'should undertake responsibilities commensurate with its economic position and strive for harmonious co-existence within the world economy, as well as working to contribute to the world community not only economically but also in the scientific and technological, cultural and economic fields'.

With this background in mind, the Group recommended a number of specific measures that the government should undertake in order to achieve this objective, having certain principles in mind. The principles concern the following objectives: balanced economic growth in Japan; expansion of imports to help maintain and strengthen the free trading system; and efforts for sustained and balanced growth of the world economy. The principles are commensurate with these objectives; they are:

(i) the policies should be based on market mechanisms, i.e. the guidelines should be 'freedom in principle, restrictions only as exceptions' – accordingly, further improvements in market access and thorough promotion of deregulation should be carried out;

(ii) the policies should have a global perspective, i.e. although Japan should rectify its economic structure on its own initiative, at the same time it must seek the cooperation of all countries if world growth is to be promoted; and

(iii) the policies should have a long-term perspective, i.e. since the process of reforming the economic structure as well as improving the basic character of the Japanese economy is a long-term one, 'efforts to this end must be made continuously and from a long-term perspective', but, of course, the relevant policies must be initiated as soon as possible.

The recommendations of the Maekawa Report can be summarised as follows:

(i) Expanding domestic demand. The transformation of the Japanese economy from one of 'export-led growth' to one driven by 'domestic demand' necessitates that the government should 'put firmly into place domestic demand expansion policies that have large multiplier effects and will lead to increased private consumption'. In this respect, three major areas were designated:

(1) Promoting housing policies and urban redevelopment. The Group stressed that efforts are required to make fundamental reforms in the Japanese housing policies and to strengthen and broaden measures to promote housing. Moreover, particularly in large urban centres, the creation of new residential areas closer to offices by the redevelopment of existing areas and the construction of new neighbourhoods should be promoted. Also, urban facilities should be expanded and improved.

The Group specified certain actions needed to promote these efforts: the expansion scale must centre on the mobilisation of the vitality of the private sector, so steps should be taken to ease regulations and to provide 'pump-priming' financial incentives; tax deductions for the acquisition of houses should be increased; measures should be undertaken to keep land prices stable, for example the re-zoning of urban areas, the relaxation of local government residential guidelines and the easing of the restrictions on building size and land use; and efforts should be made to accelerate the settlement of problems arising from land use among those concerned.

(2) Stimulating private consumption. The Group recommended increases in wages, cuts in taxes, reductions in working hours (to be consistent with the rest of the OECD) and encouraging the active use of paid leave as a means of increasing private consumption. With regard to working hours, the group recommended the pursuit of the early realisation of the five-day working week in the

private sector, with efforts to be made for speedy implementation in the public and financial sectors.

(3) Promotion of social infrastructure investment by local governments. The Group believed that a radical increase in capital formation by local governments was essential for the nation-wide spread of the impact of more powerful domestic demand. Hence, it recommended the enlargement of independent local works using local government loans.

(ii) Transformation to an internationally harmonious industrial structure. Although the Group insisted that this should be achieved through the working of the market mechanism, it recommended that additional efforts should be pursued through the following measures:

(1) Promotion of the transformation of industrial structure and positive industrial adjustment. The Group pointed out that positive industrial adjustment must encourage the international division of labour through the acceleration of the structural reforms being promoted under current laws, giving due consideration to small and medium size industries. Moreover, coal-mining policies should be reviewed with the aim of drastically reducing the level of domestic output and increasing imports, due allowance being made for the serious impact of this on local economies. Also, it is vital to encourage technological R&D, the growing diffusion and application of information technology in the economy and society and the development of the service sector which will be accelerated by the greater availability of free time and the diversification of consumption patterns.

(2) Promoting direct investment. The Group felt that this is important since direct overseas investment plays an important role in rectifying Japan's external economic imbalances and in promoting the economic development of the host country. Given due consideration to the impact on the domestic economy and employment, the Group recommended that Japan's rapidly expanding overseas investment should be further encouraged through: enhancing the conclusion of bilateral agreements for the protection of investment; improving overseas investment insurance schemes; participating in the Multilateral Investment Guarantee Agency (MIGA); and reinforcing other governmental measures to support overseas investment. Also, it is necessary to expand

economic cooperation to improve the environment for investment in the LDCs.

The Group also felt that foreign investment in Japan should be encouraged by improved conditions for financial assistance, increased supply of information, etc. Moreover, industrial cooperation should be actively promoted, including the exchange of technology and cooperation in third-country markets; more specifically, the establishment of a 'private-sector-led institution' for industrial cooperation to enhance personnel exchanges should be encouraged.

(3) Promoting agricultural policies befitting an age of internationalisation. In order to attain this objective, the Group suggested that the government should endeavour to accomplish a thorough structural adjustment with priorities given to policies focused on fostering core farmers for the future, and price policies reviewed and rationalised towards greater use of the market mechanism. More specifically, with the exception of basic farm products, efforts should be made for a steady increase in the imports of products (including agricultural processed goods) whose domestic price differs markedly from the international market price and these price differentials should be reduced while agriculture is being rationalised and made more efficient.

Finally, where products are subject to quantitative import restrictions, efforts should be made to eliminate these while taking into consideration the developments in the relevant consultations and negotiations including the new Round of GATT.

(iii) Further improving market access and encouraging the import of manufactured goods. In order to achieve this, the Group recommended that full implementation of the Action Programme should be promoted in the areas of tariffs, import quota restrictions, standards and certification procedures, government procurement, etc. (see the following chapter). Also, the OTO should be reinforced and a study of the possibility of giving it a legal basis should be undertaken.

Further active measures should be undertaken to promote the import of manufactured goods. Apart from the usual efforts, these should include: the streamlining of distribution mechanisms; the conducting of a review of the various restrictions relating to distribution and sale; the strict reinforcement of the Anti-Monopoly Law for the prevention of unfair business transactions (this should be done with special attention to monitoring the registration of international contracts, dealing harshly with unfair or exclusive trading practices and ensuring that nothing is done to unfairly prevent parallel imports); and the strengthening of domestic arrangements to eliminate illegal acts with regard to foreign trade marks and counterfeit products.

Finally, together with the promotion of imports (via an intensification of consumer-directed campaigns and the complete availability abroad of information on the Japanese market and distribution systems), efforts should be made to promote expanded economic cooperation and private-sector technology transfers to contribute to expanded imports of manufactured products from the LDCs.

Prudent behaviour by private companies. Thinking of those private companies who tend to pursue the expansion of their market share at all costs, the Group hoped that Japanese companies will behave in awareness of their international responsibilities.

(iv) Stabilisation of exchange rates and liberalisation and internationalisation of financial and capital markets. With regard to exchange rate stability, the Group emphasised that this depends on exchange rates' reflecting the essential economic bases of the countries concerned and that stability itself depends on the elimination of the disparities in the performance of these economies. Since neither can be guaranteed, cooperation and intervention by the countries concerned can be effective tools for correction. The Group was of the opinion that, while ensuring international compatibility in basic economic policy, it is important that efforts should be made to build upon the accumulated experience in international cooperation to develop a framework for future stability.

The Group also recommended that efforts should be made to further liberalise financial and capital transactions and to expand transactions by non-residents both for financing and investment. With regard to the strengthening of the investment markets, it was recommended that investment instruments should be diversified, giving special emphasis to the development of short-term financial markets, and that international compatibility of market arrangements and trading practices, especially in taxation, is needed to ensure the expansion and strengthening of the secondary markets and the internationalisation of trading.

(v) Promotion of international cooperation and Japan's contribution to the world economy in a manner commensurate with its international status. In order to achieve this, the Group recommended the following:

(1) With regard to the promotion of international cooperation, five major areas were designated: the expansion of imports from the LDCs, especially manufactured imports (the transfer of technology and increased Japanese investment in the LDCs should help here); the alleviation of the international debt problem (by promoting international efforts to lower interest rates, by increasing financial flows to the LDCs, by strengthening the financial basis of multi-national development banks and improving their efficiency and by considering the impact of the debt problem on private financial institutions); the achievement, as early as possible, of the current medium-term target to expand the official development assistance of Japan, mobilising non-governmental organisations as well, and expanding technical assistance with special emphasis on the training of assistance personnel, improving the grant element, restraining mixed credits and promoting untied aid; the creation of new science and technology for the twenty-first century not only by promoting R&D in basic science and technology in Japan but also through international research cooperation in these fields; and efforts to promote Japanese language education and Japanese studies overseas, to support the exchange of personnel, to strengthen international broadcasting and to adapt to the 'age of internationalisation' by opening academic and research institutions to foreigners, making arrangements to accept more foreign teachers and students and 'accommodating' Japanese students returning from abroad.

(2) As for the promotion of the new Round of GATT, the Japanese government should react positively to matters of interest to the LDCs and should actively participate in the establishment of international rules in such areas as trade in services and intellectual property rights. Also, it should seek to improve the GATT rules and strengthen the GATT system in order to restore the credibility of the GATT. Moreover, the government is urged to actively conduct negotiations on tariffs on industrial products in accordance with the Action Programme.

FISCAL AND MONETARY POLICY MANAGEMENT

The Group realised that not only did the implementation of their recommendations have monetary and fiscal policy implications, but also that monetary and fiscal policy had a crucial role to play in the process. It was recommended that when any fiscal measures are carried out, they must not disturb the current fiscal reforms being pursued with regard to ending the reliance on deficit-financing bonds and also that they should 'respond flexibly in an effort to achieve economic and social balance, on a medium- and long-term basis, with creative efforts for the appropriation of fiscal resources with effectiveness and priority, for the mobilisation of private-sector vitality, and for deregulation'. The tax system should also be reviewed with the aim of making it more simple and equitable as well as more conducive to promoting economic vitality and broader choice and, at the same time, becoming more responsive to international viewpoints. More specifically, the preferential tax treatment for savings should be fundamentally reviewed in the light of these aims, with priority for the abolition of tax exemption on interest on small savings.

The Group drew attention to the fact that monetary policy had an important role to play not only to ensure currency stability but also to promote more dependence on domestic demand.

CONCLUSION

In this chapter, two sets of demands on the Japanese government were specified, one by an entirely Japanese group and the other by the United States–Japan Advisory Commission which is composed of an equal number of representatives from Japan and the USA. However, before one jumps to the conclusion that it should not come as a surprise to learn that the two sets of demands are more or less identical, it should be emphasised that the Japanese members of the two groups are entirely different, except for Okita – see the Appendix to this chapter. Moreover, it is still the case that the Joint Commission has an equal number of US representatives. Furthermore, a specification of the US Congressional bills demanding more market opening measures by Japan and President Reagan's appeals to Prime Minister Nakasone to do so in order to cool down the heat of protectionism in the House will not add much to the total list of demands since the contents are not different from those presented in this chapter – see Chapter 1 for a specification of some of the relevant Congressional and Senate special committees bills. Finally, these demands incorporate all those made by the whole of the international community on

Japan. Therefore, the specified sets of demands can be taken as a *comprehensive* list of the kinds of market opening and structural adjustments Japan is being asked to make both from within and without.

Two final points should be made. A careful consideration of the membership of the Committees shows that the Japanese side is representative of the whole society (the government, the bureaucracy, the business world and the trade unions): a true reflection of the Japanese thirst for consensus politics. On the other hand, the US representatives all come from the management side of the business world, except for the former US ambassador to Japan! The second point is that, if one considers the membership of committees over a long period of time, one finds a great deal of stability on the Japanese side and a great deal of diversity on the US side (reflecting the almost complete change of personnel that comes with each US president). This has been a sore point for the Japanese since they feel that they set up committees with the main object of settling problems, yet every now and then they find themselves dealing with new people who seem to know nothing about what went on before them – could this be yet another 'scenario' for explaining the causes of trade frictions between Japan and the USA?

APPENDIX: MEMBERSHIP OF THE TWO GROUPS

United States–Japan Advisory Commission

Chairmen
David Packard (Chairman of the Board, Hewlett-Packard, Inc.).
Nobuhiko Ushiba (Former State Minister for External Economic Affairs).

Members
Michael D. Antonovich (Chairman, Board of Supervisors, Fifth District, County of Los Angeles).
Daryl Arnold (Chairman, Western Growers Association).
James F. Bere (Chairman, Borg-Warner Corporation).
Douglaş A. Fraser (President Emeritus, United Automobile, Aerospace and Agricultural Implement Workers of America).
James D. Hodgson (Former Ambassador to Japan).
Yotaro Kobayashi (President, Fuji Xerox Co., Ltd).
Akio Morita (Chairman and Chief Executive Officer, Sony Corporation).
Saburo Okita (Former Minister of Foreign Affairs).
Seizaburo Sato (Professor of Political Science, University of Tokyo).
Ichiro Shioji (Chairman, Confederation of Japan Automobile Workers' Union).
Isamu Yamashita (Chairman, Mitsui Engineering & Shipping Co., Ltd).

The Advisory Group on Economic Structural Adjustment for International Harmony

Chairman
Haruo Maekawa (Ex-Governor, Bank of Japan).

Members
Shoichi Akazawa (President of JETRO; former Director-General, MITI).
Takashi Ishihara (Chairman, Nissan Motor Corporation, Vice-Chairman, Kaidanren).
Ichiro Isoda (Chairman, Sumitomo Bank).
Tadanobu Usami (Chairman, 'So-Doomei'; former Chairman, National Union of Textile Workers).
Yoshio Okawara (Ministry of Foreign Affairs; former Japanese Ambassador to the USA).
Saburo Okita (President, International University of Japan; former Minister of Foreign Affairs and former member, EPA).
Hiroto Oyama (Former editor, *Nikei Shimbun* Newspaper).
Hiroshi Kato (Professor, Keio University).
Yutaka Kosai (Professor, Tokyo Institute of Technology; former member, EPA).
Goro Koyama (Adviser, Mitsui Bank and its former Chairman).
Mamoru Sawabe (Chairman, Japan Horse-racing Association; former Vice-Minister of Agriculture, Fisheries and Forestry).
Setsuya Tabuchi (Chairman, Nomura Securities Company).
Minoru Nagaoka (President, Nihon Tobacco Company; formerly with the Ministry of Finance).
Takashi Hosomi (President, Overseas Economic Cooperation Fund; formerly with the Ministry of Finance).
Isamu Miyazaki (Chairman, Daiwa Economic Research Institute; former member, EPA)
Takashi Mukaibo (Former President, University of Tokyo).

6 Japan's Response to Demands for Market Opening

Apart from the presentation of a sample of earlier demands made by the EC and the USA on the Japanese government to open up its markets, the previous chapter was mainly devoted to the demands made by two major groups: the United States–Japan Advisory Commission and the Advisory Group on Economic Structural Adjustment for International Harmony (Maekawa Report). The aim of this chapter is to present Japan's response to these demands.

The presentation of the responses will be made in a manner equivalent to the presentation of the demands. Hence, the first section will describe the reactions to the sample of demands made by the EC and the USA, while two further sections will be devoted to the Action Programme (which is, in a fashion, the response to the demands made by the Joint Commission and similar bodies) and to the Japanese government's response to the recommendations of the Maekawa Report. However, it may be useful to follow the first section by a brief description of other actions taken by Japan in the period between the responses to the sample of demands made by the EC and the USA and the Action Programme.

EARLIER DEMANDS AND RESPONSES

Japan's response to the 1981 demands and actions taken by the EC and the USA was to lower its tariffs on cars as well as to declare 'voluntary export restraints' (VERs) on its car exports to the USA for fiscal years 1981 to 1983. This was in April. In September, Japan and the USA agreed to advance the implementation of tariff cuts for semi-conductors to April 1982. In October: the Japan–US Economic Relations Group submitted its final report; the Council of Ministers of Foreign Affairs met and decided on measures for the balanced recovery of domestic demand and the expansion of imports of manufactured goods by Japan; and the Japanese government sent an economic mission (the Dokō Mission) to seven European countries.

Finally, in December, Japan adopted a number of external economic measures: the tariff cuts agreed in the Tokyo Round were implemented two years in advance; some market-opening steps were taken; imports were promoted through the extension of foreign currency loans for emergency imports; some VERs were undertaken; and some industrial and economic cooperation steps were announced.

SOME LATER RESPONSES

These later responses were covered, in broad terms, at the end of Chapter 2. Hence, this section is confined to a specification of some of the necessary details in only four areas.

(a)   Standards and certification systems.   In 1983, the Japanese Diet enacted amendments (effective from 1 August 1983) to sixteen laws: the Pharmaceuticals Affairs Law (affecting pharmaceuticals, medical equipment and cosmetics), the Nutrition Improvement Law (concerning special nutrition foodstuffs), the Agricultural Chemical Regulation Law, the Fertiliser Control Law, the Agricultural Mechanism Promotion Law (affecting agricultural machinery and equipment), the Law Concerning Standardisation and Proper Labelling of Agricultural and Forestry Products (covering agricultural, forestry and fishery products such as foodstuffs and plywood), the Law Concerning Safety Assurance and Quality Improvement in Feeds, the Consumer Product Safety Law (including helmets for motor cyclists and baseball players), the High-pressure Gas Control Law, the Electrical Appliance and Material Control Law, the Law Concerning the Security of Safety and Optimisation of Transactions of Liquefied Petroleum Gas, the Measurement Law (concerning measuring devices), the Gas Utility Industry Law (regarding urban gas appliances), the Law Concerning the Examination and Regulation of Manufacture etc. of Chemical Substances (covering seven substances including polychlorinated biphenyls and naphthalenes and hexachlors benzenes), and the Road Vehicle Act and the Labour Safety and Sanitation Law (affecting machine tools and equipment, including press machines and gas masks). The purpose of these revisions was to permit self-certification by foreign companies and to make the inspection and certification procedures the same for both Japanese and non-Japanese companies. Given the range of products covered by the revisions, it could be argued that the principle of non-discrimination

between Japanese and foreigners had been somewhat extensively applied.

Consider some specific details:

(1) Cars. Japan has adopted the following measures with regard to type designation and standards for cars:

    (i) foreign car manufacturers can apply for type designation thus disposing of the need for the Ministry of Transport to inspect every single vehicle;

    (ii) the procedures and requirements for type designation have been drastically simplified by substituting documentation for actual inspection of cars, by accepting data from tests performed by foreign testing organisations (where procedures are equivalent to those in Japan) and by simplified paperwork requiring less detail than previously – this has reduced the time requirement by about a third;

    (iii) as a member of the UN Economic Commission for Europe's Group of Experts on the Construction of Vehicles (Working Party 29), Japan has already made its safety standards conform with those in Western Europe and North America – harmonisation measures asked for by these two areas have all been accepted except for emission-control requirements; and

    (iv) when drafting car standards, the views of foreign manufacturers are now being sought.

(2) Pharmaceuticals. Apart from seeking regular meetings with the American Chamber of Commerce in Japan, accepting foreign stability-test data and accepting foreign data on specifications and test methods, the new regulations allow the transfer of import approvals for pharmaceuticals from one importer to another when the foreign manufacturer is unchanged, and health drinks and herb sweets made of chamomile are now regarded as foodstuffs rather than pharmaceuticals, making their import easier than before.

(3) Electrical appliances. Four major improvements have been introduced. Foreign representatives are included in the drafting procedure for the standards for household electrical appliances (under the Electrical Appliance and Material Control Law). Work has been accomplished on harmonising Japanese technical standards for electrical appliances with those of the International Electro-technical Commission (reported in GATT in

August 1983). Japan has made arrangements for cross-acceptance of data with Canada and the USA. The new regulations now allow the transfer of type authorisation from one importer to another when the foreign manufacturer remains the same.

(b) Liberalising trade in services. This sector comprises many areas including telecommunications, information processing, engineering, consulting, education, finance, insurance, medical care, hotels and restaurants, mass media and air and sea transport. However, details worth mentioning are available for only two sectors:

(1) Telecommunications and information processing. Due to the impressive developments in computer and telecommunications technology, demands were made both within Japan and from the USA for the deregulation of the use of telecommunication networks and information-processing services. Japan's Public Communications Law was slightly amended in 1982 with the result that the use of telecommunication networks 'has largely been liberalised' (Okita, 1984). Moreover, value-added networks are now allowed for small business concerns. Also, during 1984/ 5 the whole structure of telecommunications and data-processing use was overhauled by being subjected to competition and by privatising the Nippon Telegraph and Telephone Corporation (NTT). However, some degree of control still prevails due to the protection of privacy, software copyright and national security, but Okita (1984) believed that the 'trend is towards sweeping liberalisation'.

(2) Financial services. In the financial and capital markets, non-discrimination between Japanese and foreign firms, the easing of restrictions and reducing the role played by the government are the main principles of Japanese policy. Since 1978 much progress has been achieved in the area of non-discrimination with the Revised Banking Law of 1982 (effective from April 1982) stipulating that foreign banks 'shall receive exactly the same treatment as that accorded to Japanese banks'. With regard to government control, since late 1980 (the Foreign Exchange and Foreign Trade Control Law, revised and effective from December 1980), measures have been taken to 'consolidate the framework for financial liberalisation, including the shift from regulated, in principle, to unregulated, in principle, for external transactions' (Okita, 1984). However, Okita was quick to add

that it would be utter folly to expect drastic reforms in this area since even countries like the USA and Switzerland have marked differences; to make a demand for sweeping reforms is to ask for the destruction of Japanese society. Irrespective of this, however, on 21 October 1983 (Comprehensive Economic Measures), the Japanese government announced its intention to promote further liberalisation of the financial and capital markets as well as to increase the international role of the yen. General guidelines were offered in four areas: the liberalisation of short-term capital markets, including the creation of an active market for treasury bills, greater flexibility in amounts and maturities for certificates of deposit and the creation of a market in yen-denominated bankers' acceptances; the liberalisation of the market for public and corporate bonds, including greater diversity in the types and maturities of national bonds, greater flexibility in the conditions of issue of corporate bonds, the issue of government bonds denominated in foreign currencies and relaxation of the conditions of issue of Euro-yen bonds; liberalisation of interest rates, including attempts to achieve market-determined interest rates through liberalising short-term capital and bond markets and the gradual disposing of interest rate ceilings; and the lowering of barriers between financial institutions, including the gradual removal of the distinctions between ordinary and trust banks, securities companies and other financial institutions. Agreements along these lines were reached between the USA and Japan at the end of May 1984. For a graphic representation of these developments, see Chart 2.1.

(c)   On 14 December 1984, the Japanese government announced a new 'package' of market-opening measures.   These were mainly designed to enhance imports from the LDCs. The measures included reductions in the tariffs levied on 39 agricultural and fishery products two years ahead of the schedule agreed upon during the 1973 Tokyo Round of multilateral trade negotiations. Among the 39 products were dried bananas, shark meat, papaya, prawns and squid – see Table 6.1 for details.

The measures proved controversial since the list included neither boneless chicken, a symbolic item in trade disputes between Thailand and Japan, nor tropical plywood and several other items for which South-East Asian countries were vigorously pursuing tariff reductions. It was reported that the exclusion of these items was due to the stiff opposition of the Ministry of Agriculture, Forestry and Fisheries on the grounds that these were 'sensitive' items.

The 39 products also included 18 items for which the import duties had already been removed or the tariffs on which were low and preferential. Hence the announcement of the measures on these items did not get much applause, rather a great deal of sarcastic criticism by the Japanese press. However, it should be noted that the Japanese press acts as the main vehicle of public criticism due to the fact that decisions are reached by consensus; they are the equivalent of an opposition party in the British parliamentary system. Therefore, over-reaction by the Japanese press does not mean that the announced measures were insubstantial.

Table 6.1 Imported goods covered by the December 1984 measures

List I	Tariff Rates (%)	
	Current	New
Meat and edible meat offal (except poultry liver), salted, in brine, dried or smoked (other than those of pigs or bovine animals)	10.0	7.0
Hard roe of Tara (frozen)	7.5	6.0
Baracouta (family Sphyraenidae and family Gempylidae), and Kingclip (fresh or chilled; excluding fillets)	3.8	3.0
Sea bream, barracouta (family Sphyraenidae and family Gempylidae) and Kingclip (frozen; excluding fillets)	3.8	3.0
Shark (fresh or chilled; excluding fillets)	4.1	3.5
Shark (frozen: excluding fillets)	4.1	3.5
Hard roe of tara (genus *Gadus*, genus *Theragara* and genus *Merluccius*) (dried, salted, in brine or smoked)	10.3	7.5
Ise-ebi and other shrimps, prawns and lobsters (fresh, chilled or frozen)	3.4	3.0
Cuttlefish and squid [fresh (live or dead) chilled or frozen]	6.9	5.0
Cut flowers and flower buds of a kind suitable for bouquets or for ornamental purposes (fresh, dried, dyed, bleached, impregnated or otherwise prepared)	7.5	6.0
Cashew nuts (fresh or dried)	1.9	0.0
Bananas (dried)	6.6	6.0
Pineapples (dried)	15.0	12.0
Coconuts and Brazil nuts (fresh or dried)	1.9	0.0
Grapefruit (fresh or dried)		
(June–November)	15.0	12.0
(December–May)	30.6	25.0
Pears and quinces (fresh)	8.8	8.0
Papaya, pawpaws, avocados, guavas, durian, billimbi, champeder, jackfruit, bread-fruit, rambutan, rose-apple		

Table 6.1 Continued

jambo, jambosa diambookagget, chicomamey, cheri-moya, kehapi, sugar apple, mangoes, bullock's-heart, passion-fruit, dookoo, kokosan, mangosteens, soursop and litchi (frozen, not containing added sugar)	15.0	12.0
Pepper of the genus *Piper*, pimento of the genus *Capsicum* or the genus *Pimenta* (other than packaged in containers for retail sale) (ground or mixed)	4.1	3.5
Curry	13.5	12.0
Other spices (other than packaged in containers for retail sale) (ground or mixed, other than ginger)	4.1	3.5
Palm oil	7.4	7.0
Other prepared or preserved meat or meat offal (other than guts etc., dried after simply being boiled in water) (not containing meat or meat offal or bovine animals or pigs)	10.0	7.0
Shrimps, prawns and lobsters (prepared or preserved) (other than those smoked, simply boiled in water or in brine and those chilled, frozen, salted, in brine or dried, after simply being boiled in water or in brine)	9.2	7.5
Papaya, pawpaw, avocados, guavas, durian, bilimois, chawpeder, jackfruit, bread-fruit, rambutan, rose-apple jambo, jambosa diambookagget, chicomamey, cheri-moya, kehapi, sugar-apple, bullock's-heart, passion-fruit, dookoo koksan, soursop, litchi, mangoes and mangosteen (prepared or preserved by vinegar or acetic acid, containing added sugar)	16.9	15.0
Mangoes and manogsteen (prepared or preserved by vinegar or acetic acid, not containing added sugar)	13.5	12.0
Pineapples (prepared or preserved, containing added sugar) (in can, bottle or pot, not more than 10 kilograms each including container)	*	30.0
Instant curry and other curry preparations	13.5	12.0
Bases for beverage, non-alcoholic (containing panax ginseng or its extract; not containing added sugar)	19.7	15.0
Ginseng root (packed in farms or in packages of a kind sold by retail)	7.1	6.6
Herbicides, rat poisons, anti-sprouting products, etc. (other than plant-growth regulators, disinfectants, insecticides, fungicides) (packed in forms or in packages of a kind sold by retail)	6.6	5.8
Insecticides of organic chlorine	6.6	5.8
Wood sawn lengthwise (sliced or peeled but not further prepared, of a thickness not exceeding 5 mm), veneer sheets and sheets of plywood (of a thickness not exceeding 5 mm) [of Kawarin, Tsuge or box-wood, Tagayasan (Cassina siamea ham), red sandal wood, rose wood or ebony wood, excluding ebony wood with white streaks]	10.6	8.0

*The higher of 18.75 per cent plus 27 yen per kilogram or 30 per cent.

Plywood (not surface-worked) (other than those with face
plies on both side of coniferous species, not less than
6 mm in thickness)   19.3   17.0

List II

(Items on which tariffs will be completely eliminated in FY 1985)

Normal paraffin.
Santonin.
Bovine cattle leather and equine leather (wet blue chrome grain).
Woven pile fabrics and chenille fabrics (with pile yarn of wool or fine animal
hair) (Astrakhan fabrics or seal fabrics).
Textile hosepiping and similar tubing (of flex or ramie).
Textile hosepiping and similar tubing (other than those of synthetic fibres and
of cotton).
Tarpaulins, sails, awnings, sun-blinds, tents and camping goods (of flax,
ramie, etc.).
Felt hats (combined or trimmed with precious metals, rolled precious metals,
metals plated with precious metals, precious stones, etc.).
Hats and other headgear (plated, etc.) (combined or trimmed with precious
metals, metals plated with precious metals, etc.).
Billets and slabs of iron or steel.
Handles of base metal (made of, or combined with, metals plated with
precious metals, etc.).

List III

(These will be excluded from the selected product – SP – items, resulting in the
total elimination of their tariffs in FY 1985)

Yarn of man-made fibres (containing more than 50 per cent by weight of
synthetic fibres or acetate fibres).
Yarn of man-made fibres (containing not more than 50% by weight of
synthetic fibres or acetate fibres).
Woven fabrics of jute or of other textile bast fibres.
Textile materials prepared for use in making wigs and the like.
Wigs, false beards and the like, etc. (of human or animal hair or of textiles).
Dolls.

Source: The Foreign Ministry, Tokyo.

Be that as it may, about half a year later (on 25 June 1985) the
Japanese government decided on further market opening measures.
These were highlighted by a 20 per cent across the board tariff cut on
1790 items and a more than 20 per cent reduction in the tariffs or their
removal for 72 agricultural and industrial items. The 72 items
consisted of 34 types of industrial goods, 33 agricultural commodities

(including bananas, boneless chicken and palm oil – the 'symbolic items in trade frictions between Japan and the nations of ASEAN) and five alcoholic products.

The tariff on boneless chicken is to be reduced from its present level of 18 to 14 per cent, that on palm oil from 3 per cent to nil and seasonal tariffs on bananas from 35 to 25 per cent between October and March and from 17.5 to 12.5 per cent between April and September. Tariffs on the 34 industrial products, including car parts and manufacturing tools, will be completely eliminated. For a detailed specification of these measures, see Table 6.2, and for information regarding the way in which these measures were later incorporated into an 'Action Programme', see the section below under that heading.

Table 6.2   Revised tariff schedule for farm and other goods

I. Farm products (tariff cuts to be effective from early 1986)

	Present rate (%)		New rate (%)	
Fowl without bones	18		14	
Duck	12.8		10	
Poultry (other than fowl, turkey and duck)	16		12.5	
Blood ark shell	10		8	(G)
Jellyfish	10		8	(G)
Matsutake	5		0	(G)
Bananas (fresh)				
April–September	17.5	(G)	12.5	(G)
October–March	35	(G)	25	(G)
Oak leaves	10		0	(G)
Sphagnum	10		5	
Palm oil	3	(G)	0	(G)
Castor oil	9		7.2	
Baker's wares (other than biscuits, cookies and crackers) (containing sugar)	40	(G)	30	(G)
Biscuits, cookies and crackers (containing sugar)	20	(G)	15	(G)
Baker's wares (other than biscuits, cookies and crackers) (not containing sugar)	35	(G)	25	(G)
Biscuits, cookies and crackers (not containing sugar)	17.5	(G)	12.5	(G)
Fruit prepared or preserved by vinegar or acetic acid				
(not containing added sugar)	15		16	(G)
(containing added sugar)	12.5	(G)		

Table 6.2 *Continued*

Chestnuts	20		16	
Walnuts	20		16	
Macadamia nuts	12	(G)	9	(G)
Pistachio nuts	12		9	
Pecans	12		9	
Papayas	4		3	(G)
Pineapples	35		28	
Chestnuts (peeled)	20		16	
Hijiki	10	(G)	8	(G)
Pyrethrum extract	20		10	
Tropical fruit (other than mangoes and mangosteens) (containing added sugar)	12.5	(G)	16	(G)
Tropical fruit (other than mangoes and mangosteens) (not containing added sugar)	10	(G)		
Mangoes and mangosteens (containing added sugar)	12		9	
Mangoes and mangosteens (not containing added sugar)	7.5	(G)	5.6	(G)
Vegetables prepared or preserved by vinegar or	20		15	
acetic acid (containing added sugar)	16	(G)	12	(G)
Vegetables prepared or preserved by vinegar or acetic acid	16		12	
(not containing added sugar)	12	(G)	9	(G)
Fruit preserved by freezing	28		20	
(containing added sugar)	17.5	(G)	9	(G)
Tropical fruit (other than pineapple)	35		28	
Pineapple	28		20	
Instant coffee	17.5	(G)	12	(G)
Jellyfish (prepared or preserved)	17.5		14	
Young corncobs (in can, bottle or port)	10	(G)	8	(G)
Menthol	10	(G)	9	(G)
	28% or 900 yen/kg		24.4% or 720 yen/kg	
Ho oil	1.85	(G)	0	(G)

Note: (G) indicates an item subject to the GSP under which Japan offers preferential tariff treatment to certain LDCs.

II. Alcoholic items (the measures will be effective from April 1987)

Wine from fresh grapes (bottled)	38 per cent or 280 yen/litre whichever is the less, subject to a minimum customs duty of 299 yen/litre	30.4 per cent or 224 yen/litre whichever is the less, subject to a minimum customs duty of 132.80 yen/litre
Champagne and other sparkling wines	MFN 360 yen/litre GSP 260 yen/litre	MFN 288 yen/litre GSP 208 yen/litre

Table 6.2   *Continued*

Sherry, port and other fortified grape wines	220 yen/litre	176 yen/litre
Scotch whisky and other whisky (bottled)	36 per cent or 332 yen/litre whichever is the less, subject to a minimum customs duty of 299 yen/litre	246 yen/litre
Brandy (bottled)	407 yen/litre	325.60 yen/litre

III. Manufactured goods (tariffs on all the items in this category will be completely eliminated in early 1986)

	Present rate
For purification of the exhaust gas from cars	1.2
Vehicle belts and their belting	4.9
Rubber tyres, tyre cases, interchangeable tyre treads, inner tubes and tyre flaps for all types of wheels	4.0
Parts of motor vehicles	5.7
Precious and semi-precious stones (other than unpolished unperforated or similarly worked and formed to be used for mechanical or industrial purposes)	3.2
Polished skin	11.5
Blades for machine saws (other than hacksaw blades)	3.6
Drills, bits, reamers and screw taps	4.8
Milling cutters	5.5
Gear cutters	4.9
Diamond tools	5.8
Cutting tools (used in or with machines) (hard metal and other tools)	4.2
Inter-changeable tools (for hand, machine or power-operated tools) (excluding hard metal, and diamond tools)	4.2
Knives and cutting blades (for machines or mechanical appliances)	4.2
Parts of machinery for making or finishing paper or paperboard	4.2
Accessories and parts of machine tools for working metal or metal carbides	4.2
Lead-acid batteries	5.8
Electrical lighting and signalling equipment (other than for motor vehicles; excluding vehicles of heading No. 87,09 or B7.11)	4.2
Electronic telephonic and telegraphic switchboards and exchangers	5.7
Telephonic switchboards and exchangers (other than those of electronic type)	4.2
Apparatus for carrier current line system	3.6
Radiotelegraphic and radiotelephonic apparatus (for aircraft; excluding radio navigational aid apparatus and radio remote control apparatus)	4

Table 6.2 *Continued*

Parts of radiotelegraphic or radiotelephonic transmission and reception apparatus, or of radio broadcasting and television apparatus (excluding parts of radio navigational aid, radar, or remote control apparatus)	4.2
Cathode-ray tubes for television receivers	4.2
Carbon electrothermal resistors	4.9
Parts and accessories for motorcycle, autocycle, etc.	4.8
Cameras for uses other than aircraft, photo-engraving and medical or surgical purposes (excluding for film of a width of 35 mm)	5.7
Parts and accessories for cameras	5.7
Pressure gauges	4.9
Parts or accessories suitable for use solely or principally with one or more of the articles falling within the specified headings	4.2

Source: Ministry of Foreign Affairs, Tokyo.

(d) Office of the Trade Ombudsman (OTO). OTO used to be called the Headquarters for the Promotion of Settlements of Grievances Related to the Openness of the Japanese Market. It was established in January 1982 as part of a package of market-opening measures undertaken in that year. It consists of the administrative vice-ministers from the fourteen government ministries and agencies concerned and is headed by the Deputy Chief Cabinet Secretary in the Office of the Prime Minister.

In January 1983, the OTO Advisory Council was established with the aim of overseeing the operations of the OTO and to deliberate on complaints regarding access to the Japanese market. The advisory council consists of eight members (two of whom are Akito Morita of Sony and Soichiro Honda of Honda – see Appendix to the previous chapter) with Nobuhiko Ushida as Chairman and Saburo Okita as Deputy Chairman. In April 1984, when a package of market-opening measures was introduced to tackle complaints about procedures for direct investment in Japan and related matters and OTO was put in charge of it, OTO was renamed the Office of the Trade and Investment Ombudsman.

By May 1984, OTO had received 149 complaints, 99 of which came from abroad (including 49 from the USA and 29 from Western Europe). The Ministry of Health and Welfare received 57 of these complaints while the Ministries of Finance, International Trade and Industry and Agriculture, Forestry and Fisheries received 36, 30 and 14 respectively.

Of the complaints received, all but six were processed by May 1984. Eighty-five cases were resolved in an 'import-facilitating' manner with 41 of them getting improvements in import-inspection procedures and other provisions and the remaining 44 resolved as being cases of 'misunderstanding'.

Apart from these functions, OTO has been promoting an extensive educational campaign for foreign firms and diplomatic missions in Japan as well as companies abroad through the Japan External Trade Organisation (JETRO). 'The OTO is unique in bringing together high-level officials from a broad range of government ministries for the specific purpose of opening up a market. There is nothing quite like it anywhere else in the world and it is hoped that foreign manufacturers and governments will take advantage of [its] availability' (Okita, 1984).

THE ACTION PROGRAMME OF 1985

On 30 July 1985, the Japanese government announced the outline of the so-called 'Action Programme for Improved Market Access'. The government proudly declared that when the Action Programme has been fully implemented (within three years), Japan's market will be more open than any other in the advanced industrial nations; hence the end result will be 'befitting the position' that Japan now occupies in the world economy.

The Action Programme was devised with the aim of assisting international attempts to curb protectionist sentiments and actions and to promote a new round of multilateral trade negotiations under the auspices of GATT. However, the Japanese government insisted that the programme 'represents an autonomous decision based on consideration of the contribution Japan should make and the role it should play in relation to the maintenance and reinforcement of stable world economic development and the free trade system' (dispatch by the Ministry of Foreign Affairs, Tokyo, July 1985).

The Action Programme has three main objectives. Firstly, it aims to minimise government intervention by depending, 'whenever possible', on the responsibility and choice of the consumer, being guided by 'freedom in principle, restrictions only as exceptions'. Secondly, as stated earlier, it is intended to make a positive contribution to GATT's New Round of multilateral trade negotiations. Finally, it is meant to assist the LDCs in promoting their economic development.

The Action Programme offers specific measures to make the Japanese market more accessible to foreigners. These specific measures cover six aspects: a reduction in the general level of Japanese tariffs, an easing of import quota restrictions, a better system of 'standards and certifications' for import procedures, a more open government procurement policy, a more internationalised financial and capital market, and improvements in the services sector and the promotion of imports.

A general outline of the Action programme

With regard to the reduction of the general tariff level, the programme includes the tariff reductions and eliminations package that had been announced about a month earlier, covering altogether 1853 items – see Some Later Responses, section (c) above. Moreover, the Government declared its readiness to eliminate completely its tariffs on industrial products, provided other industrialised nations agreed to do likewise in the New GATT Round. In addition, the programme included the Japanese government's intention to improve the GSP 'for the benefit of developing countries'.

The longest section of the Action Programme is devoted to the standard-cum-certification and import procedures. The document announcing the programme stated that the Japanese government had undertaken a comprehensive review of the relevant Japanese laws and regulations and decided, 'after closely examining all the requests received from the foreign governments and business circles', to take action on practically all of them. The specific measures undertaken cover 88 amendments. These include: a switch from government to self-certification, the further reduction and elimination of certification systems, and the acceptance of foreign testing data and designation of foreign testing agencies.

With regard to government procurement, the programme specifies that the number of contracts awarded through single tendering will be reduced and that the relevant provisions of the GATT Agreement on Government Procurement will be applied to government-related organisations that are normally out of the scope of the Agreement.

The programme also promises a further liberalisation of the financial and capital markets including the easing of interest rate ceilings on deposits. There is also a commitment to a more liberal system in the services area through a strict control of counterfeit commodities and commercial practices.

The Japanese government also expressed its firm determination that the implementation of the Action Programme would be carried out by the 'establishment of a responsible system within the government' which would ensure that any ensuing measures (which should take into consideration the opinions and advice of foreign governments) are also carried out. For this purpose, an 'Action Programme Promotion Committee', headed by the Chief Cabinet Secretary, would be set up to oversee this course of action. Furthermore, legislative revisions based on the programme would be drafted and passed to the ordinary session of the Diet at the end of 1985.

It should also be added that, together with the Action Programme, the government promised to undertake measures to expand domestic demand further. A special 'working group' will be set up with this objective in mind. Moreover, ODA (overseas development assistance) will be increased and improved via a new 'Medium-term Target' for the expansion of aid to the LDCs and investment into and from Japan will be promoted to help in the vitalisation of the industrialised economies.

Finally, one should mention that Prime Minister Nakasone went on television to appeal to the Japanese people to purchase a minimum of $50 worth of foreign goods to help ease trade frictions.

Details of the Action Programme

Let us now turn to the details of the programme.

Tariffs (see Table 6.3):

Table 6.3   Tariff reductions and elimination under the Action Programme, 1985. (List of principal items broken down according to country/region)

Developed countries

	Agriculture, forestry and fishery products	Industrial and mining products
US	Walnuts (20%→16%) Duck meat (12.8%→10%) Pecans (12%→9%) Wine of fresh grapes (bulk) (Y80/1→Y64/1)	Monochrome film (6%→3.9%) Paper products (3.1–8.5%→2.5–6.8%) Aramid fibre (10%→8%) Aluminium polished skin sheets for aircraft (11.5%→0%)

Table 6.3   *Continued*

	Wine of fresh grapes (bottled) (down 20%)	Certain telecommunications and radio equipment (4–5.7%→0%) Automobile parts (4.2%→0%) Menthol (down 20%) Aluminium products (11.5%→9.2%) Lead-acid batteries (5.8%→0%)
Canada	Sphagnum (moss) (10%→5%) Rye whiskey (28%→22.4%)	Methanol (4.9%→3.9%) Paper products (3.1–8.5%→2.5–6.8%) Tyres (4%→0%) Certain telecommunications and radio equipment (4–5.7%→0%) Safety glass (5.5%→0%)
EC	Instant coffee (Germany, France, Netherlands) (17.5%→14%) Bakery products (UK) (35–40%→25–30%) Wine (bulk, bottled) (France, Germany, Netherlands) (see US column) Whisky (UK) (down 20%) Brandy (bulk) (down 20%) Beer (down 20%)	Menthol (Germany) (down 20%) Women's outer garments (France, Italy, UK) (20–14%→16–11.2%) Neckties (silk) (Italy, France, UK) (16.8%→13.4%) Medical instruments (Germany) (5.8%→4.6%) Skis (France, Italy, Germany) (6%→4.8%) Ski parts and accessories (France, Germany) (6%→4.8%) Automobile parts (4.2%→0%) Furniture (4.8%→3.8%) Parts of pumps for liquids (3.6%→0%)
EFTA, etc.	Bakery products (Austria) (35–40%→25–30%)	Cork (Portugal, Spain) (3.7–5.4%→3–4.3%)

Table 6.3 *Continued*

| | Wine (bulk, bottled) (Portugal, Austria) (see US column) Champagne and other sparkling wine (down 20%) Sherry, port wine (down 20%) | Paper products (Finland, Sweden) (see US column) Aluminium products (Sweden) (11.5%→9.2%) Cameras (Sweden) (5.2%→0%) Medical instruments (Sweden) (4–5.8%→3.2–4.6%) Embroidery (including motif) (Austria) (22.4%→17.9%) |
| Oceania | Macadamia nuts (Australia) (10%→6%) Abalone (in airtight containers) (Australia) (12%→9.6%) Papaya (Fiji) (4%→3%) Sphagnum (moss) (10%→5%) Wine (bulk, bottled) (Australia) (see US column) | Methanol (New Zealand) (4.9%→3.9%) Precious stones (opal) (Australia) (3.2%→0%) Medical instruments (Australia) (4.9–5.8%→3.9–4.6%) |

Developing countries

	Agriculture, forestry and fishery products	*Industrial and mining products*
ASEAN	Fowl without bones (Thailand) (18%→14%) Bananas (Philippines) Apr.–Sept. 17.5%→12.5%; Oct.–Mar. 35%→25% Palm oil (Malaysia) (3%→0%) Pineapples preserved by freezing (Thailand) (35%→28%) Castor oil (Thailand) (9%→7.2%)	Ethyl alcohol (down 20%) Women's outer garments (20–14%→16–11.2%) Men's outer garments (20–14%→16–11.2%) Man-made fibres (6–20%→4.8–16%) Handkerchiefs (8–11.3%→6.4–9%)
Republic of Korea	Blood ark shell (10%→8%)	Woven fabrics of man-made fibres (10%→8%)

Table 6.3 *Continued*

	Matsutake (5%→0%) Chestnuts (20%→16%)	Stockings (10–11.2%→8–9%) Men's and boy's outer garments (11.2–14%→9–11.2%)
	Hijiki (10%→8%) Leaves of oak (10%→0%)	Women's outer garments (14%→11.2%) Handkerchiefs (of cotton) (8.4%→6.7%)
Latin America	Fowl without bones (Brazil) (18%→14%) Bananas (see ASEAN column) Instant coffee (Colombia, Brazil, etc.) (17.5%→14%) Wine (bulk, bottled) (see US column)	Ferro-silicon (3.7%→3%) Ethyl alcohol (40%→32%) Precious stones, semi-precious stones (down 20%)
Middle East, Africa	Macadamia nuts (Kenya) (10%→6%) Pyrethrum extract (Kenya) (20%→10%) Instant coffee (Tanzania) (17.5%→14%)	

Note: Regarding the items below, on (1) the Japanese Foreign Minister and on (2) and (3) the Minister of Agriculture, Forestry and Fisheries made the following statements on 28 June at the Japan–ASEAN Economic Ministers' Conference.

(1) So-called boneless chicken: Japan intends to make further efforts to eliminate the tariff differential between so-called boneless chicken and legs of fowls with bone-in during the period of the Action Programme.

(2) Bananas: Although further reduction of the tariff is difficult, it will be kept in mind as a problem to be examined in the future.

(3) Plywood: Reduction of tariff on plywood will be examined, keeping in mind the request to rectify the tariff differential between broadleaf tree plywood and coniferous plywood.

Source: Ministry of Foreign Affairs, Tokyo, June 1985.

(i) New GATT Round. Apart from stating the nation's willingness to completely eliminate its tariffs on industrial goods on the proviso that other industrialised nations did likewise in the new GATT Round, Japan promised to promote tariff negotiations in agricultural and fishery products, giving due consideration to the 'special characteristics' of agriculture and to 'rectifying "tariff escalation"'.

(ii) Tariff Elimination/Reduction before the New GATT Round. About 1850 items (80 per cent of 2302 dutiable items – about 530 are already duty-free) are included for this purpose. It is promised that these measures will be implemented from the earliest possible date in 1986, with 1 April designated for certain commodities. There will be individual tariff reductions of more than 20 per cent, with complete elimination on some, on 36 agricultural and fishery items including: bananas, blood ark shell, boneless chicken, castor oil, chestnuts, frozen fruits, instant coffee, macadamia nuts, matsutake, palm oil, papaya, walnuts and whisky. Tariffs on 110 processed agricultural products and 1670 industrial mining products will be reduced by about 20 per cent across the board; included here are aramid fibre, some high technology items and film and paper products – there is a proviso here that these reductions may be suspended in 'cases where domestic industries suffer substantial injury from an import surge'. Tariffs will be completely abolished for 36 industrial and mining products including cameras, car parts and telecommunications and radio equipment. Also, a unilateral elimination of tariffs on 32 products with rates of or below 2 per cent will be made on 1 April 1987. Finally, Japan promises to promote negotiations with those interested in eliminating tariffs on some high technology products.

(iii) Improving the GSP. It should be apparent that the proposed tariff reductions will disadvantage the GSP (see El-Agraa, 1985a for a fuller discussion of the GSP system), so Japan has decided to reduce the tariffs on the relevant items covered by the GSP with immediate effect in the financial year beginning in 1986. It also promised substantial improvements in the GSP from April 1987 by: improving the ceiling system; expanding the import quotas and promoting an equalisation of benefits to the countries included in the GSP; and by improving the GSP itself by reducing the number of exceptions to the tariff preferences, completely eliminating tariffs and by giving special consideration to the least developed nations within the system.

Standards/certification systems and import procedures. The Japanese government is to make 88 amendments in the relevant laws concerning standards/certification systems. The most significant of these are: a reduction in the number of items under this system (ten amendments); the replacement of government with self-certification (fourteen amendments); and the acceptance of foreign test data and the 'active' use of foreign test agencies (nineteen amendments).

The government also decided on: the curtailment or relaxation of standards/ certification requirements (five amendments); the achievement of greater transparency in procedures (eight amendments); conformity with international standards (eleven amendments); the reduction of the number of items subject to import procedures (three amendments); and the simplification and acceleration of import procedures (six amendments).

Examples of the main items in which these specific measures apply were given in the official presentation of the Action Programme:

Cosmetics.   A system of comprehensive approval standards will be established with regard to the ingredients that may be used in combination in 15 types of cosmetic products such as hair liquids and nail varnish. Only blanket approval will become necessary for each type of product so that only notification will be necessary for individual items; this is expected to reduce the number of approvals by about 60 per cent, greatly accelerating the procedures involved.

Cars.   Previously, types of car of which 500 units or less were imported were granted simplified certification systems. Further improvements will be made here and the quantity involved will be doubled to one thousand units; this will be done under a new 'Preferential Handling Procedure for Imported Vehicles'. It is indicated that this will put 'virtually all imported vehicles within the scope of the simplified certification system'.

Subject to certain conditions, the new procedure will also allow the acceptance of data provided by manufacturers regarding the emission of exhaust gas and testing for noise levels. It is claimed that these and other measures will reduce the inspection periods for imported vehicles, which previously lasted between sixty to seventy days from the date of landing in Japan, to such an extent that it will be possible to commence sales preparations immediately.

A number of improvements will also be made to the type designation system for motor vehicles imported in quantities in excess of one-thousand units. It will no longer be necessary to provide safety and durability data when applications are being made. Moreover, instead of the system of sample inspection, there will be a strengthening of the machinery for accepting overseas vehicle inspections.

Electrical appliances.   The list of items under government safety checks (Category A under the Electrical Appliance and Material Control Law) has been revised with a large number of items being transferred to Category B (consisting of products checked for compliance with standards under the manufacturers' own responsibility). This automatically extends the range of items subject to self-certification.

These measures will triple the number of items under Category B from the 1985 level of 72 items. The standards employed to ensure the safety of electrical appliances and materials will be altered to achieve compatibility with the standards of the International Electrotechnic Commission that are in use in Western Europe. When this has been achieved (within three years), European manufacturers exporting to Japan will no longer need to produce goods 'specifically configured to Japanese standards'.

Medical equipment. Here, approval conditions will be eliminated (within three years) from 33 categories, at a rate of eleven categories per year. Provided safety conditions are ensured and the equipment concerned has established technical reputation, the categories affected will include clinical microtomes, medical centrifugal subsiders and equipment used by specialist personnel. Moreover, under the 'Japanese industrial standards' (JIS; regarding size specification, etc.), 36 new standards will be established within three years. Conformity with these standards will eliminate the necessity for approval; thus the number of imported items subject to approval requirements will be reduced by about 25 per cent. The items under consideration will include medical equipment using high-pressure oxygen, electric scalpels and mercury thermometers.

Pharmaceuticals. Foreign test data will be accepted for all categories except for areas where the results for Japanese and non-Japanese may vary: comparative clinical trials; dose finding tests; and absorption, distribution, metabolism and excretion tests. Moreover, standard processing times will be set for the certification of pharmaceuticals and medical equipment with the intention of accelerating procedures, and applicants will be notified of the time required for processing.

JIS mark approval for foreign goods. Before 1985, where JIS labels were to be displayed on foreign products, it was necessary for a Japanese official to go to the country concerned to carry out factory inspection. The implementation of the new measures will enable approval applications for JIS marks to be screened on the basis of data prepared by a foreign testing agency. Moreover, the appropriate Minister will be able to designate the foreign test agencies whose test data will be accepted for electrical appliances and materials and LPG (liquefied petroleum gas) containers. Both measures should promote the acceptance of foreign test data and make for better access for foreign products to the Japanese market.

The Japanese government also announced its intention to use the drafting of the Action Programme 'as an opportunity for promoting technical cooperation with the developing countries with a view to establishing in those countries a system of standards that are compatible with international standards'. The intended enhancement of cooperation will take the form of accepting increased numbers of trainees and the establishment of new courses as well as the expansion of programmes whereby Japanese specialists are sent to the LDCs.

Government Procurement.   There are several intended actions here: the number of contracts awarded through single tendering will be reduced by repetitive tendering, revised bidding conditions etc.; Japan will unilaterally extend the bidding time from the 30 days specified in the 'GATT Government Procurement Code' to 40 days in order to facilitate the placing of orders by foreign suppliers; qualification procedures for bidding will be improved and simplified; the Japanese government will establish a unified government liaison office, within the Ministry of Foreign Affairs, to provide information and to process complaints from foreign suppliers; and, in order to expand opportunities for foreign suppliers, the Japanese government will unilaterally apply the provisions of the 'GATT Government Procurement Code', to sixteen agencies in addition to the 45 agencies already covered. These are:

- Water Resources Development Public Corporation (National Land Agency);
- New Tokyo International Airport Authority (Ministry of Transport);
- Japan Highway Public Corporation (Ministry of Construction);
- Environmental Pollution Control Service Corporation (Environment Agency);
- Japan International Cooperation Agency (Ministry of Foreign Affairs);
- Pension Welfare Service Public Corporation (Ministry of Health and Welfare);
- Labour Welfare Projects Corporation (Ministry of Labour);

- Employment Promotion Projects Corporation (Ministry of Labour);
- Japan Consumer Information Centre (Economic Planning Agency);
- Japan Information Centre of Science and Technology (Science and Technology Agency);
- Japan Foundation (Ministry of Foreign Affairs);
- National Stadium (Ministry of Education);
- University of the Air Foundation (Ministries of Education and Posts and Telecommunications);
- Japan Racing Association (Ministry of Agriculture, Forestry and Fisheries);
- Japan External Trade Organisation (Ministry of International Trade and Industry); and
- New Energy Development Organisation (Ministry of International Trade and Industry).

(iv)   Services and the Promotion of Imports

- *Services*. Three items are covered. The first of these is the question of foreign lawyers: under the Japanese Lawyers Law, foreign lawyers are not permitted to practise, or offer consulting services, in Japan. A bill to revise this law to enable foreign lawyers to practice in Japan is promised for the next regular session of the Diet and efforts will be made to secure its early passage. The second, is the problem of counterfeit products. Japan has promised to step up its efforts to eradicate counterfeit products by stronger enforcement of regulations and the establishment of anti-counterfeit officers. Finally, there is the matter of commuter air services, i.e. regular short-distance flights. The Japanese government will relax the 5.7 tons weight limit imposed on aircraft used for commuter air services by un-scheduled air transportation companies, thus promoting the sale of foreign aircraft in Japan. Moreover, the regulation specifying that an aircraft must have a crew of three will be relaxed to enable the marketing of aircraft designed for a crew of two, which will presumably help foreign aircraft firms.
- *Import promotion*. This item covers the expansion of import credit on manufactured products as well as government procurement of imported goods. Here, the Japanese government has promised to support the efforts of the private sector to increase imports by various means including: a further reduction in the interest charged by the Export-Import Bank of Japan from 7.1 per cent to a

minimum of 6.5 per cent on import credit for manufactures and the introduction of foreign currency lending for such products. Moreover, the government will itself endeavour to buy foreign goods for its procurement.

● *Investment promotion.* This is concerned with the promotion of investment in Japan through an expansion of the credit extended by the Japan Development Bank. The Japanese government promises the implementation of a number of measures to aid foreign corporations wishing to make direct investments in Japan. The measures will include a reduction in the interest rate charged by the JDB (on credit for enhancing the inflow of direct investment in Japan) from 7.5 to 7.1 per cent.

(v) Financial and capital markets. This section of the Action Programme covers three major areas:

● *Liberalisation of the financial and capital market.* The government promised: the elimination of the ceiling on interest rates on large denomination time deposits (in excess of one million yen) in Autumn 1985 – this will be accompanied by relaxation in the regulation of interest rates on inter-bank deposits; the gradual raising of the ceiling on 'money market certificates' (MMCs) issues from Autumn 1985 with a lowering of the minimum denomination and an extension of the maximum maturity of MMCs to two years by the Spring of 1987; and a gradual raising of the ceiling on issues of 'certificates of deposits' (CDs) from Autumn 1985 with an extension of the maximum maturity to one year by the Spring of 1987.

In addition, measures will be taken to promote the efficiency and diversity of the financial and capital markets. These include the development of the short-term government debt market, the establishment of a bond futures market in October 1985, the development of the Tokyo primary market, and permission for securities companies to deal in Yen denominated 'bank acceptances' (BAs). Moreover, in response to requests by foreign banks and in the light of a review of practices in inter-bank markets, transactions without collateral were incorporated into the call money market by the end of July 1985.

● *Improvement of access.* This field is concerned with two major areas: the membership of foreign securities firms in the Tokyo Stock Exchange (TSE) and the participation of foreign banks in Trust Banking in Japan. With regard to the former, an *ad hoc* committee on membership of the TSE decided in March 1985 to increase the full membership of the TSE to 83 seats; the committee was expected to reach a conclusion in Autumn 1985. As to the latter, it is promised that licences to engage in trust banking activities by nine eligible foreign banks (announced in June 1985) will be issued promptly upon the submission of applications – note that the total number of Japanese banks active in this area is eight.

● *Euroyen market.* Here, further efforts are promised for the development of this market. Moreover, in line with similar measures for Euroyen bonds issued by non-residents in June 1985, the Euroyen bonds issued by residents will be diversified; this will include the authorisation, from the Spring of 1986, of floating rate notes.

(vi) Import restrictions. This is a very brief section dealing with agricultural and industrial products. The Action Programme specifies that Japan will make efforts to improve market access for agricultural products through active participation in the negotiations and consultations under the GATT as well as with interested countries. Also, Japan will deal with the question of import restrictions on leather and leather shoes, in the 'appropriate manner', within the context of GATT.

Implementation and Promotion Committee

In order to ensure an effective and forceful implementation of the Action Programme, the Implementation and Promotion Committee (IPC, short for the Committee to Promote the Implementation of the Action Programme) was established within the Government Ruling Parties Headquarters for the Promotion of External Economic Measures. This, of course, meant that the Committee for Drafting and Promoting the Action Programme on Standards and Certification Systems was dissolved.

The IPC is responsible for drawing up the details of the Action Programme after the outline of the programme in each area is decided and for following up the implementation. Also, it has the power to ask for the cooperation, where necessary, of administrative inspection. However, this may seem like a loose arrangement, so specific measures were mentioned:

● With regard to the areas of standards and certification systems and import procedures, a Sub-committee on Standards and Certification Systems was established. This consisted of certain members of the IPC who were members of the Committee for Drafting and Promoting the Action Programme on Standards and Certification Systems. The areas of responsibility of this Committee are: to conduct a very strict examination when there is a need for the establishment of new standards and certification systems, including the enlargement and strengthening of existing systems, and to scrutinise the appropriateness of the contents of such systems; to examine and approve the standard processing period determined by each ministry and agency; and to examine and approve the result of the examination by each ministry and agency concerned with standard and certification systems as well as other tasks assigned to the IPC dealing with standard and certification systems and import procedures outlined in the Action Programme.

● With regard to government procurements, advisory offices will be set up in each ministry and agency concerned and a 'united office' dealing with common external affairs will be established in the Ministry of Foreign Affairs with the object of complementing the advisory offices. The 'united office' will receive all enquiries from foreign suppliers and deal with them through such organisations as the liaison and coordination committees established within the ministries and agencies concerned.

The Chairman of the IPC (who may seek the opinion of informed people both within and outside the Committee, including, when needed, members of the Advisory Committee on External Economic Issues) will be the Chief Cabinet Secretary. The rest of the Committee consists of the Deputy Chief Cabinet Secretary (in working capacity), the Vice-Minister for Economic Planning, the Deputy Chairman, all the Vice-Ministers of all the Japanese ministries and agencies and the Director-General of the National Police Agency.

The management of the IPC will be aided by a conference to be established and whose membership comprises the Director-Generals from the relevant bureaux in the different ministries and agencies. The Conference will be chaired by the Director-General of the Coordination Bureau of the Economic Planning Agency, but the Director of the Cabinet Councillor's Office of the Cabinet Secretariat will become the chairman when standards, certification and import procedures are under consideration. The Conference will consist of the Director-Generals, or those with equivalent ranks, of the different ministries and agencies to which the Committee members belong.

Finally, an Improvement Surveillance Officer for Standards and

Certification will be posted in each of the government ministries and agencies. The task of this force is to ensure the effective implementation of measures for improving standards, certification and import procedures. They should achieve this by such means as the thorough diffusion of detailed relevant information down to the primary working level.

THE RESPONSE TO THE MAEKAWA RECOMMENDATIONS

The response by the Japanese Government to the Maekawa Report was immediate; it was announced a day later (on 8 April, 1986) as the declaration of the Ministerial Conference for Economic Measures (MCEM) – Declaration, hereafter. This is not surprising given what was stated in the previous chapter: Prime Minister Nakasone established the Maekawa Committee to report to him in good time before the Tokyo Summit in May.

The Declaration reiterated the pronouncements made in the Maekawa Report: it is critical that the Japanese government should take effective measures to 'consolidate' the economy's health and to promote economic growth through the expansion of domestic demand, hoping that the world economy will get a boost through the balanced growth of the Japanese economy. Of course, the Declaration had to take into consideration two crucial developments: the coordinated action by the Group of Five (G5) to appreciate the yen and the Deutschmark and depreciate the US dollar, and the dramatic fall in the price of oil. Hence, the Declaration had the following preamble:

> It is essential therefore, that, as well as continuing to work for appropriate and flexible fiscal and financial policy management, the government strive to see that the advantages accruing from the yen's appreciation and lower oil prices work their way throughout the entire economy and benefit everyone alike. At the same time, while further promoting improvements such as relaxing restrictions so that the private-sector economy can develop vigorously, it is imperative that the government work to promote housing construction. In addition, it is necessary to improve the economic climate so that small businesses can respond positively to the harsh changes under way in the economy.

Given these policy directives, the Japanese government committed itself to the implementation of 'carefully thought out measures' in six major areas.

Flexible monetary policy management

Given that the Bank of Japan (BOJ) lowered its official discount rate by 0.5 per cent on 30 January 1986 and by another 0.5 per cent on 10 March and that these triggered off reductions in the interest rate on savings, the short-term prime rate and other rates, it was felt that the Japanese interest rates were generally low across the board. Hence, with the rate of interest approaching the 5 per cent mark, it was inevitable to conclude that the 'government is to work for flexible management of its monetary policies while continuing to watch economic trends in Japan and overseas and the international currency situation' while discouraging excessive speculative transactions.

Promoting implementation of public works

The government committed itself to ensuring the highest ever ratio of contracts met during the first half of FY 1986, giving due consideration to the economic situation in each area, the state of social infrastructure, project priorities and other factors. Moreover, local governments will be asked to take the necessary measures to ensure the smooth implementation of public works.

Passing along the benefits of Yen appreciation and lower oil prices, and setting reasonable prices

The nine major electric power firms will be asked to pass along these benefits 'with provisional rate reductions and other means, study of modalities to begin immediately and actual implementation to begin in June'. The sum involved was projected to be about 1 trillion yen, provided the trends in exchange rates and oil prices continued.

The price bands set for livestock products will have their median reduced by 2.3 per cent for dairy cattle beef (which provides 70 per cent of Japan's consumption of beef), 5.6 per cent for pork and 4 per cent for butter to be effective from FY 1986.

With regard to imported beef, the discount for retail prices will be raised to 20–30 per cent (from 10–20 per cent), effective from May 1986 and efforts will be made to promote the scope of 'meat day' sales.

A 'beef week' was set for the Golden Week holidays (29 April to 5 May 1986) and beef is to be put on special sale in major cities. Moreover, additional measures for the distribution of beef will be implemented during FY 1986.

Efforts will be made to reduce the directional disparities in international air fares.

In order to reduce user costs in international telecommunications, efforts will be made to encourage rate reductions by September 1986 at the latest.

Efforts will be made to reduce other public utility fees, and where such reductions are difficult to carry out efforts will be made to pass the benefits through long-term rate stability, improved service and other modalities, taking due factors into account.

Finally, businesses will be asked to adjust their pricing and other policies to take into consideration the effects of the appreciation of the yen and the reduction in the price of oil. Among the many measures suggested are the holding of major import bazaars with the help of JETRO and the Manufactured Imports Promotion Organisation (MIPRO), the encouragement of local merchant associations to hold import fairs, the promotion of advertising and other information programmes about imported manufactures, and the surveying of price trends for leading imported consumer goods and others (37 products – see Table 6.4).

Promoting urban redevelopment by easing restrictions

The priority will be for promoting the re-zoning of Tokyo, except where it is necessary to preserve a pleasant residential environment for low rise housing areas, by designating current Category 1 Exclusive Residential District within the area bounded by Tokyo Loop Road 7 as Category 2 Exclusive Residential District. Also, standards will be reviewed to allow for major increases in total floor space regulations in specially designated and comprehensive planning areas. Moreover, efforts will be made to relax slant plain restrictions in order to fully utilise the use of urban space for urban redevelopment.

With regard to the creation of new urban areas, priority will be given to re-zoning in areas adjacent to urbanisation control areas where major population increases are expected, areas around new rail stations and other areas where major new urban development investment is foreseen. At the same time, efforts will be made to promote the lifting of the reserved population framework. Moreover, as well as

Table 6.4 Imported consumer products subject to research of price and other trends

Tuna	Salmon	Octopus
Shrimps	Processed meat products	Natural cheese
Canned vegetables (sweet corn)	Lemon	Grapefruit
Bananas	Soya bean oil	Chocolate (cocoa beans)
Chocolate (confectionery)	Wood	Formula feed
Whisky	Wine	Electric razors
Articles of aluminium for domestic use	Jeans	Shirts
Undergarments	Sports shoes	Socks
Ties	Passenger cars	Tyres
Fountain pens	Balls for gymnastic use	Golf clubs
Tennis rackets	Film	Gramophone records
Books, magazines, umbrellas	Handbags	Wrist-watches

Source: Ministry of Foreign Affairs, Tokyo.

reviewing the criteria for licensing for development, efforts will be made to expedite and streamline development approval procedures. In addition, local governments which had not yet 'corrected their excesses' in accordance with the reviews of housing development guidelines to date will be instructed to make serious efforts to rectify them; in doing so, efforts are to be made to rectify the amount of land which must be set aside for roads, parks, schools and other public facilities and to raise the effective ratio of housing area in total development areas and costs. Efforts will also be made to utilise funding by the private sector for 'landfill projects' by, for example, raising the private sector's funding ratio in outstanding public–private projects that will contribute to the revitalisation of the public sector. Finally, efforts will be made to promote the effective utilisation of public land by relying on the vitality of the private sector; this should be facilitated by the passage of the Bill to Partially Amend the National Properties Law and the Bill to Partially Amend the Local Government Law (both Bills were before the Diet prior to its dissolution at the end of May 1986 for a double election) enabling the introduction of a land trust system for public land.

Promoting housing construction and private-sector capital investment

With regard to the promotion of housing construction, the interest rates on loans from the Housing Loan Corporation will be lowered together with efforts to promote lending by moving up the application periods for individual housing loans, extending the application periods, increasing the number of times applications can be accepted for rental housing by the private sector and raising the price of housing eligible for public financing. Also, efforts will be made to make people more fully aware of (hence, more likely to take advantage of) the tax deductions for encouraging the acquisition of housing and the expansion of special exemption in the gift tax for this purpose; both were enacted in the reform of the tax system in February 1986. Moreover, financial institutions in the private sector will be asked to consider the lowering of their interest rates and to ensure stable supplies of funds for housing loans to individuals. In addition, apart from training and deploying remodelling advisers, developing and spreading remodelling technology and providing more information (for example, by holding home rebuilding fairs in order to promote home enlargement or remodelling), international houseware shows will be held to stimulate demand for housing-related goods. Finally, comprehensive measures to encourage the construction of wooden buildings will be promoted.

As to additional capital investment, efforts will be made to encourage electrical power and gas companies to accelerate their orders and expand their capital investment, including spending for maintenance work. The orders of the electrical power companies were about 700 billion yen in the first half of FY 1986; they will be asked, in response to strong public demand, to inject an additional 100 billion yen to their current plans for purchasing underground transmission cables (to be positively supported by the appropriate administrative bodies) in each of the following two fiscal years. The gas companies will also be asked to make efforts to accelerate their orders during the first half of FY 1986, to strengthen security and to introduce other improvements. Moreover, the NTT will be asked to increase its investment in FY 1986 by about 150 billion yen by accelerating its plans for network digitalisation and expanding its plans to purchase underground transmission cables. Also, when the Urban Railways Construction Act (then being proposed to the Diet) is passed, large-scale works to reinforce transportation capabilities (such as the quadrupling of railway lines) will be promoted through using the Railways Construction Fund System.

With regard to the utilisation of the vitality of the private sector for public works, apart from enhancing a quick passage through the Diet of the Law for Special Measures Relating to the Construction of the Bay of Tokyo Crossway, efforts will also be made to get work going on a full scale of the new Kansai International Airport. Also, with the passage of the Law for Provisional Measures Relating to the Promotion of Improvements at Designated Facilities Utilising the Abilities of Private-Sector Operators, basic directions will be promptly drafted in an attempt to contribute to the smooth implementation of such designated areas as the open research facilities, the international exhibition and concert halls and port and harbour operational facilities. Likewise, efforts will be made to vigorously promote local projects involving the energies of the private sector, including the further promotion of the 'technopolis concept'. Finally, efforts will be made to promote the more efficient use of national forests by the building in them of second houses and recreational facilities for those who work there, and to make effective use of forests owned by the public sector.

Small businesses

Interest rates on loans for the Small and Medium Enterprises Special Loan System and the Management Improvement Loan System for Small Enterprises are to be lowered with the aim of facilitating fund raising by small businesses. Also, as well as making efforts to rigorously enforce the Law to Prevent Sub-Contractor's Payment Delays, parent firms will be advised to abstain from 'unduly passing the burden' of the appreciation of the yen onto their sub-contractors. Moreover, in order to maintain business orders for small sub-contractors affected by the appreciation of the yen, efforts will be made, through the Sub-Contracting Business Promotion Council, to 'flexibly' introduce sub-contracting companies to potential customers. Furthermore, in order to enhance consultations and advice for sub-contracting companies and to make efforts to encourage and strengthen the capabilities of such special consultative organisations as the Commercial Association and the Chamber of Commerce and Industry and to establish a consultative capability at the National Federation of Small Business Organisations, efforts will be made to establish consultative facilities at prefectural offices and to strengthen cooperation between the national and local governments. In addition, the Minister of International Trade and Industry is to appoint experienced and knowledgeable businessmen and other experts as Local Small Business Activity Promotion Advisers to provide advice and suggestions on how local manufacturing firms especially hard hit by the appreciation of the yen and other factors can best shift into other lines of business. Also, as well as working to ensure that local small business executives and other people are fully aware of and using the emergency measures for management stabilisation and business conversion measures provided for under the Temporary Law on Business Conversion and Adjustment Measures for Small and Medium-Sized Enterprises, prefectures will be asked to establish Local Production Policy Promotion Councils with membership drawn from small business associations, financial institutions and people with knowledge and expertise to study what should be done in each region. Moreover, as well as accelerating the implementation of plans to build industrial parks, wholesale markets and other facilities using finance from the modernisation loans for small business organisations to promote domestic demand in each region, the prefectures will be urged to take measures to ensure the smooth implementation of these plans. Finally, in carrying out advanced implementation of public works, efforts will be made to expand the contract opportunities for small and medium size businesses.

Two more areas were covered under the general section on small businesses: metal mining and employment policies. The Declaration stated that, as well as moving the financing period up for Metal Mining Stabilisation Financing designed to cover exploration, safety policies and other aspects of mining, the Mining Council will make an immediate study of ways to help these companies respond to the sudden deterioration in their industries. Under the industry designation criteria revised in March 1986, efforts will be made to 'flexibly' designate regions and industries in line with the actual situation in each region and industry and to promote the active use of Employment Adjustment Grants. Finally, for older people and those who lost their jobs at designated depressed industries or regions (due to depression), efforts will be made to promote their prompt rehiring through the use of Designated Job-Seeker Employment Development Grants, the implementation of designated 'job-seeker' development opportunities and vocational training such as Entrusted Training and Intensive Training.

CONCLUSION

Unless one is prepared to state that both the Action Programme and the Declaration are mere rhetoric by the Japanese government, the only conclusion that can be reached is that the Japanese government has undertaken a number of major measures to increase imports. Some of the measures have already been implemented: the coordinated appreciation of the yen (together with the Swiss Franc and the Deutschmark) and depreciation of the dollar, the increase in Japan's contribution to overseas development assistance, the reduction of tariffs on a number of agricultural and industrial products and the genuine efforts to increase domestic demand and promote the purchase of foreign goods. Moreover, although a number of political commentators may describe Prime Minister Nakasone's recall of the Diet for a special session to discuss the proposed measures to help small businesses overcome the hardship imposed on them by the appreciation of the yen as a mere gesture to enable him to dissolve the House and prepare for a double election, the fact remains that those measures will be discussed soon after the elections are over, particularly so with a workable majority for the LDP. The readiness of the Japanese government to draw up a supplementary budget of about 3 trillion yen to help boost the domestic economy may be cast in the same vein. The only scepticism that may remain is that, in spite of the concreteness of some of the measures proposed, the outside world, particularly businesses and politicians in the USA, may deem the Action Programme and the Declaration as yet another 'package'. Indeed, James Baker, the US Treasury Secretary's reaction was to utter but the expected: he stated that the Action Programme was only a plan and can, therefore, be judged only on the basis of 'its prompt implementation and its final result toward the opening of Japan's markets', and Senator Danforth was adamant that the US Congress should 'enact legislation insisting on results and imposing penalties on Japanese products if the results are not forthcoming'. There also remains the problem of the 'package approach'; the United States–Japan Advisory Commission (1984) felt that it is of decreasing usefulness since the:

> contents of each package are for the most part selected to respond to foreign pressures. They appear to the Japanese people as concessions to appease the [USA] and other countries rather than as actions beneficial to Japan itself. Any appearance of reciprocity

is rare. With the knowledge that another package will in time be forthcoming, the tendency for Japanese bureaucrats is to limit their commitments in order to save something for the future. In the [USA], each package is examined for what was left out and should be extracted in the next package. The consequence is a confrontational tugging, which reduces rather than increases mutual confidence. Over time, the packages also do less to draw attention to Japan's market-opening progress. Previously announced measures appear to be repeated in later packages, and explanations of what has been added are often highly technical and raise questions as to why a previous measure was only half the step in the first instance.

However one should not end the chapter there: it has to be emphasised that the Action Programme, incorporating measures regarding tariff reductions in agricultural products announced three months earlier, the Declaration with its emphasis on increasing domestic demand, and the dramatic appreciation of the yen relative to the dollar in spite of rhetoric to the effect that it has not appreciated enough (those who are arguing so are asking for an appreciation which will completely wipe out the US trade deficit – see Chapters 3 and 4), should be clear indications of the fact that they are not just another 'package' with the promise of more to take into account what has not been included. Japan has made great efforts to adopt measures which should lead to 'harmony with the international community', and those who seek instant results in an area where results take a very long time to materialise, *if other things remain the same*, can only be castigated as being simply irresponsible, be they economists, politicians, or anyone who is trying to make instant history.

7 Neo-protectionism: A Comprehensive Theoretical Appraisal

Before proceeding to the concluding chapter, it is vital to have a theoretical discussion of neo-protectionism since it lies at the very heart of Japan's trade frictions with the outside world. A theoretical discussion of 'orthodox' protectionism is not warranted since the specialist reader should be well versed here, but neo-protectionism is still not well-understood, in spite of my own efforts in this area – see El-Agraa (1984) for a full discussion. Moreover, the crucial aspects of orthodox protectionism are highlighted within the discussion of aspects of neo-protectionism.

INTRODUCTION

The history of the world economy has, during the past two decades or so, experienced two interesting developments. On the one hand, there has been a tremendous drive for international economic integration. Indeed, there are more schemes under that heading than could reasonably be discussed in a single large book (see El-Agraa, 1982; 1987). On the other hand, there has been a revival of protectionism – see the various publications by the Cambridge Economic Policy Group (CEPG) between 1978 and 1981 setting out their protectionist stance, and Page (1979) for a global empirical assessment. Page, who tried to estimate the changes in non-tariff distortions of trade barriers between the period prior to 1974 and after, reached the conclusion that:

about 40% of trade by all market economies was controlled before 1974; this has risen to just under a half [see Table 7.1]. Most trade in non-manufactures was already managed in 1974; the rise since then has been small. In manufactures, however, the share has risen from 13% to almost a quarter. For imports by the EC countries, the changes are from 36% to 45% for all goods, and from virtually nothing to 16% for manufactures. ... For all goods, the share of trade controlled by the European countries is slightly lower than

Table 7.1   Managed trade by country (percentages of 1974 trade)

	All goods			Manufactures		
	1974	1979	1980	1974	1979	1980
Belgium/Luxembourg	27.5	33.4	34.0	0.7	9.1	10.0
Denmark	29.5	42.8	43.2	0	21.1	21.7
France	32.8	42.6	42.7	0	16.0	16.2
Germany	37.3	47.1	47.3	0	17.9	18.3
Ireland	26.8	33.5	34.0	1.5	11.0	11.7
Italy	44.1	52.2	52.3	0	16.1	16.4
Netherlands	32.5	39.8	40.1	0	12.8	14.8
United Kingdom	38.5	47.4	47.9	0.2	17.0	17.4
EC (9)	35.8	44.5	44.8	0.1	15.7	16.1
Australia	17.9	34.8	34.8	7.8	30.0	30.0
Austria	20.8	30.3	30.3	0	13.1	13.1
Canada	22.4	18.3	18.3	11.4	5.8	5.8
Finland	32.9	33.6	33.6	3.1	3.5	3.5
Greece	100.0	100.0	100.0	100.0	100.0	100.0
Iceland	20.6	31.2	31.2	1.3	15.7	15.7
Japan	56.1	59.4	59.4	0	4.3	4.3
Norway	16.3	33.7	33.7	0	24.6	24.6
Portugal	25.5	27.5	27.5	10.5	11.7	11.7
Spain	32.2	52.3	52.3	0	37.1	37.1
Sweden	24.7	36.3	36.3	3.1	19.4	19.4
Switzerland	16.9	18.3	18.3	2.1	3.4	3.4
Turkey	100.0	100.0	100.0	100.0	100.0	100.0
United States	36.2	44.4	45.8	5.6	18.4	21.0
OECD (22)	36.3	43.8	44.3	4.0	16.8	17.4
Other developed (3)	97.5	97.9	97.9	97.7	97.8	97.8
Oil exporters (15)	54.0	65.3	65.3	45.8	59.8	59.8
Non-oil developing (81)	49.8	46.8	46.9	25.0	22.7	22.8
World (122)	40.1	47.5	47.8	12.9	23.0	23.6

Source: S. A. B. Page, 'The revival of protectionism and its consequences for Europe', *Journal of Common Market Studies*, vol. 20, no. 1, 1979, p. 29.

the average for the world, but the increase since 1974 has been greater (Page, 1979, p. 28).

A proliferation of integration schemes simultaneously with increasing protectionism might not seem like contradictory tendencies for those who believe that 'free trade areas', 'customs unions', 'common markets', etc. are essentially inward-looking groupings which discriminate against the relevant 'outsiders'. However, this point of view needs to be examined with a great deal of caution: economic integration promotes free trade among the participating nations; under the rules of the General Agreement of Tariffs and Trade (GATT, Article XXIV), such groupings are not allowed to erect a common tariff barrier *in excess* of the average pre-integration tariff level; and the world has experienced general reductions in the levels of tariffs under the Dillon, Kennedy and Tokyo Rounds of tariff negotiations conducted under the auspices of GATT.

Although protectionism is not a new phenomenon, its modern revival is entirely due to the present recession and, in the case of Britain, to the policy recommendations propagated by the CEPG. A careful study of the history of the world economy will clearly show that there is a strong correlation between the level of unemployment and protectionism, and the present debate regarding Japan's trade frictions is an obvious manifestation of this, particularly in the case of the USA. If this appears to be too much of a generalisation, all that needs to be recalled is that Britain had a current account surplus from 1800 to 1880 and the US was in a similar position between 1915 and 1960 yet no single nation complained, but now that Japan is going through a similar phase in its 'balance of payments stages', the whole world has broken loose. Why? Simply because when the UK and the USA went through the equivalent stages, unemployment was not a problem for the outside world, rather it was a problem within those two economies themselves. Hence, it is this crucial difference regarding Japan's stage corresponding with unemployment in the 'outside world' that mainly accounts for the current trade frictions between Japan and the outside world and for the revival of protectionism in the USA. It should be added, however, that the emphasis is on trade frictions, not the size of Japan's surplus on current account, since it is the structural aspect of that surplus that should be of concern; it was argued in Chapter 3 that the rest of the surplus is easily explained in terms of overvalued currencies and economic mismanagement in the USA and most of the EC countries.

The Cambridge revival has an interesting twist to it in that it is presented as a panacea for 'ailing economies' such as the United Kingdom and the United States of America. The idea is that these economies suffer from Kaldorian (Kaldor, 1966) 'premature maturity': a rejuvenation of industry is entirely dependent on the notion that all the necessary conditions for 'infant industries' are prevalent in these, and similar countries. Moreover, the economic rationale for this neo-protectionism is presented in Keynesian macroeconomic terms with unemployment at the very heart of the model and neoclassical concepts thrown out of the window in no uncompromising terms. Hence, the reader, although assumed to be familiar with the economic analysis of tariff (and similar trade impediments) imposition, is distracted by this new formulation and different set of assumptions. Finally, a further distraction is introduced in that protectionism is presented as an alternative policy option to devaluation, when the world monetary system is now operating a freely flexible exchange rate regime, albeit a managed one.

The purpose of this chapter is to attempt a thorough appraisal of neo-protectionism in all possible economic frameworks: macroeconomic, general equilibrium and political economy.

THE MACROECONOMIC MODEL

In spite of earlier efforts (e.g. Hicks, 1953; Brown, 1961; El-Agraa, 1978a, 1978b, 1978c, 1979 and El-Agraa in El-Agraa and Jones, 1981), Godley has recently stated that Keynesian economics was never *properly* incorporated into international trade theory. He emphasised that even before the 'monetarist counterrevolution' international trade was one field where neoclassical concepts remained dominant and proceeded to claim that this helps to explain why 'virtually the entire profession . . . supports the principle of free trade' (Godley, 1981a, p. 2). He went on to point out that the most significant respect in which international trade theory has always been un-Keynesian is that it is built on the premise that output and full employment are taken for granted; that employment in aggregate might be altered by the existence of international trade is hardly considered. He found this state of affairs extraordinary: 'It appears to me rather to be the case not merely that international trade performance influences aggregate demand and employment but that it has a dominant, almost an exclusive role in doing so. . . . The argument turns on the crucial role of the foreign trade multiplier' (Godley, 1981a, p. 3).

The aim of this section is to formulate the CEPG *basic model* as accurately as possible so that Godley's claims can be stated much more clearly and succinctly; hence they can be more accurately evaluated.

The model

The CEPG's most elaborate model is to be found in two articles published in *Economica* (Godley and Cripps, 1976) and *The Cambridge Economic Policy Review* (CEPR) (Godley and May, 1977). The model stated in these papers remains the basic one in spite of later additions (CEPR, 1978–81; McCullum and Vines, 1981) since the elaborate models do not alter, to any significant extent, the conclusions of the basic model (Godley, 1981a). Hence, clarity of exposition necessitates confining discussion to the basic formulation.

The CEPG model postulates an economy measured in *current prices* so that every element expresses a money flow per unit of time such that:

$$Y \equiv G + dS + PE + X - M, \tag{1}$$

where Y is national income, G is government expenditure, dS is the change in the value of stocks, PE is private expenditure on both consumption and fixed investment, X is exports and M imports.

This national income identity can be expressed as a flow of funds identity by subtracting the tax yield from both sides and rearranging:

$$G - T \equiv (Y - T - dS - PE) + (M - X), \tag{2}$$

i.e. in each period of time the *ex post* public sector deficit is, by definition, equal to the total of the private sector's net acquisition of financial assets plus (minus) the deficit (surplus) on the current account.

The tax yield (T) and the level of stocks (S) are simple functions of Y such that:

$$T = tY, \tag{3}$$

and

$$S = \beta Y, \tag{4}$$

where β is *probably* (Godley's own word and emphasis) a function of interest rates. Imports are related to Y such that:

$$M = mY, \tag{5}$$

where m is 'formally not a parameter but a variable' (Godley, 1981a,

p. 4). Because the various elements are expressed in current prices, the magnitude of m will depend not only on Y but also on the price of imports relative to the price of domestic production as well as 'other systematic factors and time trends'.

To complete the system, it is assumed that equilibrium exists between the desired stock of financial wealth (W^*) and disposable Y such that:

$$W^* = a(1 - t)Y, \tag{6}$$

where a is partly dependent on interest rates as well as an adjustment process given by

$$W - W_{-1} = \varphi(W^* - W_{-1}). \tag{7}$$

Substituting, one can derive the 'steady state solution' to the model:

$$Y = (G + X)/(t + m). \tag{8}$$

This equation gives a remarkably strong result. There were only two relationships in the model with parameters directly affected by interest rates – equations (4) and (5). Since in stable equilibrium the higher the interest rates the lower probably the stock levels relative to income and stock *changes* (of both financial and tangible assets) are *nil*, all terms in φ, a and β have fallen out. Equation (8) thus shows that income flows are in the end entirely independent of interest rates, money and monetary policy, except to the extent that these affect X and m *indirectly* via the exchange rate.

This is the CEPG's basic model. The elaborate version incorporates short-run dynamics and long-run growth feedbacks 'without in any way altering the essential conclusions' (Godley, 1981a, p. 5). Godley emphasised that equation (8) lies at the heart of his thinking about income determination: the expression $Y = (G + X)/(t + m)$ 'is as important to me as is the identity of $MV = PT$ to a monetarist. It expresses a quintessential causal process relating income determination exclusively to fiscal stance measured by G/t (*not* by the *ex post* borrowing requirement $G - T$) and to trade performance measured by X/m (*not* by $X - M$, the *ex post* current balance of payments' (Godley, 1981a, p. 6).

He also emphasised that it is a significant property of equation (8) that while it is based on the assumption that the stock–flow relationships in the domestic economy are all in equilibrium (changes in stocks of tangible financial assets held by the private sector having a value of zero) 'there is no mechanism whatever which ensures that the current balance of payments $(X-M)$ or the public sector deficit $(G-T)$ looked at *ex post*, or the flow of national income (Y), should take on any particular value' (Godley, 1981a, p. 6).

Assuming that borrowing from abroad must normally approximate to zero, the model suggests that fiscal policy must be conducted in such a way that the current account must also approximate to zero. Manipulating equation (8) in this way by incorporating $X = M = mY$ it follows that a necessary and sufficient condition for achieving a zero balance of payments is that the fiscal stance (measured by the term G/t) must equal trade performance (measured by X/m), since:

$$Y = G/t = X/m. \tag{9}$$

This equation suggests what role has to be played by fiscal policy in order to ensure that the balance of payments is equal to zero. It also indicates that if fiscal policy is operated subject to a balance of payments constraint, Y will be *uniquely* determined by trade performance.

Several points need emphasising regarding this construct. Firstly, the model, being Keynesian, suggests that there is no natural tendency for equilibrium Y to settle at the full employment level. Secondly, international trade performance is very crucial for determining whether or not Y is at the level required to ensure full employment. Thirdly, since governments operate in such a way as to ensure near zero on current account, a time series analysis of $(X-M)$ throws no light on how X/m is working as a process, hence it is an 'egregious and very vulgar error to suppose that if a country shows over a period of years a balance of payments close to zero it has no balance of payments problem' (Godley, 1981a, p. 7). Fourthly, if government policy were aimed at keeping the current account within limits which can be financed, there is 'no natural mechanism whatever for correcting a malignant trend in the ratio X/m should it be progressively reducing output and employment. There is in particular no reason why the exchange rate should change in any particular way when the balance of payments is close to zero' (Godley, 1981a, p. 8). Finally, the ratio X/m is 'paramount', in Godley's thinking, to protectionism since if it were too low to generate full employment for whatever reason then, in Godley's own words, 'by hook or by crook' it should be raised by import controls since devaluation is both unnecessary and difficult to operate in a world of freely flexible exchange rates.

To conclude this section, it is important to stress that the CEPG does not envisage protectionism as a 'beggar thy neighbour' type of policy, particularly since they see it in a 'macroeconomic' sense, not as a way of 'shoring up this or that failing industry under general conditions of stagnation' (Godley, 1981a, p. 9). X/m can be raised without improving the *ex post* current account since fiscal expansion (G/t) should be directed towards domestic activity without reducing aggregate imports.

The CEPG sees the effect of such a policy on the rest of the world in the following way:

> If the composition as well as the total of imports is unchanged under a policy of protection combined with fiscal expansion, then obviously the policy has no impact whatever on the rest of the world. If the composition of imports changes so that more come from countries whose domestic output is balance of payments constrained (X/m is less than full employment output) and less from unconstrained countries, then the policy is clearly beneficial on balance to the rest of the world. *Contrary to what is often assumed, the effect would be to increase production and trade in the rest of the world.* Since the exports of constrained countries would be increased, their imports would be increased by a corresponding amount, and their domestic output substantially increased as well. These increased imports by constrained countries would come in part from unconstrained countries and in part from other constrained countries who in turn would increase *their* imports and output. At the end of the day *there will clearly be a net addition to world trade and production*, and it is even the case that there should be no net loss of exports by unconstrained countries taken as a whole, although a change in the country pattern of their exports will be essential. If, and only if, protection by one country has the effect of reducing imports from constrained countries and by implication increasing them from unconstrained countries, will there be a net reduction in world trade and production (Godley, 1981a, pp. 9, 10; my emphasis).

It should be apparent that this particular argument does not flow naturally from the basic model; the model must *explicitly* incorporate at least three countries: the home country (UK or USA), countries with constraints on X/m and countries without such constraints. However, it is impossible to develop such a model since specifying the conditions in a manner equivalent to the basic CEPG model will create a problem of overdetermination: if two countries set their fiscal policies such that their current accounts are balanced, then the third country's current account will also be balanced. Hence, instead of pursuing this line, let us carefully examine the implications of the CEPG's model.

Implications of the model

We have seen that the basic equation, given balance of payments equilibrium, results in $Y = G/t = X/m$. When 'protection' is introduced it takes the form of a lowering of m. With X remaining fixed, Y rises as a result. The increase in Y raises T hence creating a budget surplus which must be eliminated (if the budget is to remain balanced) by either an increase in G or a fall in t. This further raises income. Hence, at the end of this sequence M has returned to its initial value:

$$dY = dG/(t+m) - dm(G+X)/(t+m)$$

where d stands for a change in the relevant element. Assuming reflation by way of G and that

$$dG = t\,dY$$

from which

$$dY = -dm(X+G)/m(t+m)$$

hence

$$d(mY) = m\,dY + Y\,dm$$

$$d(mY) = -dm(X+G)/(t+m) + dm(X+G)/(t+m) = 0.$$

Therefore, the exports of the rest of the world, in *total*, remain unaltered and the initial fixed-X assumption is validated.

It is of the utmost importance to note that this validation depends on the crucial assumption that the 'authorities' introduce the required expansion in G (or the reduction in t) at a vital moment before the cut in m leads to a reduction in imports from the rest of the world (a fall in X). If this operation is not carried out to perfection, the cut in M

(hence in X) will materialise well before X is restored to its initial level. Hence any 'imperfection' in carrying out this operation will provide an atmosphere which is conducive to retaliation by the outside world. It should also be emphasised that this 'imperfection' cannot be underrated by asserting that the authorities must raise G *first* since in this model that would require an increase in T first, with similar consequences. Hence any 'imperfection' in carrying out this operation will invite reactions from the outside world.

Criticisms

The CEPG's formulation can be criticised in its own right: the way it lumps together the private sector in terms of its consumption and fixed investment behaviour implies that consumers adopt the same attitude to private consumption expenditure as to fixed investment expenditure; the ruthless manner in which the price mechanism is dealt with; the rigidity with which international investment, which is as normal an activity as commodity trade, is excluded from the model; and, *most importantly*, the assertion that a one-period model (short-to-medium term) analysis, which is what the Keynesian framework is all about, can be used to formulate a *long-term stable equilibrium* model.

I do not intend to discuss these matters here because I deem it important that discussion should not deviate from the *basic* formulation otherwise one may be accused of switching grounds or misrepresenting the model, an accusation which has been made against the attempts by Corden *et al.* (1975) and Hindley (1977). Instead, it may be useful to use a two-country model to make a point about reciprocity or international interdependence. If the current account must balance it follows that $Y_1 = m_2 Y_2 / m_1$ and $Y_2 = m_1 Y_1 / m_2$. This tells us only that $Y_1/Y_2 = m_2/m_1$, i.e. the two countries can either fight each other by lowering their import coefficients, which is likely to reduce the gains from (balanced) trade, or the two countries can act together to raise their aggregate expenditures in equal proportions until they reach full employment. This is a result that will be discussed in the conclusion.

There is, of course, a dynamic version of the two-country model: country 1 lowers m_1 in period (0) thus making itself better off in relation to country 2's income of period (-1), but making country 2 worse off in period $(+1)$, and as a result country 1 returns in period $(+2)$ to where it was at the beginning.

Another point that a cynical observer of the CEPG model may make is that there is no need to use an identity and several behavioural equations in order to arrive at equation (8). Starting from this equation, one need stress simply that it is based on the equality $G - T + X - M = 0$, along with the assumption that $T = tY$ and $M = mY$. This implicitly assumes that investment always equals savings in a steady state, or in terms of Godley's notation, private expenditure always equals disposable income: a dubious and hardly Keynesian assumption.

From here, it can be claimed that the CEPG assumes that the government wishes to assure long-run equilibrium in the current account and will carry out the necessary fiscal policy to achieve current account balance, since nothing in the model generates such balance. The required fiscal policy, from equation (9), is $G = Xt/m$ or $t = mG/X$, or some other combination that fulfils (9). This determines a long-run equilibrium $Y = X/m$. However, this income (Y) may be less than full employment Y. Under the above assumptions, Y can be raised only by reducing m, since the country has no control over X. This can be accomplished by protectionism. However, as stated above, the assumption that X cannot be influenced by this country is a dubious one: it takes at least two countries to play the protectionist game; hence the minimum needed is the two-country model just discussed. Note also that such a reformulation can be described as cynical simply because almost all models of steady growth finally reduce to such simple relationships that the behavioural equations on which they are based completely disappear (for example, the Harrod–Domar model); hence, it would be unfair to single out the CEPG model in this respect.

Conclusions

The conclusions of this section are:

(i) The CEPG's protectionist stance is correct *provided* that one accepts their basic model and, most importantly, provided that the authorities are able to carry out the 'protectionist operation' to perfection – an impossible task. However, the basic model, being Keynesian, is only suitable for the short and, arguably, the medium terms, not for the long term, and the 'operation' requires such skill in its execution that any imperfection will produce an atmosphere which will result in retaliation by the outside world. If retaliation does occur then the logical conclusion is that it would ultimately result in the complete elimination of international trade.

(ii)   An international trade policy the essence of which is the negotiation of joint reflation by member nations of the world economy is superior to protectionism. Even with the requirement of balance of payments equilibrium, reflation produces better results for all concerned, but this is a conclusion with which the CEPG concurs even though they do not believe that the 'capitalist' world will endorse.

(iii) Even if the CEPG's 'protectionist operation' can be carried out to perfection it should be apparent that the world would be hostile to such a policy particularly since the joint reflation alternative strategy is not only superior but also reflects faith in the international community.

A GENERAL-EQUILIBRIUM MODEL

It is rather odd that a one-period (*short-to-medium term*) Keynesian framework should be employed to formulate a *long-term stable equilibrium* model. Therefore, in spite of the CEPG's assertions to the contrary, the application of neoclassical concepts for an appraisal of their proposition is inevitable. The purpose of this section is to do precisely that in a brief and concise fashion.

Before embarking on such an analysis, however, it would seem that if the profession is to assess the CEPG's protectionism objectively, the discussion should be conducted in abstract terms. I shall, therefore, refer to their protectionism as the '*employment-tariff proposition*'. This abstraction has the added advantage of clearly indicating that the discussion is really about protection and employment rather than a comparison of the impact of protectionism and exchange rate changes on the level of employment.

One can readily utilise production-possibility-frontiers (PPFs) and community-utility-functions (US) for a rigorous analysis of the 'tariff-employment proposition'. Before doing so, however, it is important to state that the term import controls implies quantitative or import quota restrictions, but since it has been convincingly demonstrated that, under the assumptions of competitive supply from abroad, perfect competition in domestic production and perfect competition among quota holders, quotas are equivalent to tariffs in the sense that a tariff rate will produce an import level which, if

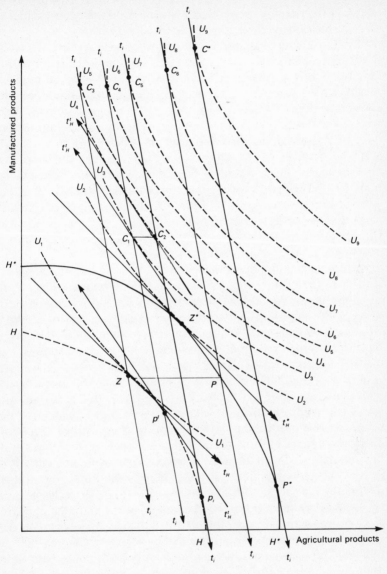

Figure 7.1

alternatively set as a quota, will produce an identical discrepancy between foreign and domestic prices, I shall, to simplify the analysis, use tariffs as the appropriate means for imposing import restrictions. I shall also ignore firstly the ingenious new developments in the theory of tariffs which incorporate the analysis of 'tariff seeking', 'tariff evasion or smuggling' and 'revenue seeking' as these complicate the analysis without fundamentally changing the conclusions of this section and secondly such problems as raised by the new literature on tariff formation in democracies (Brock and Magee, 1981).

In the presence of unemployment in an autarkic situation, the country under consideration will be producing at a point such as Z in Figure 7.1. Z lies inside the country's full employment PPF, H^*H^*. It also lies on domestic terms of trade, t_H, which are equal in slope to those that would have materialised in the full employment autarkic situation, t^*; this can be justified on similar grounds to those propounded for the vent-for-surplus theorems.

A point of equilibrium is Z since U is at a tangent to t_H at that point. Had there been full employment, the autarkic production and consumption points would have been those indicated by Z^*. Hence, Z satisfies the autarkic Pareto-optimality conditions since one can visualise it as lying on a less-than-full-employment PPF, HH, or at the corner of the fixed production combination given by point Z, i.e. the corner of the rectangular PPF with OZ as its diagonal.

Now suppose that this country is exposed to international trade with the terms of trade depicted by t_i. If Z were due to a vent-for-surplus situation, production will, as a result, move to point P on H^*H^*, i.e. the production of agricultural products will be expanded to take advantage of the favourable international terms of trade with the production of manufactured products being maintained at the Z level. Consumption will move to C_6 where U_8 is at a tangent to the international terms of trade line passing through P. The move from Z to P and C_6 is equivalent to the 'first phase' or the Smithian phase of the vent-for-surplus. Note that if full advantage is taken of the favourable international terms of trade, production will move to P^*, fulfilling the international Pareto-optimality conditions. Also note that the right-angled triangles (not drawn) with (C_6, P) and (C^*, P^*) as two of their corners give the level of exports (agricultural products) and imports (manufactured products) for the respective situations.

If the initial level of employment is fixed (and unalterable), unimpeded international trade will leave production at Z while consumption moves to C_3 where U_5 is at a tangent to the international terms of trade passing through Z.

Finally, if unemployment is due to some fundamentally structural cause with full employment completely out of the question but the *existing* level of employment has an element of factor mobility about it between the two producing sectors, Z can be seen as a point lying on HH (the less-than-full-employment PPF) since the whole of HH lies within H^*H^*. Hence, unimpeded international trade will move production to P_i and consumption to C_5 where U_7 is at a tangent to the international terms of trade.

Now, given the situation of a less-than-full-employment PPF, assume that this country declines to operate a system of unimpeded free trade by adopting tariff impositions on manufactured products. A tariff rate which results in the domestic terms of trade depicted by t'_H will take production to point P' and consumption to point C_1 on U_3. A production subsidy which has the equivalent production effect (i.e. move production to P') will move the consumption point to C_4, while a consumption tax equivalent to the tariff will move consumption to C_2 instead of C_1.

Therefore, in the presence of unemployment, all the main propositions of orthodox trade theory remain intact: free trade is better than no trade; restricted trade is superior to no trade; production subsidies are superior to tariffs; and consumption taxes of tariff equivalence are superior to tariffs. However, to conclude from this that the 'employment-tariff proposition' is fallacious will be premature since a careful reading suggests that there is a further point that should be considered. The proposition could be interpreted to mean that the protection afforded to the import-competing sector of the economy (manufactured products) will induce employment into the sector resulting in a boost for the industry which will render it more efficient and potentially very competitive internationally. In other words, the manufacturing sector in this country exhibits characteristics of an infant-industry and should therefore be seen in that context only – presumably that is what the proponents of the proposition mean by 'unsuccessful' and 'ailing' countries (industries).

Let us assume that this restatement is a correct interpretation of the proposition. Then consider Figure 7.2 which is a simplified version of Figure 7.1 with two new PPFs: [H_1H_1 and H_2H_2]. Recall that with impediments on international trade, this country could be producing at P' and consuming at C_1 or, alternatively, producing and consuming at Z in the case of a prohibitive tariff rate. Hence the initial less-than-full-employment PPF is either HH or the rectangle with OZ as its diagonal. As a result of protecting the manufacturing sector in period t, the country finds itself with a PPF such as H_1H_1 or H_2H_2 since

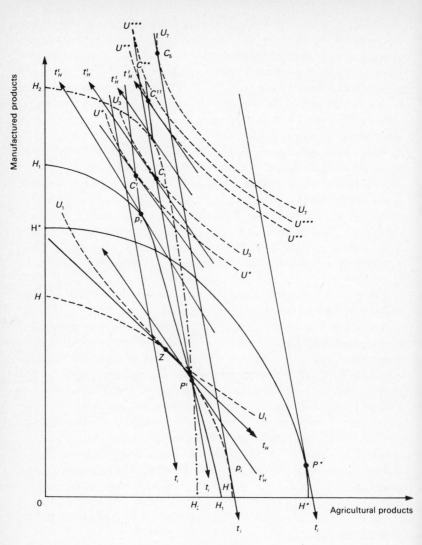

Figure 7.2

expanded employment and production in the manufacturing sector has reduced the average cost of production here. If this country continues to face the same international terms of trade subject to the tariff, it should be apparent that the country will end up worse off than initially if the new *PPF* is H_1H_1 since C' lies on a lower social utility curve than C_1; it is equally obvious that the country will be better off if the PPF happens to be H_2H_2 since C'' lies on a higher social utility curve than C_1. The likelihood of the PPF becoming H_2H_2 or one in that region will depend on the *extent* of the boost given to employment and efficiency in the protected manufacturing sector.

It should be stressed that if the international terms of trade move in favour of the protected industry during the period under consideration, the possibility of improvement may or may not be strengthened depending on whether or not the pattern of trade is reversed since what we have is in effect the reverse of the 'immiserizing growth' case first developed by Johnson (1967) and generalised by Bhagwati (1968); there, it is the worsening in the international terms of trade due to the expansion of the *exporting* sector which, under extreme conditions, results in the misery.

Before concluding this section a few points are in order. Firstly, the same analysis and results will ensue if the initial point was Z (rather than P) due to a prohibitive tariff. Secondly, this need not be a 'small-country' analysis, since offer curves could be constructed from HH for this country and from the equivalent PPFs for the rest of the world to determine the terms of trade. Thirdly, the pattern of trade after the realisation of the benefits of protection will be reversed particularly if the rest of the world was also following the same policy measures with regard to agricultural products. Finally, the size of the trade triangles could be examined in the context of the 'employment-tariff proposition' but it should be obvious that such a consideration would not add anything new of significance.

Conclusion

I have demonstrated that orthodox international trade theory is quite capable of producing a rationale for the proposition that protected growth *can* enhance the 'unsuccessful' economy and may eventually provide full employment for that country (HH moving out all the time). It should be stressed that the rationale is based on an 'infant-industry' argument set in the context of growth in conditions contrary to those needed to produce 'immiserizing growth'. It is therefore pertinent to ask: does this mean that the 'employment-tariff proposition' is correct?

In order to answer this question properly we have to consider the different components of the proposition. Firstly, I have demonstrated that it is quite simply wrong to claim that orthodox trade theory cannot provide a rationale for free trade in the presence of unemployment. Secondly, I have shown the general validity of the propositions that consumption taxes of tariff equivalence and production subsidies are superior to tariff protection. Thirdly, let us remember that the infant industry argument itself does not provide a rationale for tariff protection (since a production subsidy to take production to P initially would have led to consumption at C^{**} in Figure 7.2) except in circumstances where the investment market is short-sighted, underdeveloped or non-existent and that is why international trade theorists conceded it for those developing countries where financial institutions are virtually non-existent and government revenue is not high enough to provide the necessary production subsidies. Fourthly, the 'infant-industry' argument requires that the sacrifice of consumption during the 'maturing' period should be less than the final gain. Finally, the proposition that free trade destroys 'unsuccessful' countries is simply and categorically wrong. We can therefore conclude that *only one* aspect of the proposition (protection creating employment and expanding the economy) is *broadly theoretically* correct *provided* convincing answers are advanced to the following questions:

(1) Why is it that import controls can be justified as a means of protection in the UK and the USA rather than the more efficient production subsidies or consumption taxes of tariff equivalence?

(2) Why is it that the production-possibility-frontier, after the infant industry has matured, will be like H_2H_2 rather than H_1H_1?

(3) Why is it that the new employment in the protected industry comes only from the pool of the unemployed rather than from the 'exportables' sector?

(4) What is the reason for the belief that the UK or the USA is an 'unsuccessful' or 'ailing' economy in the sense of not having the ability to fully utilise its industrial base due to the existence of 'infant-industry' type conditions?

In short, the 'employment-tariff proposition', contrary to the statement made by its proponents, makes *theoretical* sense, albeit not in *generally valid* terms, but the justification for the policy recommendations depends entirely on *practical considerations*: it does not flow naturally from the theoretical base! Therefore the onus is on the proponents to provide a sound empirical justification for their proposition.

A POLITICAL ECONOMY APPROACH

Let us now analyse the 'employment-tariff proposition' in a political economy framework. The framework is based on Johnson's (1965) 'scientific tariff' approach, a detailed exposition of which is to be found in El-Agraa (1984); I shall provide here only a basic summary of it.

Johnson's method is based on four major assumptions: (i) governments use tariffs to achieve certain non-economic (political, etc.) objectives; (ii) actions taken by governments are aimed at offsetting differences between private and social costs – they are, therefore, rational efforts; (iii) government policy is a rational response to the demand of the electorate; and (iv) countries have a preference for industrial production.

In addition to these assumptions, Johnson makes a distinction between private and public consumption goods, real income (utility enjoyed from both private and public consumption, where consumption is the sum of planned consumption expenditure and planned investment expenditure) and real product (defined as total production of privately appropriable goods and services).

These assumptions have important implications. Firstly, competition among political parties will make the government adopt policies that will tend to maximise consumer satisfaction from both 'private' and 'collective' consumption goods. Satisfaction is obviously maximised when the rate of satisfaction per unit of resources is the same in both types of consumption goods. Secondly, 'collective preference' for industrial production implies that consumers are willing to expand industrial production (and industrial employment) beyond what it would be under free international trade.

Tariffs are the main source of financing this policy simply because GATT regulations rule out the use of export subsidies and domestic political considerations make tariffs, rather than the more efficient production subsidies, the usual instruments for protection.

Protection will be carried to the point where the value of the marginal utility derived from collective consumption of domestic and industrial activity is just equal to the marginal excess private cost of protected industrial production.

The marginal excess cost of protected industrial production consists of two parts: the marginal production cost and the marginal private consumption cost. The marginal production cost is equal to the proportion by which domestic cost exceeds world market cost; in a very simple model this is equal to the tariff rate. The marginal private consumption cost is equal to the loss of consumer surplus due to the fall in consumption brought about by the tariff rate which is necessary to induce the marginal unit of domestic production; this depends on the tariff rate and the price elasticities of supply and demand.

In equilibrium, the proportional marginal excess private cost of protected production measures the marginal 'degree of preference' for industrial production. This is illustrated in Figure 7.3 where: S_W is the world supply curve at world market prices; D_H is the constant-utility demand curve (at free trade private utility level); S_H is the domestic supply curve; S_{H+U} is the marginal private cost curve of protected industrial production, including the excess private consumption cost (*FE* is the first component of marginal excess cost – determined by the excess marginal cost of domestic production in relation to the free trade situation due to the tariff imposition (*AB*) – and the area *GED* (= *IHJ*) is the second component which is the dead loss in consumer surplus due to the tariff imposition); the height of *VV* above S represents the marginal value of industrial production in collective consumption and *VV* represents the preference for industrial production which is assumed to yield a diminishing marginal rate of satisfaction.

One can adapt Johnson's framework and generalise it to tackle the 'employment-tariff proposition' provided the reservations stated earlier regarding the use of tariffs as the instrument for import controls still apply.

In Figure 7.4 I have introduced the first generalisation by ridding the model of its 'small' country nature, i.e. I have made the world supply curve, S_W, less than infinitely elastic so that the international terms of trade are no longer given and invariable, hence the free trade world supply curve is given by AS_W. Now the imposition of an *ad valorem* tariff rate of *NA/A0* will shift the world supply curve upwards to NS_w^t under tariff imposition. Higher tariff rates will result in an upward shift of NPS_w^t. It is therefore still true that the tariff imposition will have the two cost components (ot their equivalent) indicated by the triangles *GEF* and *GED* (= *HIJ*).

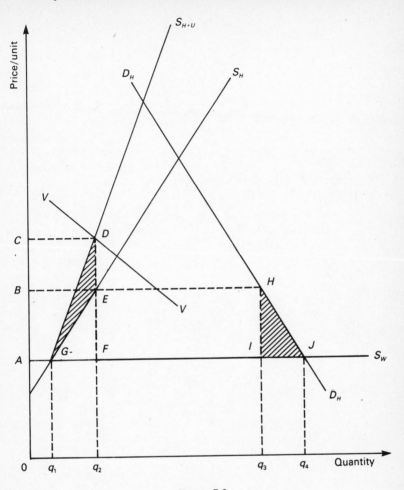

Figure 7.3

The second generalisation is implied by the change of S_H to S_H^P and S_{H+U} to S_H^S with P standing for 'private' and S for 'social' so that S_H^P and S_H^S are the 'private' and 'social' supply curves respectively. Note that the imposition of a tariff increases the level of domestic production above the free trade level. This extra production generates extra employment since we have a pool of unemployed labour. Hence, although it is valid that the triangle *GEF* is an excess cost of production (since in the world market the country will pay only

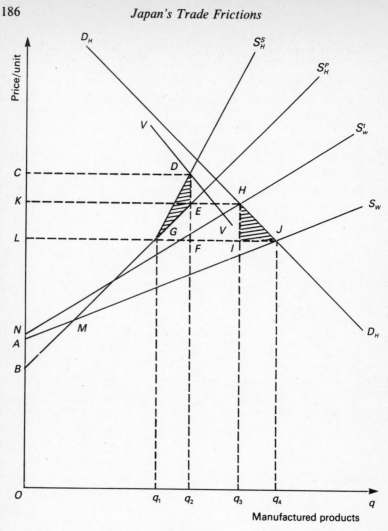

Figure 7.4

q_1GFq_2), the employment equivalent of the output q_1q_2 is a *pure* benefit to society. This means that the *VV* curve can now be interpreted as the society's marginal valuation of the reduced unemployment (increased employment). *VV* is therefore still above the level of free trade employment and slopes downwards indicating a diminishing marginal rate of employment valuation as the size of the unemployment pool diminishes. So this is the third generalisation since in the Johnson version of the model VV has an element of arbitrariness about it: its position *is not precisely* determined.

Figure 7.4 has been drawn in such a way that $0q_2$ is an equilibrium level of output and employment in the manufacturing sector since VV intersects S_H^S at that output level. $0q_2$ requires an *ad valorem* tariff rate of $NA/A0$. It should be apparent that the tariff rate is dependent on the slopes of the supply and demand functions, the difference between VV and the free trade employment level and the difference in the costs of production between the home country and the world.

The final generalisation needed to tackle the 'employment-tariff proposition' is that the extra output and employment in this sector made possible in period t by the tariff imposition will, at some future date, make the industry more efficient, i.e. the industry will be reinvigorated and galvanised into a state of maturity having been in an 'infant-industry' state initially. This means that in, say, period $t+1$, S_H^p will shift downwards by the full margin of savings in costs. Imagine a vertical 'specific' downward shift of S_H^p in Figure 7.4. This will bring with it a new S_H^p and, assuming VV remains constant, the 'natural', i.e. free trade, level of employment, will increase, the new tariff rate will be smaller and the level of imports will shrink in comparison with the initial tariff-ridden situation.

If the extra employment in period $t+1$ is reinforcing, the home country supply curve will continue to shift downwards resulting in more employment, lower tariff rates and shrinking imports. And if the process continues long enough, a situation may be reached where the home country becomes self-sufficient in manufactured goods. Whether the country becomes a *net exporter* in the end will depend on the relative slopes of VV and $D_H D_H$ and the world price: suppose the world price of manufactured products settles at $0L'$ per unit (Figure 7.5) and that the home country's supply curve shifts down to $S_H^{p'}$, the country will then produce $0q_6$, consume $0q_5$ and export $q_5 q_6$ at the world price, hence reversing the original pattern of trade.

A few questions could be raised: why does the VV curve remain static in a dynamic world? why does the demand curve remain unaltered? and what is happening to the world supply curve? With regard to the VV curve, it could be argued that it may shift downwards as the level of employment in this sector is increased. It is obvious that this will not alter the basic conclusions reached. It could also be argued that $D_H D_H$ will expand in that supply creates some of its own demand. Again, it should be apparent that that will only increase the size of imports or reduce the level of exports when the

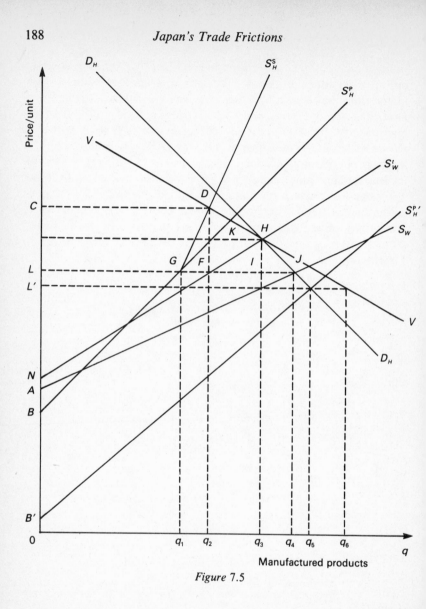

Figure 7.5

pattern of trade is finally reversed. Also, if the world becomes less efficient in the process due to loss of exports, the basic conclusions are still valid. Finally, since this analysis can be applied to other sectors as well then the (initially) 'exportables' sector could be subjected to a reverse situation giving the contrary results.

Before concluding this section it should be pointed out that if production subsidies are allowed, the initial equilibrium level of output (see either Figure 7.4 or 7.5) will be that given by the intersection of VV and S_H^P, since consumers will face the free international price and will therefore consume $0q_4$, hence S_H^P is both the 'private' and 'social' supply curve and S_H^S or S_{H+U} will disappear altogether. Production subsidies are possible in this version of the model in contrast to Johnson's because we are mainly concerned with the import-competing sector of the economy.

Finally, it should be obvious that if one accepts this model, it can be demonstrated that protecting the import-competing sector will provide it with an atmosphere conducive to expansion.

Conclusion

I have demonstrated that the political economy (scientific tariff) approach can be used in a generalised and dynamic sense to provide a theoretical rationale for the 'employment-tariff proposition'. However, this rationale is based on an infant-industry type of argument.

In order to answer the question of whether the proposition is correct or mistaken in this context, I should reiterate some of the points made in concluding the previous section which are of particular relevance here. Firstly, production subsidies are superior to import restrictions. Secondly, it should be recalled that the 'infant-industry' argument itself does not provide a rationale for protection except in very special circumstances in certain developing nations. Finally, the 'infant-industry' argument requires that the sacrifice of consumption during the 'maturing' period should be less than the final gains from protection.

It should, however, be added that in this model it could be argued that free trade is destructive since the free trade level of employment, if we accept the VV curve, is well below what is socially desirable, so in this sense the 'employment-tariff proposition' is correct. To determine whether or not the proposition is correct in absolute terms, as opposed to in principle only, will necessitate providing convincing answers to a set of questions most of which are exactly those posed in the previous section:

(1) Why should import controls be preferred in the UK and the USA to the more efficient production subsidies?

(2) Does the new employment in the protected industry come only from the pool of the unemployed or from the 'exportables' sector? Is total demand increased during the protection period?

(3) Are there reasons for believing that the UK or the USA is characterised by the existence of infant-industries?

(4) If the whole world claims the same infant industry situation and if increased employment in the import-competing sector comes partly from the 'exportables' sector, where does the 'employment-tariff proposition' lead to?

In short, as concluded in the previous section, the proposition can be given *theoretical* relevance in a political economy framework but the panacea of import controls depends entirely on *practical considerations*: it does not flow naturally from the theoretical model. Therefore, again, the onus is on the advocates of the proposition to provide a *sound empirical* rationale for their policy recommendation.

CONCLUSION

Since each section finished with its own conclusion, it is both pointless and space-wasting to repeat those conclusions here. Hence, all that needs to be stated here is that this chapter has attempted to tackle the '*employment-tariff proposition*' within three theoretical frameworks: macroeconomic, general equilibrium and political economy. The macroeconomic model, apart from its unsuitability for analysing a long-term steady equilibrium problem, clearly demonstrates that the 'protectionist operation' is impossible to carry out without contradicting the very basis on which the model is built. The general equilibrium model leaves us with the classical question regarding why countries like the UK and the USA can be justified in adopting a protectionist stance rather than employing the more efficient alternative of production subsidies. And the political economy framework raises this very question. In short, both the latter models raise the usual questions about the nature of the claim that *advanced nations* are subject to the necessary conditions which international trade theorists have reluctantly accepted as the only basis for conceding protection to infant industries in certain developing nations. Hence, it is the responsibility of the proponents of this proposition to advance a sound empirical justification for why 'ailing' advanced nations should be considered to be similar to very poor underdeveloped countries.

Needless to add, the conclusions reached in this chapter should be borne in mind when discussing enhanced protectionism in the rest of the world as a response to Japan's huge trade surplus.

8 Conclusions

I hope I have clearly demonstrated in this book that when Japan's trade relations are considered in their only appropriate context, the global-cum-historical context, there is no single or simple explanation for the trade frictions between Japan and the rest of the world, particularly with the EC and the USA. A simple explanation is unwarranted since the USA is responsible for the major part of its trade deficit with Japan (and with the outside world). Of course, Japan may appear to be accountable for about two-thirds of its trade surplus with the rest of the world, i.e. Japan may be held responsible for that part of the surplus caused by an under-valued yen prior to the joint action by G5 (or G7 after the Tokyo Summit in May 1986). However, a significant portion of this sum is simply a mirror image of the consequences of an over-valued US dollar. Hence, particularly in the case of the USA, there is no escape from the fact that it is responsible for almost its entire trade deficit. The British and French cases are not different from that of the US since they both had over-valued currencies. What remains to be investigated is whether the sectoral approach to solving trade frictions (the latest in this is the approach referred to as market-oriented sector-specific – MOSS) is appropriate and also what fundamental solutions should be contemplated in order to tackle Japan's basic problem of dependence on the outside world for its raw materials and energy supplies.

MACROECONOMICS OF TRADE FRICTIONS

It is really astonishing that the debate on trade frictions does not reflect an understanding of very basic economics. At a very elementary level, students are taught that a nation's trade account balance on goods and services (the difference between exports – X – and imports – M) is determined by the difference between the levels of national savings (S) and national investment (I); hence, only measures that affect either will eventually alter the trade balance. In a simple form this can be expressed as:

$$X - M = S + (T - G) - I,$$

which is a national income accounting *identity*. It tells us that the discrepancy between X and M must match the difference between national savings (which are equal to savings by the private sector – S – plus the surplus in the government budget – the difference between government tax revenue, T, and public expenditure, G) and I. Note that the difference between $S+(T-G)$ and I is equal to net foreign investment (ignoring unilateral transfers). Hence, a trade surplus is always a reflection of a net outflow of foreign investment. Also note that, since this is an income accounting identity, efforts made to influence any one of these aggregates must automatically affect one or more of the other aggregates in a *consistent* manner.

What is the significance of this simple accounting relationship for trade frictions? Cooper (1986) gives a very clear answer:

> This relationship is of fundamental importance in assessing overall trade performance. While lifting the Japanese citrus quota will almost certainly raise Japan's imports of citrus, and will probably raise overall Japanese imports (but by less than the increase in citrus imports), it would not reduce the large Japanese trade surplus except insofar as lifting the quota affected national savings and/or investment, i.e. probably not at all, or only negligibly. Given a large savings-investment imbalance, a rise in one particular import will be offset by a decline in other imports and/or a rise in exports. Paradoxically, it is even conceivable that a stripping away of all Japan's protective practices ... would lead to a *rise* in the trade surplus rather than a decline, if the sudden import competition reduced Japanese investment more than it reduced savings; but since "saving" includes corporate earnings, it could equally plausibly reduce the trade surplus by reducing corporate profits but at the same time stimulating corporate investment, in order to survive in the new, more competitive environment. The point is that to assess the overall impact one must look beyond the commodities immediately affected by the change in policy, whether it be import restriction or export promotion.

What is the precise implication of this for Japan's trade frictions? In order to illustrate its importance, consider the case of Japan's trade frictions with the USA. Since 1981, the USA has been experiencing a fast growing deficit on the trade account, whereas Japan and some European nations (Switzerland and West Germany) have been accumulating large surpluses. In 1984, the US had a record trade deficit of $95 billion which amounted to 2.6 per cent of GNP. At the same time gross private savings were 18.4 per cent of GNP, the highest on record since 1945. Gross investment was 17.4 per cent of GNP which is typical for a boom year. However, the government (including both state and local governments) budget deficit was 3.4 per cent of GNP, a smaller percentage than in 1983 but 'nearly an historic high', excluding the Second World War percentage. Given the above identity, these developments meant that the USA had to have a large trade deficit.

In Japan, the conditions were more or less the opposite. The Japanese private savings and investment rates were in excess of those in the USA. Moreover, the two were on the whole about equal to each other until 1975, after which time investment fell sharply and has remained low, by Japanese standards (see Chapter 2), ever since. Also, recall that in the early 1970s Japan greatly extended its social welfare programmes, and when this was occurring at the same time as the slowing down in the rate of growth of Japanese GNP, large deficits in the government budgets ensued, reaching over 4 per cent of GNP in 1979. Since then the Japanese government has been committed to reducing this deficit (see Chapters 5 and 6). However, private savings have remained in excess of investment; hence, the large trade surpluses since 1981 (see Chapter 2).

An analysis of US and Japan S/I trends for the period 1970–84 was undertaken by Bergsten and Cline (1985). Their results are given in Table 8.1, where all data are expressed as percentages of GNP. They conclude:

The table immediately highlights the atypical nature of the recent US external deficit. From 1970 to 1982, the average US current account balance was zero. But in 1983, the current account fell to a deficit of 1.3 percent of GNP, and in 1984 the deficit widened to 2.8 percent. . . . For Japan, the divergence from long-term averages has been in the opposite direction. From 1970 through 1982, the global current account averaged a surplus of only 0.6 percent of GNP – a smaller figure than normally associated with the image of Japan as a surplus country – but in 1983 the surplus reached 1.8 percent, and in 1984 it was 2.6 percent. . . . The rising bilateral imbalance between the two countries has paralleled this divergent trend toward sharply higher current account deficits in the [USA] and current account surpluses in Japan.

The table indicates the sharp difference between the level of private saving in Japan and the [USA]. Gross private saving (not

Table 8.1 Savings, investment and current account as % of GNP for Japan and the USA, 1970–84

	Private saving			Private investment (D)	Government balance		Saving-investment balance (G=C−D+F)	Current account (H)
	Personal (A)	Business (B)	Total (C)		Structural (E)	Actual (F)		
United States								
1970	5.6	10.4	16.0	14.5	−1.5	−1.1	0.4	0.2
1971	5.6	11.1	16.7	15.4	−2.1	−1.8	−0.5	−0.1
1972	4.4	11.5	16.0	16.4	−2.0	−0.3	−0.7	−0.5
1973	6.0	11.2	17.2	17.3	−1.5	0.6	0.5	0.5
1974	5.9	10.4	16.4	15.9	−0.6	−0.3	0.2	0.1
1975	6.1	12.2	18.2	13.3	−2.4	−4.1	0.8	1.2
1976	4.8	12.3	17.1	15.0	−1.8	−2.1	0.0	0.2
1977	4.1	13.0	17.0	16.9	−2.0	−0.9	−0.8	−0.8
1978	4.1	13.2	17.3	17.9	−1.6	0.0	−0.6	−0.7
1979	4.0	12.8	16.8	17.5	−0.9	0.6	−0.1	0.0
1980	4.2	12.4	16.5	15.3	−1.4	−1.2	0.0	0.0
1981	4.6	12.6	17.2	16.4	−0.9	−0.9	−0.1	0.2
1982	4.4	12.6	17.1	13.5	−1.9	−3.8	−0.2	−0.3
1983	3.6	13.7	17.3	14.3	−2.7	−4.1	−1.1	−1.3
1984	4.3	14.2	18.4	17.4	−3.4	−3.4	−2.4	−2.8

Japan

Year								
1970	11.5	22.0	33.1	33.9	1.9	1.8	1.0	1.0
1971	11.6	21.0	30.8	29.5	1.7	1.2	2.5	2.5
1972	11.9	20.4	31.9	29.6	0.6	−0.1	2.2	2.2
1973	14.0	18.4	32.0	32.6	0.3	0.6	0.0	0.0
1974	16.8	13.3	29.7	31.1	0.7	0.4	−1.0	−1.0
1975	16.1	13.0	28.6	26.0	−1.9	−2.7	−0.1	−0.1
1976	16.5	14.2	30.2	25.9	−2.9	−3.7	0.7	0.7
1977	15.2	14.5	29.2	23.8	−3.1	−3.8	1.6	1.6
1978	14.7	16.2	30.3	23.1	−4.9	−5.5	1.7	1.8
1979	13.2	16.0	28.6	24.8	−4.3	−4.8	−0.9	−0.9
1980	13.8	15.5	28.7	25.2	−4.1	−4.5	−1.0	−1.0
1981	14.0	14.9	28.2	23.8	−3.5	−4.0	0.4	0.4
1982	12.5	15.4	27.3	23.0	−2.8	−3.6	0.6	0.6
1983	12.8	15.2	26.4	21.1	−2.2	−3.5	1.8	1.8
1984	12.5	15.9	26.1	20.9	−1.3	−2.6	2.6	2.6

Note: The sum of gross business savings and household savings exceeds private savings because of statistical discrepancy.

Source: C. F. Bergsten and W. R. Cline, *The United States–Japan Economic Problem* (Washington DC: Institute for International Economics, 1985)

deducting capital consumption allowance) has been in the range of 30 percent of GNP in Japan, compared with approximately 17 percent ... in the [USA]. The largest difference has been in household saving, which for Japan has been nearly three times as high (14 percent of GNP) as in the [USA] (4 percent ...). Gross business saving shows a much smaller difference (averaging approximately 17 percent ... in Japan and 12 percent in the [USA]).

The uninitiated may wonder how these trends in savings and investment emerge as trade surpluses or deficits. In a simple model, given the Japanese budget deficit (i.e. these private savings were not being absorbed by the government), the excess of private savings over investment in Japan had to look for investment opportunities abroad. This act exerted pressure on the yen which had to depreciate, thus making Japanese commodities more competitive in the world market. On the other hand, the combination of a government budget deficit and an excess of investment over private savings in the USA pushed interest rates up. This made the USA more attractive to foreign investors and the inflow of foreign capital led to the appreciation of the dollar, and hence to a loss of competitiveness of US goods both abroad and in the US market itself. Therefore, the transmission of the discrepancies between private savings and investment into trade deficits or surpluses is facilitated by changes in the rates of exchange. This could not have happened under the Bretton Woods system of fixed exchange rates; in that system the excess of private savings over investment led to a reduction in the level of national income and activity (a recession) until the decline in private savings, the enlargement in the government budget deficit (due to lower tax revenues) and the improvement in the trade balance (due to lower imports) restored the equality between national savings and investment – note also that the economic recession may exert downward pressure on the level of both wages and prices; hence, the nation's international competitiveness may improve in the process.

The moral of this is that it is simply an error to assume that trade surpluses (and economic growth and employment) are determined or greatly affected by foreign 'trade practices', be these good or bad. This fundamental mistake is a good example of what economists call the 'fallacy of composition': adding up a number of independent measures, each with well-defined consequences, will not in fact produce the desired overall impact. In short, the Japanese government could try to please the outside world by eliminating every single 'design' pointed at as causing a restriction in Japanese imports, yet the net effect on the trade surplus may be nothing or even an addition to it; trade imbalances arise from overall macroeconomic elements, not from any unfair international trade policies regarding *particular* commodities. Of course, from the perspective of an individual industry, these macroeconomic considerations may seem unimportant relative to the policies for each commodity that countries may adopt. But it should be clear that such a limited perspective is simply a defeatist one.

Given this macroeconomic background, the responses by Japan to demands by the outside world for market opening (see Chapter 6) has been admirable: not only has Japan made changes in its policies with regard to specific commodities, which should please specific sectors but may have no trade balance effect, but also, and more importantly, Japan has enacted measures to gear its economy towards more emphasis on domestic demand. This means that the Japanese authorities are adopting measures that directly affect private savings and investment behaviour; hence, they are undertaking the most appropriate measures for affecting the trade surplus. It should be mentioned that some of the measures stated in the previous chapter have already been carried out. For example, on 14 May 1986, the Japanese government approved the return of 1085.9 billion yen to gas and electricity consumers from windfall profits accruing to the nine electric power companies and three major gas suppliers from the appreciation of the yen and the fall in the price of oil: this was intended to add to consumers' disposable income and affect their consumption/savings behaviour and, hence, affect the Japanese economy's macroeconomic dimensions. Another example is the Japanese government's adoption on 30 May 1986, of an emergency package extending financial relief to the small- and medium-sized firms hardest hit by the appreciation of the yen. The package: (i) instructed three governmental financial institutions, including the Smaller Business Finance Corporation, to reduce interest rates to these firms in order to enhance their transformation from reliance on exports to reliance on domestic demand by reducing the interest on the special loans for this purpose from 5 to 4.85 per cent; (ii) created a special loan plan in which cooperatives of small local companies hit hard by the appreciating yen will be given access to interest-free loans to facilitate their conversion; (iii) indicated that the government will provide special loans carrying an interest of 6.4 per cent per annum for small firms to lessen their interest burdens on previous loans from the three govern-mental financial institutions; and (iv) included measures to induce gas companies, beef importers and liquefied gas distributors and retailers to reduce their charges so as to return to the consumers windfall profits due to the appreciating yen.

It should be pointed out, however, that in December 1986, the OECD, in its projections to 1988 (OECD, 1986), reached the conclu-sion that the trade balance for the USA will continue to worsen while Japan's and West Germany's will continue to improve. Japan's trade surplus will rise from just over 44 billion dollars in 1984 to 76.7 billion dollars in 1988, the respective surpluses for West Germany being just under 23 billion dollars and about 45 billion dollars. The deficit for the USA will increase from 112.5 billion dollars in 1984 to about 137 billion dollars in 1988 – see Table 8.2. These projections did not take into consideration any of the measures discussed in this chapter. Be that as it may, the analysis in Chapter 3 clearly indicated that Japan will continue to have a trade surplus for some time, but that the magnitude of this surplus will diminish as a percentage of GDP; the decline is due to the recent co-ordinated appreciation of the Japanese yen and depreciation of the US dollar. It should be added, however, that the literature on the *J* curve indicates that the balance on current account will first improve because import prices will adjust more quickly than export prices before revaluation eventually leads to a deterioration in the balance – see NIESR (1968), p. 11. However, this does not mean that Japan's trade frictions will pass away since, despite the decline of the trade surplus in percentage terms, the absolute figure may remain substantial. Moreover, Japan will con-tinue to have a deficit with the Middle East, unless some of the measures recommended in the following section bear fruition, with the implication that Japan will continue to have a surplus with the rest of the world to compensate for its deficit with its major oil suppliers.

THE WAY FORWARD

Notwithstanding the number of market-opening measures under-taken by the Japanese government during the past two decades, most particularly the recent measures including the expansion of domestic demand, a careful study of Japan's international trade situation (see Chapters 2–5) suggests that some fundamental global perspective is needed if Japan is to alleviate its fears regarding its almost complete

	1980	1981	1982	1983	1984	1985	1986	1987	1988 I
Current balances ($ billion)									
United States	1.9	6.3	−9.1	−46.6	−106.5	−117.7	−138.1	−136.4	−133.4
Japan	−10.7	4.8	6.8	20.8	35.0	49.2	81.6	77.4	72.3
Germany	−15.7	−5.5	4.1	4.1	7.0	13.2	32.4	26.3	20.7
OECD	−68.7	−24.7	−28.8	−28.0	−65.8	−57.5	−19.7	−34.0	−47.3
OPEC	103.4	47.6	−22.1	−11.5	−9.6	−4.7	−51.5	−42.4	−28.7
Non-oil LDCs	−67.4	−84.9	−59.5	−23.7	−9.4	−16.3	−7.1	−1.9	−3.7
World discrepancy	−32.8	−62.0	−110.5	−63.2	−84.8	−78.5	−78.2	−78.2	−79.7
Current balances (% GNP)									
United States	0.0	0.2	−0.3	−1.4	−2.8	−2.9	−3.3	−3.1	−2.9
Japan	−1.1	0.4	0.6	1.8	2.8	3.7	4.1	3.7	3.3
Germany	−1.9	−0.8	0.6	0.6	1.2	2.0	3.6	2.6	2.0
Trade balances ($ billion)									
United States	−25.5	−28.0	−36.5	−67.1	−112.5	−124.4	−144.1	−141.3	−136.8
Japan	2.1	20.0	18.1	31.5	44.3	56.0	86.2	82.3	76.7
Germany	10.4	18.0	26.4	22.4	22.9	28.9	53.5	48.9	44.8
Net investment income ($ billion)									
United States	30.4	34.1	29.9	23.1	18.8	25.3	22.5	18.0	14.4
Japan	0.9	−0.8	1.7	3.1	4.2	6.8	10.8	16.5	20.2
Germany	2.3	0.2	−1.6	1.3	2.0	1.8	0.7	2.5	3.8
Net foreign assets position ($ billion)									
United States	199.9	173.7	158.9	121.2	19.7	−99.0	−153.3	−285.2	−389.9
Japan	22.2	21.8	21.9	36.8	63.7	104.6	208.6	294.8	350.7
Germany	40.1	29.1	30.1	35.6	41.4	51.9	69.6	99.1	116.7

Source: OECD Economic Outlook 40, December 1986.

dependence on the outside world for its energy supplies and for a substantial portion of its raw materials. A solution to these problems is most likely to encourage Japan to continue its present policy measures, and this should contribute to the creation of stable and 'harmonious' international trade relations between Japan and its trading partners. In other words, one could simply put forward the obvious and sensible policy recommendation package of: efforts to achieve an equilibrium exchange rate parity for the US dollar must be sustained; a substantial reduction in the US budget deficit must be carried out; Japan should carry out its commitments to the Action Programme and the recommendations of the Maekawa Report, and seriously pursue the MOSS programme; and efforts should be made not only to ensure that the new round of GATT negotiations is successful for promoting global free and fair trade but also to pursue a sensible reform of the international monetary system. However, these efforts are not enough to alleviate Japan's permanent worry about dependence on other nations for its raw materials and crude energy supplies: permanent solutions require more drastic changes.

As was clearly shown in Chapter 2 (Table 2.12), the only 'area' with which Japan has been having a consistent balance of trade deficit is the Middle East, reflecting its heavy dependence on the import of crude Middle Eastern oil. A permanent solution to Japan's international trade relations must take this factor into consideration. On the other hand, Japan conducts a major part of its external trade with the EC, SE Asia and the USA; hence Japan will have to develop a special kind of trading relationship with these areas. These considerations create certain problems, given the on-going debate on 'Pacific Basin' cooperation-cum-integration. The reason is that the Middle East dimension necessitates that a:

> regional approach should . . . be regarded as supplementary to and supportive of . . . genuine global solutions . . . [to] the world economic problems. Emphasis [should be] on the progressive nature of any open regionalism, considering that the real alternative to regionalism is not . . . global free trade . . ., rather *ad hoc* pressures for bilateral trade restrictions (Kitamura, 1984).

Since the Middle East is an 'area' of particular interest to Japan, the 'Pacific Basin' concept leaves out a very important dimension of Japan's international trade relations. This is in spite of the fact that there already exist: (i) the PECC (Pacific Economic Cooperation

Conference) which is a tripartite structured organisation with representatives from governments, business and academic circles and with the secretariat work being handled between general meetings by the country next hosting a meeting; (ii) the PAFTAD (Pacific Trade and Development Conference) which is an academically oriented organisation; (iii) the PBEC (Pacific Basin Economic Council) which is a private-sector business organisation for regional cooperation; and (iv) the PTC (Pacific Telecommunications Conference) which is a specialised organisation for regional cooperation in this particular field.

What is therefore needed is a *very involved* type of economic integration simultaneously accompanied by vigorous efforts for promoting international cooperation in general. The theoretical implications as well as the practical problems of such a proposal have been discussed elsewhere (see El-Agraa, 1980; 1982; 1983a; 1984, and El-Agraa and Jones, 1981), but in this particular context it should be emphasised that one of the implications of such a form of co-operation-cum-integration, if it is to exclude the Middle East, is that the nations of ASEAN, Australia, Canada, New Zealand, the USA, etc. must stand ready not only to supply Japan with its energy needs but to do so on a *permanent and irrevocable* basis. This suggests that a serious consideration of the concept of 'Pacific Basin' would entail that: the USA should provide Japan with its own oil (the embargo of US exports of Alaskan oil will have to be seriously reconsidered with this object in mind) and import its needs from countries with which it has 'special relationships' (such as Mexico or some of the Middle East countries); and Canada should supply Japan with natural gas. Of course, another way of tackling the Middle East problem is through a huge increase in nuclear power, which would have certain trade implications for the Japan–Australia relationship, but may be politically unthinkable in the light of Japan's stance with regard to excessive dependence on nuclear energy and its safety aspects, and the Chernobyl nuclear disaster in the USSR. Moreover, a drastic expansion in the production of nuclear power still leaves the problem of the supply of raw materials. In short, if the concept of 'Pacific Basin' cooperation-cum-integration is to be taken seriously by Japan, with the purpose of finding a permanent solution to its problems, it will have to be a very involved form of economic (and political) integration. Unfortunately, given the diversity of the peoples of the Pacific Basin nations and the marked differences in these countries' level of economic development and political systems, one feels that what is most likely to emerge, in the very long term, will be no more than a forum for cultural exchanges and some coordination of ODA contributions. This is in spite of the fact that: Canada and the USA are presently negotiating the formation of a 'free trade area'; Australia and New Zealand are already members of a 'free trade area'; and Brunei, Indonesia, Malaysia, the Philippines, Singapore and Thailand are members of ASEAN. The reason is that the economic integration of parts of a whole does not necessarily mean that the whole can be integrated into one. That is why Akamatsu (1937; 1961) coined the term 'flying-geese' to describe the pattern of development that may ensue from further cooperation-cum-integration within the Pacific Basin area. Therefore, one would be perfectly justified in ruling out this concept, in the form suggested at present, as a possible permanent solution to the Japanese 'problem'.

So what is the way forward? Clearly, no single act is going to solve Japan's problem since the dimensions of the situation are multifarious. No modification of existing GATT rules, however desirable any proposed changes might be, will result in a permanently acceptable outcome for Japan. Hence, my solution is a practical but a complex and demanding one which takes into consideration what has just been stated and what was discussed elsewhere in this book and in El-Agraa (1982; 1986a).

It should be clear by now that Japan will be running a surplus on current account for a while due to the present stage in the development of its balance of payments in accordance with its own economic development. I hope I have clearly demonstrated that only a third of Japan's current trade surplus is of this long-term nature since the other two thirds are attributable to an over-valued US dollar and to economic mismanagemant in the USA in particular. I also hope that I have clearly shown that it is not the trade imbalance as such which has been the cause of trade frictions, rather its happening simultaneously with high levels of unemployment in the USA and almost the whole of the rest of the OECD. Hence, the first part of the solution is the obvious one of a substantial increase in Japanese direct investment in the countries with which Japan has a huge trade surplus, most particularly in the USA since this will ensure not only new employment opportunities in the USA but also the use of local materials for production purposes. Fortunately, Japan's direct investment in the manufacturing sector in the USA in 1984 ($657 million) was in excess of its total for the three years from 1981 to 1983 ($321 million, $316 million and minus $31 million respectively). The picture is different for the *overall* direct investment figures ($2768 million in 1981, $1991 million in 1982, $1657 million in 1983 and $3481 million in 1984), since the 1984 figure, although in excess of that in any of the previous three years, is only just over a quarter more than that of 1981.

The second part to the solution requires an understanding of some 'special' relationships between the USA and Japan. It should be recalled that after Japan's surrender at the end of the Second World War, the USA allowed Japan free access to its markets and technology without demanding reciprocity in the economic field. This was contrary to the position of the USA with regard to Western Europe where the creation of the EC was advocated on the understanding that the multinational companies of the USA had to be treated as European domestic firms and that NATO had to be established with the limited aim of defending any member nation against an attack by the Soviet Union. The only demand made on Japan was the stationing of US military capabilities in Japan. Many experts would argue that these 'special relationships' have been the main cause of the outstanding economic performance of Japan. The point to emphasise is that Japan and the USA do have a special relationship which will continue to prosper, particularly with the weakening of the special relationship between the USA and Western Europe. Hence, Japan and the USA should make efforts to strengthen this special relationship and, for my second point, preferably give it a formal structure.

The third part of the solution simply requires an understanding of the fact that Japan relies heavily on SE Asia for its imports of raw materials. SE Asia is an area with fast growing NICs and has a great potential for more NICs (for example, China). Hence, it is in Japan's interest to promote a special relationship with this area. Of course, Japan has a commitment to the so-called 'Fukuda Doctrine' which led to the creation of a fund of $1 billion in 1977 to assist the ASEAN 'Industrial Projects', which should be continued and reinforced, but the recommendation made here extends beyond that. At the same time, the USA is also very involved in this region, not only because of its global defence strategy but also because of its interest in a share of this market. Therefore, both Japan and the USA, who have a great interest in formalising their special relationship, need to become involved in special commitments within SE Asia.

If one takes these three considerations together, it may be concluded that the concept of Pacific Basin cooperation-cum-integration is the only genuine solution to the problems of Japan and the USA (as well as the other nations in this area). Given what is stated above about the nature of the nations of the Pacific Basin, that would be a broad generalisation: what is needed is a very strong partnership between Japan and the USA within a much looser association with the rest of SE Asia. Hence, what is being advocated is a form of involved economic integration between Japan and the USA (and Canada, if the present negotiations for a free trade area of Canada and the USA lead to that outcome), within the broad context of 'Pacific Basin Cooperation', or, more likely, within a free trade area with the most advanced nations of SE Asia: Australia, New Zealand, South Korea, the nations of ASEAN, etc. – see Kojima (1971) and Drysdale (1985) for a full discussion of this aspect of my proposal. In short, my suggested solution is one of a very involved partnership between Japan and the USA within the context of a free trade area of the most advanced nations of the Pacific Basin; hence, the implication is that the present discussion of 'Pacific Basin cooperation-cum-integration' is not a practical one except for promoting cultural understanding (which is, of course, very desirable in itself and is not in contradiction to my proposal).

However, this does not mean that the scheme proposed here should be a protectionist one. Members of this scheme should promote cooperation with the rest of the world through their membership of the GATT and should coordinate their policies with regard to overseas development assistance, both financially and in terms of the transfer of technology, for the benefit not only of the poorer nations of SE Asia, but for the whole developing world. In this sense, the rest of the world has nothing to fear from the proposed solution since it may enhance, for example, EC exports in the markets of the member nations of this scheme and reduce the contribution of Western Europe to ODA. Moreover, this solution may even bring about a drastic change in the attitude of West Europeans towards some major desirable changes in their own efforts for economic integration and political unification.

Bibliography

ACKLEY, G. and ISHI, H. (1976) 'Fiscal, monetary, and related policies', in H. Patrick and H. Rosovsky (eds), *Asia's New Giant: How the Japanese Economy Works* (Washington, DC: Brookings Institution).

AKAMATSU, K. (1937; 1961) 'A theory of unbalanced growth in the world economy', *Weltwirtschaftliches Archiv*, Band 86, Heft 2.

ALLEN, G. C. (1965) *Japan's Economic Expansion* (London: Macmillan).

AMERICAN CHAMBER OF COMMERCE IN JAPAN (1982a) 'Report on 1981/82 trade-investment barrier membership survey', *ACCJ Position Papers*, March 8, Tokyo, Processed.

AMERICAN CHAMBER OF COMMERCE IN JAPAN (1982b) 'US–Japan trade and investment', *ACCJ Position Papers*, May 18–22, Washington, DC, Processed.

AOKI, M. (ed.) (1984) *The Economic Analysis of the Japanese Firm* (Amsterdam: North-Holland).

ARTHUR D. LITTLE, INC. (1979) *The Japanese Non-Tariff Trade Barrier Issue: American Views and Implications for Japan–US Trade Relations* (Cambridge, Mass.: Arthur D. Little, Inc.).

BALASSA, B. (1984) 'Trends in international trade in manufactured goods and structural change in industrial countries', *World Bank Staff Working Paper*, no. 611 (Washington, DC: World Bank).

BALASSA, B. and BALASSA, C. (1984) 'Industrial protection in developed countries', *World Economy*, vol. 7, no. 2, June.

BALDWIN, R. E. (1971) *Non-tariff Distortions of Trade* (Washington, DC: Brookings Institution; London: Allen & Unwin).

BANK OF JAPAN (1978) *The Japanese Financial System* (Tokyo: BOJ).

BANK OF JAPAN (1981) *Outline of Foreign Exchange Control in Japan* (Tokyo: BOJ).

BANK OF JAPAN (various years) *Economic Statistics Annual* (Tokyo: BOJ).

BANK OF JAPAN (various years) *Balance of Payments Monthly* (Tokyo: BOJ).

BANK OF TOKYO (1981) *The Activities of the Bank of Tokyo Group in the Field of International Financings* (Tokyo: BOT).

BARDS, W. J. (1979) *Japan and the United States: Challenges and Opportunities* (New York: New York University Press).

BAYLISS, P. T. (1985) 'Competition and industrial policy', in A. M. El-Agraa (ed.), *The Economics of the European Community*, second edition (Oxford: Philip Allan).

BERGSTEN, C. F. (1982) 'What to do about the US–Japan economic conflict', *Foreign Affairs*, no. 58, Summer.

BERGSTEN, C. F. and CLINE, W. R. (1985) *The United States–Japan Economic Problem* (Washington, DC: Institute for International Economics).

BHAGWATI, J. N. (1986) 'Distortions and immiserizing growth', *Review of Economic Studies*, vol. 35.

205

BILSON, J. F. O. (1984) *Macroeconomic Stability and Flexible Exchange Rates* (Cambridge, Mass.: National Bureau of Economic Research).

BLACK, S. W. (1984) 'Changing Causes of Exchange Rate Fluctuations', *Brookings Discussion Papers in International Economics*, no. 12 (Washington, DC: Brookings Institution).

BLUMENTHAL, T. (1970) *Savings in Postwar Japan* (Cambridge, Mass.: Harvard University Press).

BOLTHO, A. (1975) *Japan: an Economic Survey*, 1953–1973 (Oxford: Oxford University Press).

BORRUS, M., MILLSTEIN, J. and ZYSMAN, J. (1982) *International Competition in Advanced Industrial Sectors: Trade and Development in the Semiconductor Industry*, Report prepared for the Joint Economic Committee, 97 Cong., 2 sess., Washington, DC.

BROCK, W. A. and MAGEE, S. P. (1981) 'Tariff formation in a democracy', in J. Black and B. Hindley (eds), *Current Issues in Commercial Policy and Diplomacy* (London: Macmillan).

BRONTE, S. (1979a) 'Inside the Tokyo Ministry of Finance: the most powerful men in Japan', *Euromoney*, June.

BRONTE, S. (1979b) 'The dilemma of Japan's City Banks', *Euromoney*, September.

BRONTE, S. (1981a) 'The Japanese revel in their freedom to invest abroad', *Euromoney*, March.

BRONTE, S. (1981b) 'Where Japanese exports face unfair competition', *Euromoney*, July.

BRONTE, S. (1982) *Japanese Finance: Markets and Institutions* (London: Euromoney publications).

BROWN, A. J. (1961) 'Economic separatism versus common markets in developing countries', *Yorkshire Bulletin of Economic and Social Research*, vol. 13.

CAMBRIDGE ECONOMIC POLICY REVIEW (1978–81)

CARMOY, GUY DE (1978) 'Subsidy policies in Britain, France and West Germany: an overview', in S. J. Warnecke (ed.), *International Trade and Industrial Policies* (London: Macmillan).

CAVES, R. E. and UEKUSA, M. (1976) 'Industrial Organization in Japan', in H. Partick and H. Rosovsky (eds), *Asia's New Giant: How the Japanese Economy Works* (Washington, DC: Brookings Institution).

CEPG, in *Cambridge Economic Policy Review*.

CLARK, R. (1979) *The Japanese Company* (New Haven: Yale University Press).

CLINE, W. R. (ed.) (1982a), *Trade Policy for the 1980s* (Washington, DC: Institute for International Economics).

CLINE, W. R. (1982b) *Reciprocity: a New Approach to World Trade Policy* (Washington, DC: Institute for International Economics).

CLINE, W. R. (1984) *Exports of Manufactures from Developing Countries: Performance and Prospects for Market Access* (Washington, DC: Brookings Institution).

CONGRESSIONAL BUDGET OFFICE (1984a) *Baseline Budget Projections for Fiscal Years 1985–1989* (Washington, DC: CBO).

CONGRESSIONAL BUDGET OFFICE (1984b) 'The effects of changes in interest rates on different sectors of the US economy', Staff Memorandum, June, Processed (Washington, DC: CBO).

CONGRESSIONAL BUDGET OFFICE (1984c), *The Economic and Budget Outlook: an Update* (Washington, DC: CBO).

CONGRESSIONAL BUDGET OFFICE (1985a) *The Economic and Budget Outlook: Fiscal Years 1986–1990*, Report to the Senate and House Committees on the Budget, Part 1 (Washington, DC: CBO).

CONGRESSIONAL BUDGET OFFICE (1985b) *The Economic and Budget Outlook: an Update* (Washington, DC: CBO).

COOPER, R. N. (1968) *The Economics of Interdependence: Economic Policy in the Atlantic Community* (New York: McGraw-Hill).

COOPER, R. N. (1978) 'US policies and practices on subsidies in international trade', in S. J. Warnecke (ed.), *International Trade and Industrial Policies* (London: Macmillan).

COOPER, R. N. (1986) 'Industrial policies and trade distortions: a policy perspective', in A. M. El-Agraa (ed.), *Protection, Cooperation, Integration and Development: Essays in Honour of Professor Hiroshi Kitamura* (London: Macmillan).

CORDEN, W. M., LITTLE, I. M. D. and SCOTT, M. F. G. (1975) *Import Controls Versus Devaluation and Britain's Economic Prospects*, Trade Policy Research Centre, Guest Paper, no. 2.

COUNCIL OF ECONOMIC ADVISERS (1985) *Economic Report of the President 1985*, February, Washington, DC.

DESTLER, I. M. (1986) 'Protecting Congress for protecting trade?', *Foreign Policy*, no. 62, Spring.

DESTLER, I. M., FUKUI, H. and SATO, H. (1979) *The Textile Wrangle, Conflict in Japan–American Relations, 1969–71* (New York: Cornell University Press).

DRYSDALE, P. (1985) 'Building the foundations of a Pacific Economic Community', in T. Shishido and R. Sato (eds), *Economic Policy and Development: New Perspectives* (Dover, Mass.: Auburn House).

EC DELEGATION IN TOKYO (1984) *Japan and the European Community: a Stocktaking*.

ECONOMIC AND FOREIGN AFFAIRS RESEARCH ASSOCIATION (various years) *Statistical Survey of Japan's Economy* (Tokyo: EFARA).

ECONOMIC PLANNING AGENCY (various publications for various years) especially *Economic Survey of Japan* (Tokyo: EPA).

EL-AGRAA, A. M. (1978a) 'On Trade Diversion', *Leeds Discussion Paper*, no. 66.

EL-AGRAA, A. M. (1978b) 'On Trade Creation', *Leeds Discussion Paper*, no. 67.

EL-AGRAA, A. M. (1978c) 'Can Economists Provide a Rationale for Customs Union Formation?', *Leeds Discussion Paper*, no. 68.

EL-AGRAA, A. M. (1979) 'Common Markets in Developing Countries', in J. K. Bowers (ed.), *Inflation, Development and Integration: Essays in Honour of A. J. Brown* (Leeds University Press).

EL-AGRAA, A. M. (ed.) (1980) *The Economics of the European Community* (Oxford: Philip Allan).

EL-AGRAA, A. M. (ed.) (1982) *International Economic Integration* (London: Macmillan).

EL-AGRAA, A. M. (ed.) (1983a) *Britain Within the European Community: the Way Forward* (London: Macmillan).

EL-AGRAA, A. M. (1983b) *The Theory of International Trade* (Beckenham: Croom Helm).

EL-AGRAA, A. M. (1984) *Trade Theory and Policy: Some Topical Issues* (London: Macmillan).

EL-AGRAA, A. M. (1985a) 'Japan's trade frictions: realities or misconceptions?', *Bulletin of the Graduate School of International Relations*, International University of Japan, vol. 2.

EL-AGRAA, A. M. (ed.) (1985b) Second Edition of *The Economics of the European Community* (Oxford: Philip Allan).

EL-AGRAA, A. M. (ed.) (1986a) *Protection, Cooperation, Integration and Development: Essays in Honour of Professor Hiroshi Kitamura* (London: Macmillan).

EL-AGRAA, A. M. (1986b) 'Women in higher eduction: a comparative statistical look', *Bulletin of the Graduate School of International Relations*, International University of Japan, vol. 3.

EL-AGRAA, A. M. (ed.) (1987) Second edition of *International Economic Integration* (London: Macmillan).

EL-AGRAA, A. M. and ICHII, A. (1985) 'The Japanese education system with special emphasis on higher education', *Higher Education*, vol. 14.

EL-AGRAA, A. M. and JONES, A. J. (1981) *Theory of Customs Unions* (Oxford: Philip Allan).

EMMINGER, O. (1985) 'The Dollar's Borrowed Strength', *Group of Thirty Occasional Papers*, no. 19 (New York: Group of Thirty).

EXPORT-IMPORT BANK OF JAPAN, *Annual Reports* (Tokyo: EIBOJ).

FEDERATION OF BANKERS ASSOCIATIONS OF JAPAN (1982) *Banking System in Japan* (Tokyo: Federation of Bankers Association of Japan).

FEIGENBAUM, G. A. and McCORDUCK, P. (1983) *The Fifth Generation: Artificial Intelligence and Japan's Computer Challenge to the World* (New York: J. Brockman).

FELDMAN, R. A. (1982) 'Dollar appreciation, foreign trade, and the US economy', Federal Reserve Bank of New York, *Quarterly Review*, vol. 7, no. 2.

FELDSTEIN, M. S. and HORIOKA, C. (1980) 'Domestic savings and international capital flows', *Economic Journal*, vol. 90.

FREITAS, L. P. (1984) 'Views from abroad: Japan', *Journal of Accounting, Auditing & Finance*, vol. 4, no. 3, Spring.

FRENKEL, J. A. (1984) *The Yen/Dollar Agreement: Liberalising Japanese Capital Markets* (Washington, DC: Institute for International Economics).

GATT SECRETARIAT (1984) *International Trade 1983/84* (Geneva: GATT).

GODLEY, W. (1981a) 'Protection as the only way to full employment: some notes on the macroeconomic theory of international trade', paper delivered to a conference in Bordeaux, June.

GODLEY, W. (1981b) Interview with Wynne Godley, *Marxism Today*, July.

GODLEY, W. and CRIPPS, F. (1976 'A formal analysis of the Cambridge Economic Policy Group Model', *Economica*, vol. 43.

GODLEY, W. and MAY, R. M. (1977) 'The macroeconomic implications of devaluation and import restriction', *Cambridge Economic Policy Review*, no. 3.

GOVERNMENT-RULING PARTIES, JOINT HEADQUARTERS FOR THE PROMOTION OF EXTERNAL ECONOMIC MEASURES (1985) *The Outline of the Action Programme for Improved Market Access*, July 30, Tokyo.

GROUP OF FIVE (1985) 'Announcement of the Ministers of Finance and the Central Bank Governors of France, Germany, Japan, the United Kingdom and the United States', September 22, Processed, New York.

HAGER, W. (1982) 'Industrial policy, trade policy, and European social democracy', in J. Pinder (ed.), *National Industrial Strategies and the World Economy* (New Jersey: Allanheld, Osmun; Beckenham: Croom Helm).

HAMADA, K. and KUROSAKA, Y. (1984) 'The relationship between production and unemployment in Japan: Okun's Law in comparative perspective', *European Economic Review*, vol. 25.

HAMILTON, C. (1985) 'Voluntary export restraints: ASEAN systems for allocation of export licences', in C. Findley and R. Garnaut (eds), *The Political Economy of Protection Policy in ASEAN and Australia* (London, Sydney: Allen & Unwin).

HANABUSA, M. (1979) *Trade Problems Between Japan and Western Europe* (Farnborough: Saxon House).

HOSOMI, T. and OKUMURA, A. (1982) 'Japanese industrial policy', in J. Pinder (ed.), *National Industrial Strategies and the World Economy* (New Jersey: Allanheld, Osmun; Beckenham: Croom Helm).

HOSOMI, T. and FUKAO, M. (1985) *A Second Look at Foreign Exchange Market Interventions*, April (Tokyo: Centre for International Finance).

HICKS, J. R. (1953) 'An Inaugural Lecture: the Long-Run Dollar Problem', *Oxford Economic Papers*, vol. 5; reprinted in R. E. Caves and H. G. Johnson (eds), *Readings in International Economics* (London: George Allen & Unwin).

HINDLEY, B. (1977) 'Britain's Economy as seen by the Cambridge Group', in H. Corbet *et al.*, *On How To Cope With Britain's Trade Position*, Trade Policy Research Centre, Thames Essay, no. 8.

HOSOYA, C. (1979) 'Relations between the European Communities and Japan', *Journal of Common Market Studies*, vol. 18, no. 2.

HYDEN, E..W. (1980) 'Internationalising Japan's financial system', *Occasional Paper*, North-East Asia–US Forum on International Policy (Stanford: Stanford University).

HYDEN, E. W. (1981) 'The working Japanese interest in syndicated loans', *Euromoney*, September.

IMLAH, A. H. (1958) 'British balance of payments and export of capital', in A. H. Imlah (ed.), *Economic Elements in the Pan Britanica* (Cambridge, Mass.: Harvard University Press).

INDUSTRIAL BANK OF JAPAN, *Quarterly Review*, various issues.

INDUSTRIAL BANK OF JAPAN (various years), *Annual Reports* (Tokyo: IBOJ).

ISARD, P. and STEKLER, L. (1985) 'US international capital flows and the Dollar', *Brookings Papers on Economic Activity*, no. 1 (Washington, DC: Brookings Institution).

JACQUEMIN, A. (1983) 'Industrial policies and the Community', in P. Coffey (ed.), *Main Economic Policy Areas of the EEC* (The Hague: Martinus Nijhoff).

JACQUEMIN, A. (ed.) (1984) *European Industry: Public Policy and Corporate Strategy* (Oxford: Oxford University Press).

JAPAN ECONOMIC AND FOREIGN AFFAIRS RESEARCH ASSOCIATION (various years) *Statistical Survey of Japan's Economy* (Tokyo).

JAPAN ECONOMIC INSTITUTE (1984) *Yearbook of US–Japan Economic Relations in 1983* (Washington, DC: JEI).

JAPAN EXTERNAL TRADE ORGANISATION (1981) *Economic Cooperation of Japan, 1979* (Tokyo: JETRO).

JINUSHI, S. (1972) 'Social security system in transition', *Developing Economies*, December.

JOHNSON, C. (1977) 'MITI and Japanese international economic policy', in R. A. Scalapino (ed.), *The Foreign Policy of Modern Japan* (Los Angeles: University of California Press).

JOHNSON, C. (1982) *MITI and the Japanese Miracle: the Growth of Industrial Policy, 1925–1975* (Stanford: Stanford University Press).

JOHNSON, H. G. (1965) 'An economic theory of protectionism, tariff bargaining and the formation of customs union', *Journal of Political Economy*, vol. 73.

JOHNSON, H. G. (1967) 'The possibility of income losses from increased efficiency or factor accumulation in the presence of tariffs', *Economic Journal*, vol. 77.

KALDOR, N. (1966) *Causes of the Slow Rate of Economic Growth of the United Kingdom*, inaugural lecture (Cambridge: Cambridge University Press).

KALT, J. P. (1985) 'The impact of domestic regulatory policies on international competitiveness', mimeo, March.

KANAMORI, H. (1985) 'Microelectronics and the Japanese economy', in T. Shishido and R. Sato (eds), *Economic Policy and Development: New Perspectives* (Dover, Mass.: Auburn House).

KAWAGUCHI, H. (1970) ' "Overloan" and the investment behaviour of firms', *Developing Economies*, December.

KEIDANREN (1985) 'Smoothing the way for imports: Keidanren presses for regulatory reform', *Keizai Koho Centre Brief*, no. 20, February, Tokyo.

KEIZAI KOHO CENTRE (Japan Institute for Social and Economic Affairs) (1982) *Japan 1982: An International Comparison* (Tokyo: Keizai Koho Centre).

KINDLEBERGER, C. P. (1986) 'Economic development and international responsibility', in A. M. El-Agraa (ed.), *Protection, Cooperation, Integration and Development: Essays in Honour of Professor Hiroshi Kitamura* (London: Macmillan).

KITAMURA, H. (1976) *Choices for the Japanese Economy* (London: Allen & Unwin).

KITAMURA, H. (1984) 'Japan and Asian-Pacific economic integration', paper presented to the American Economic Association, December.

KLEIN, L. R. and OHKAWA, K. (eds) (1968) *Economic Growth – the Japanese Experience since the Meiji Era* (Homewood, Ill.: McGraw-Hill).

KOJIMA, K. (1971) *Japan and a Pacific Free Trade Area* (Tokyo: Tokyo University Press).

KOJIMA, K. (1973) 'A macroeconomic approach to foreign direct investment', *Hitotsubashi Journal of Economics*, vol. 14, no. 1.

KOJIMA, K. (1977) *Japan and a New World Economic Order* (Tokyo: Charles E. Tuttle).

KOJIMA, K. (1978a) *Direct Foreign Investment: a Japanese Model of Multinational Business Operations* (Beckenham: Croom Helm).

KOJIMA, K. (1978b) 'Macroeconomic versus international business approach to direct foreign investment', *Hitotsubashi Journal of Economics*, vol. 23, no. 1.

KOMIYA, R. (ed.) (1966) *Postwar Economic Growth in Japan* (Los Angeles: University of California Press).

KRUEGER, A. O. and TUNCER, B. (1982) 'An empirical test of the infant industry argument', *American Economic Review*, vol. 64.

KRUGMAN, P. R. (1984) 'The US response to foreign industrial targeting', *Brookings Papers in Economic Activity*, no. 1. (Washington, DC: Brookings Institution).

LAWRENCE, R. Z. (1984) *Can America Compete?* (Washington, DC: Brookings Institution).

LEHMANN, J-P. (1984) 'Agenda for action on issues in Euro-Japanese relations', *World Economy*, vol. 7, no. 1.

LOOKWOOD, W. W. (ed.) (1965) *The State and Economic Enterprise in Japan* (Princeton: Princeton University Press).

LOOKWOOD, W. W. (ed.) (1968) *Economic Development of Japan* (Princeton: Princeton University Press).

LOOPESKO, B. E. (1984) 'Relationships among exchange rates, intervention and interest rates: an empirical investigation', *Journal of International Money and Finance*, December.

McCULLUM, J. and VINES, D. (1981) 'Cambridge and Chicago on the balance of payments', *Economic Journal*, vol. 91.

MADDISON, A. (1969) *Economic Growth in Japan and the USSR* (London: Macmillan).

MAEKAWA COMMITTEE (1986) *The Report of the Advisory Group on Economic Structural Adjustment for International Harmony* (Tokyo: Ministry of Foreign Affairs), April 7.

MARRIS, S. (1985) *Deficits and the Dollar: the World Economy at Risk* (Washington, DC: Institute for International Economics).

MASHIMOTO, M. (1982) *Growth Potential of the Japanese Economy in the 1980s* (Tokyo: Japan Economic Research Centre).

MINAMI, R. (1972) 'Transformation of the labour market in postwar Japan', *Hitotsubashi Journal of Economics*, June.

MINAMI, R. (1973) *The Turning Point in Economic Development: Japan's Experience* (Tokyo: Tokyo University Press).

MINISTRY OF FOREIGN AFFAIRS (1981) *Japan's Foreign Policy: Questions and Answers* (Tokyo: Ministry of Foreign Affairs).
MITCHELL, B. R. and DEANE, P. (1962) *Abstract of British Historical Statistics* (Cambridge: Cambridge University Press).
MITCHELL, B. R. and JONES, H. G. (1971) *Second Abstract of British Historical Statistics* (Cambridge: Cambridge University Press).
MITI (1985a) *MITI Handbook* (Tokyo: MITI).
MITI (1985b) *Report on Japanese Macroeconomic Policy*, report by a private advisory committee to the Director General, Industrial Policy Bureau (Tokyo: MITI).
MIYAZAKI, Y. (1967) 'Rapid economic growth in postwar Japan', *Developing Economies*, June.
MIYAZAWA, K. (1964) 'The dual structure of the Japanese economy and its growth pattern', *Developing Economies*, June.
MIZOGUCHI, T. (1970) *Personal Savings and Consumption in Postwar Japan* (Tokyo: Tokyo University Press).
MORITANI, M. (1982) *Japanese Technology* (Tokyo: Simul Press).
MOROHOSHI, R. (1978a) 'Government will mobilise all means to spur business', *Japan Economic Journal*, March.
MOROHOSHI, R. (1978b) 'Import-lease system is explored as new way to cut payments surplus', *Japan Economic Journal*, March.
NAMIKI, N. (1978) 'Japanese subsidy policies', in S. J. Warnecke (ed.), *International Trade and Industrial Policies* (London: Macmillan).
NATIONAL ASSOCIATION OF MANUFACTURERS (1985) *US Trade, Industrial Competitiveness and Economic Growth* (Washington, DC: the Association).
NELSON, R. E. *et al.* (eds) (1982) *Government and Technical Progress: a Cross-Industry Analysis* (New York: Pergamon Press).
NIESR (1968) 'The Economic situation: the home economy', *N.I.E.S.R. Review*, vol. 44.
NODA, K. (1975) 'Big Business Organisation', in E. F. Vogel (ed.), *Modern Japanese Organisation and Decision-Making* (Los Angeles: University of California Press).
NOGUCHI, Y. (1982) 'The government-business relationship in Japan: the changing role of fiscal resources', in K. Yamamura (ed.), *Policy and Trade Issues of the Japanese Economy: American and Japanese Perspectives* (Tokyo: Tokyo University Press).
NOMURA RESEARCH INSTITUTE (1985) 'A long-term outlook for the Japanese Economy (Fiscal 1984 to 1995)', August 26, Tokyo.
OECD (1972) *Monetary Policy in Japan* (Paris: OECD).
OECD (various years) *Economic Survey of Japan* (Paris: OECD).
OECD (various years) *OECD Economic Outlook* (Paris: OECD).
OHKAWA, K. (1972) *Differential Structure and Agriculture* (Tokyo: Tokyo University Press).
OHKAWA, K. (1985) 'Investment criteria in development planning', in T. Shishido and R. Sato (eds), *Economic Policy and Development: New Perspectives* (Dover, Mass.: Auburn House).
OHKAWA, K. and ROSOVSKY, H. (1973) *Japanese Economic Growth* (Stanford: Stanford University Press).

OHKAWA, K. and SHINOHARA, M. (eds) (1979) *Patterns of Japanese Economic Development: a Quantitative Appraisal* (New Haven: Yale University Press).

OHMAE, K. (1985) *Triad Power: the Coming Shape of Global Competition* (New York: Free Press).

OKITA, S. (1984) 'Role of the Trade Ombudsman in liberalising Japan's market', *World Economy*, vol. 7, no. 1.

OZAWA, M. (1984) 'Japan's new class society: consumption patterns reveal growing class distinctions', Long-Term Credit Bank of Japan, Tokyo.

OZAWA, M. (1986) 'Japanese consumer mysteries', *Economic Eye*, Keizai Koho Centre, Tokyo, June.

PAGE, S. A. B. (1979) 'The revival of protectionism and its consequences for Europe', *Journal of Common Market Studies*, vol. 20.

PAINE, S. H. (1971) 'Wage differentials in the Japanese manufacturing sector', *Oxford Economic Papers*, vol. 23.

PARTICK, H. and ROSOVSKY, H. (eds) (1976) *Asia's New Giant: How the Japanese Economy Works* (Washington, DC: Brookings Institution).

PARTICK, H. and ROSOVSKY, H. (eds) (1985) 'The Japanese economy in transition', in T. Shishido and R. Sato (eds), *Economic Policy and Development: New Perspectives* (Dover, Mass.: Auburn House).

PEMPEL, T. J. (1978) 'Japanese foreign economic policy: the domestic bases for international behavior', in P. J. Katzenstein (ed.), *Between Power and Plenty: Foreign Economic Policies of Advanced Industrial States* (Madison: University of Wisconsin Press).

PETRI, P. A. (1984) *Modelling Japanese–American Trade: a Study of Asymmetric Interdependence* (Cambridge, Mass.: Harvard University Press).

PINDER, J. (ed.) (1982) *National Strategies and the World Economy* (New Jersey: Allenheld, Osmun; Beckenham: Croom Helm).

PUTMAN, R. D. and BAYNE, N. (1984) *Hanging Together: the Seven Power Summits* (Cambridge, Mass.: Harvard University Press).

RAPP, W. V. and FELDMAN, R. A. (1979) 'Japan's economic strategy and prospects', in W. J. Barnds (ed.), *Japan and the United States: Challenges and Opportunities* (New York: New York University Press).

REICH, M. R., ENDO, Y. and TIMMER, P. (1985) 'The political economy of structural change: conflict between Japanese and United States agricultural policy', Processed (Cambridge, Mass.: Harvard University Press).

ROSTOW, W. W. (1960) *The Stages of Economic Growth: a Non-Communist Manifesto* (Cambridge: Cambridge University Press).

ROUSCH, C. T., Jr. (1984) *The Benefits of Eliminating the Alaskan Crude Oil Export Ban*, August (Washington, DC: Federal Trade Commission).

SATO, R. (1985) 'Nothing new? an historical perspective on Japanese technology policy', in T. Shishido and R. Sato (eds), *Economic Policy and Development: New Perspectives* (Dover, Mass.: Auburn House).

SAXONHOUSE, G. R. (1983a) 'What is all this about "Industrial Targeting" in Japan?', *World Economy*, vol. 6, September.

SAXONHOUSE, G. R. (1983b) 'The micro- and macroeconomics of foreign sales to Japan', in W. R. Cline (ed.), *Trade Policy in the 1980s* (Washington, DC: Institute for International Economics).

SCALAPINO, R. A. (ed.) (1977) *The Foreign Policy of Modern Japan* (Los Angeles: University of California Press).

SCOTT, B. R. (1985a) 'US competitiveness: concepts, performance, and implications', in B. R. Scott and G. C. Lodge (eds), *US Competitiveness and the World Economy* (Boston, Mass.: Harvard Business School Press).

SCOTT, B. R. (1985b) 'National strategies', in G. C. Lodge and B. R. Scott (eds), *US Competitiveness and the World Economy* (Boston, Mass.: Harvard Business School Press).

SEMICONDUCTOR INDUSTRY ASSOCIATION (1985) *Japanese Market Barriers in Microelectronics*, June 14 (San Jose, Calif.: SIA).

SHAPIRO, E. (1985) 'The financial system, financial regulation, financial innovation', in T. Shishido and R. Sato (eds), *Economic Policy and Development: New Perspectives* (Dover, Mass.: Auburn House).

SHINOHARA, M. (1970) *Structural Changes in Japan's Economic Development* (Tokyo: Tokyo University Press).

SHISHIDO, T. (1985) 'Japanese technological development', in T. Shishido and R. Sato (eds), *Economic Policy and Development: New Perspectives* (Dover, Mass.: Auburn House; Beckenham: Croom Helm).

SHISHIDO, T. and SATO, R. (eds) (1985) *Economic Policy and Development: New Perspectives*, Essays in Honour of Dr. Saburo Okita (Dover, Mass.: Auburn House; Beckenham: Croom Helm).

SPINDLER, J. A. (1984) *The Politics of International Credit: Private Finance and Foreign Policy in Germany and Japan* (Washington, DC: Brookings Institution).

STAIGER, R. W., DEARDORFF, A. V. and STERN, R. M. (1985) 'The effects of protection on the factor content of Japanese and American foreign trade', March 29, Processed (Ann Arbor: University of Michigan).

STATISTICAL BUREAU, PRIME MINISTER'S OFFICE (various years) *Japan Statistical Yearbook* (Tokyo: Statistical Bureau).

STRIER, F. (1981) 'Multipartite policy consensus building in Japan, West Germany, France and the United Kingdom: analysis and implications to the United States', March, US Department of Commerce, Office of Economic Policy.

SUZUKI, Y. (1980) *Money and Banking in Contemporary Japan: the Theoretical Setting and Its Application* (New Haven: Yale University Press).

THIRLWALL, A. P. (1983) 'A strategy for the United Kingdom', *Journal of Common Market Studies*, vol. 22, no. 1.

THUROW, L. C. (1985) 'The case for industrial policies in America', in T. Shishido and R. Sato (eds), *Economic Policy and Development: New Perspectives* (Dover, Mass.: Auburn House).

THUROW, L. C. (1986) 'How low must the $ go?', *Los Angeles Times*, May.

UNITED STATES–JAPAN ADVISORY COMMISSION (1984) *Challenges and Opportunities in United States–Japan Relations*, Tokyo and Washington, DC.

US GENERAL ACCOUNTING OFFICE (1979) *United States–Japan Trade: Issues and Problems* (Washington, DC: USGAO).

US INTERNATIONAL TRADE COMMISSION (1983) *Foreign Industrial*

Targeting and the Effects on US Industries. Phase 1. Japan, USITC publication no. 1437, October (Washington, DC: USITC).

US TRADE POLICY GROUP, various publications (1983–5).

US TRADE REPRESENTATIVE (1985) 'US statement on Japanese market access', addressed to OECD Trade Committee, 11 June (Washington, DC: USTR).

VOGEL, E. F. (ed.) (1975) *Modern Japanese Organisation and Decision-Making* (Los Angeles: University of California Press).

WARNECKE, S. J. (ed.) (1978) *International Trade and Industrial Policies* (London: Macmillan).

WILLIAMSON, J. (1985) *The Exchange Rate System* (Washington, DC: Institute for International Economics).

YAKUSHIJI, T. (1984) 'The government in a spiral dilemma: dynamic policy interventions *vis-à-vis* auto firms', in M. Aoki (ed.), *The Economic Analysis of the Japanese Firm* (Amsterdam: North-Holland).

YAMAMURA, K. (1967) *Economic Policy in Postwar Japan* (Los Angeles: University of California Press).

YAMAMURA, K. (ed.) (1971) *Small Business in Japan's Economic Progress* (Tokyo: Tokyo University Press).

YAMAMURA, K. (ed.) (1982) *Policy and Trade Issues of the Japanese Economy: American and Japanese Perspectives* (Tokyo: Tokyo University Press).

YOSHITOMI, M. (1985a) 'Japan as capital exporter and the world economy', *Occasional Paper*, no. 18 (New York: Group of Thirty).

YOSHITOMI, M. (1985b) 'Japan's view of current external imbalances', in C. F. Bergsten (ed.), *Imbalances in the World Economy* (Washington, DC: Institute for International Economics).

ZYSMAN, J. (1983) *Governments, Markets, and Growth: Financial Systems and the Politics of Industrial Change* (New York: Cornell University Press).

Author Index

216

Subject Index